Balkan Traditional Witchcraft
by
Radomir Ristic

Translation by Michael C. Carter, Jr.

Balkan Traditional Witchcraft
by
Radomir Ristic

Translation by Michael C. Carter, Jr.

PENDRAIG PUBLISHING, LOS ANGELES

Balkan Traditional Witchcraft was translated into English from the original Serbian by Michael C. Carter, Jr.

Pendraig Publishing, Sunland, CA 91040
© Radomir Ristic 2009. All rights reserved.
Published 2009.
Printed in the United States of America
ISBN 978-0-9796168-5-3

CONTENTS

Publisher's Note: While every effort has been made to provide illustrations of the highest quality in this book, there are a number of photographs that were scanned from very old sources - in some cases newspapers - and consequently show evidence of the half-tone printing method used in conventional print media during the early to mid twentieth century. While the quality of these pictures is less than ideal, they have been included for their historical value.

FOREWORD

Following world trends in the area of Pagan religions, Witchcraft, and various customs associated with Wicca, it is very hard not to notice the attempts of a number of authors to prove, to a greater or lesser extent, the existence of a history or heritage for the system or Tradition that they follow. How successful they will be, only time will tell.

Many modern systems are built on a foundation of solid facts and good reasoning, including the work of notable individuals, or the founders of certain trends, but also the work of independent scholars whose works left a well-documented path for future generations.

This is the case with Stregeria, the traditional Italian Witchcraft, the existence of which is rarely refuted, even today. This is a result of the efforts of Charles Godfrey Leland (1824-1903), who, in northern Italy, gained the trust of one Italian Witch, and after several years of friendship, received a number of manuscripts which he later translated and published under the familiar name of "Aradia, or the Gospel of the Witches". Today, we can also find similar things in well-known traditional systems from British, Scottish, Welsh, Irish and French Witchcraft. In addition to a number of scientifically confirmed and published materials, these traditions can be proud of their historical continuity, which, in some smaller cities and rural areas, can be found in their unchanged forms up to present day.

To avoid confusion, we must stop for a moment and explain that the Witchcraft of today can be divided into two basic groups, although the actual situation is much more complex. The first group consists of Wicca, a relatively new form of Witchcraft from the 1950s, founded by Gerald Gardner. This is a revised form of Traditional Witchcraft which contains many additions, such as ceremonial magic, Kabbalah, Masonic symbols, Pagan mysticism, eastern philosophies, etc. Gardner is not the source of all Wiccan Traditions, but he was the first, and those that came after used the name as well. Certain types of Traditional Witchcraft may be considered pre-Gardnarian, and retain their "purity", originality, and historical continuity. This is often taken to mean that they have not been revised in any way, and have no additions from other systems, but as far as we know, this is not strictly true; in many cases there appear to be elements of other traditions and religions. We should also mention that these systems or traditions are considered "pre-gardnerian", but that doesn't mean that they were created or "revealed" as a predecessor to the Gardnarian Tradition. None of this means that one form of Witchcraft is better than another, or is in any way less valuable. This is but a simple classification that helps us to distinguish these two groups.

The fundamental reason that we mention this classification in the first place is to gain a better understanding of the concept of "Traditional Witchcraft" itself, because that is the only type of Witchcraft in what we classify as Balkan, or to be precise, Old Balkan Witchcraft. At a first glance, it may seem that the term "Balkan Witchcraft" is too broad; however, it is the only possible one at the moment. The reason for this is the fact that today's borders of the Balkan region are the product of politics, and for Witchcraft, those borders have no meaning at all.

Witchcraft in the Balkans is a product of cultural heritage of many peoples. When we speak of people, we must understand that they have roots deep in the past and their foundations are based on the indigenous people of the area. Among them are Illyrians, Thracians, Dacians, Paeones, and many other smaller groupings. Later, we could include the arrival of Celts, Romans, Slavs and Turks. Wars, migrations and trade resulted in the mixing of genes and cultures. We also cannot disregard the influence of adjacent nations. Overall, today we have one general combination of different elements that together form the Balkan system. The system itself was created sometime in the Middle Ages, probably by mixing shamanism on the one hand and heretical Christianity on the other. The influence of heretical Christianity was primarily from the Bogomils, a Christian sect that taught a dualistic heresy that was similar, if not the same, as the Cathars from the south of France.

It is very difficult to classify currents within Balkan Witchcraft itself. It is certain that the Vlash current has survived the centuries wonderfully, and it manages to retain its' strength. There is also the Slovene current, but it is very hard to determine to what extent it is "pure". It is fairly easy to recognize the influences of indigenous and Celtic cultures. Then we have the Visocka (Bosnian) current, which has elements of both Vlash and Slovene. Other currents exist, of course, but it is impossible to track them down and find any serious traces, because they also include characteristics of larger currents.

Maybe the honest classification would be that two main traditions exist, Vlash and Slovene. When speaking of the Vlash current, it is necessary to say that today's Vlash people "most probably" represent Romanized Slovene people, according to ethnologist Petar Vlahovic. To all this we must add that there are obvious influences of the indigenous peoples of the time, such as the Thracians, Dacians, and Celts, who took part in their ethno-genesis. It is very difficult to say who they are exactly, even in the present day, because there is no agreement between scholars; this issue is quite politicized, which makes it difficult to identify those ethnic groups which existed in Eastern Serbia.

It is necessary to say up front that this book does not, in any case, pretend to be scientific, although it relies on scientific materials, especially on the material of ethnologists. It was written in the way I thought necessary, so it could be read and understood by all.

As you will see, this book represents the sum of two things. The first thing is material field-collected in the modern day, the second is scientific material and facts collected by ethnologists, ethnographers, and historians. This, of course, includes the testimonies of earlier authors who wrote about their travels, like M. Milicevic and Kazimirovic, as well as other authors and journalists like Jasna Jojic-Pavlovski.

It is important to emphasize that some of the rituals and incantations have been modified to make sense to modern eyes, while attempting to make the "damage" as minimal as possible. Most of these changes involve incantations that would be unintelligible for many people without revision. We have tried to preserve the essence and structure of the parts revised, trying to retain everything that is important so everyone can clearly see how they originate and how they are formed..

The whole system is presented in parts that are interpreted in a specific order, so that all that parts in the end give one complete entity. We start at the beginning with the term itself, and look at its history through initiations, ritual trance, Witch supplies and the structure of rituals, and holidays and important dates. Another very special part we will explore is that of the supernatural beings and animals that have always been very important for Balkan Witches. One chapter is dedicated to herbs too, which is literally unavoidable in a region with rich vegetation, and knowledge about them represents the very core of the magical practice of Balkan Witches. But we must emphasize one more thing.

Whenever the study of some phenomenon begins, the beginning always defines and explains the term itself and identifies specifically what is being studied. From this point on, we can say that we are speaking of Witchcraft, specifically the Witchcraft that is present in the Balkans.
However, the term "Witchcraft" today covers many things and

it is very imprecise, which leads many people into confusion. In modern usage, this term addresses at least two things. Firstly, Witchcraft means anything to do with magic, that is, any group of actions designed to bring about desired results in a mysterious way. Subsequently, all forms of spells, invocations, shaman's ritual practices, healers, etc, are assigned to the term Witchcraft. This is wrong, of course. It is better to assign all of that to the term "sorcery".

The second use of this term refers to the Renaissance Witches hunted by the Inquisition, familiar from books or movies. Some of those unlucky women were actually Witches. The thing that separates them from the first cited group is the fact that they were not just practicing magic but were believed to be part of a structured magical system, which is to say, they were passing through initiations, had a characteristic methodology of work and a final a goal that was not pragmatic, but had some religious connotation. This view of Witches is correct, which is not very difficult to conclude if we consider serious Western literature on this subject matter.

Because of all that, this book will strive to describe Balkan Traditional Witchcraft and to show clear differences between Witchcraft on the one hand, and folk magic, or sorcery on the other. To be able to present this, it is first necessary to identify several very important components. The first one is initiation, the second is the presence of ritual trance, and the third is a logical working system. Then comes ritual structure, respect for higher powers which are the subject of the cult and finally, the existence of some important dates and holidays.

From all of this, we can conclude that this book isn't meant just to inform readers about Balkan traditional Witchcraft, but to simultaneously give all the necessary information on how to practice it. Here, you will find instruction on initiation as a first step, the methods of getting into trance, the ways of creating rituals, when and how they are performed and many other things.

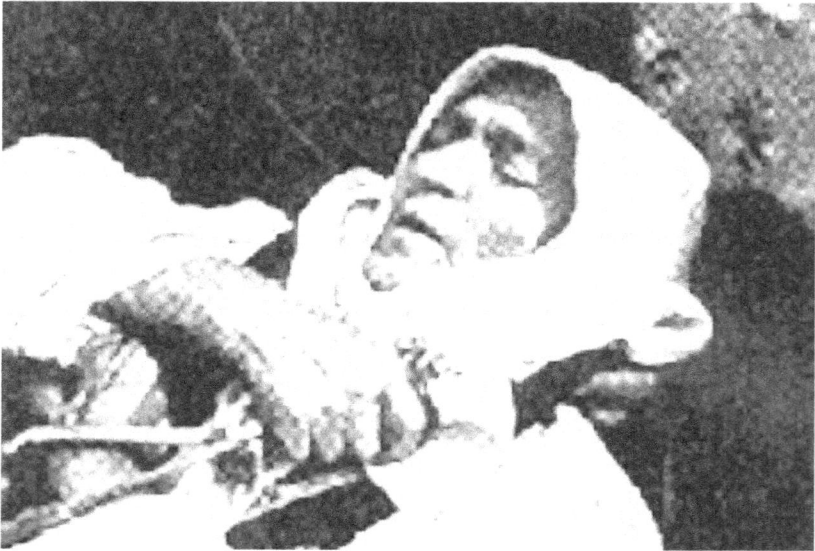

Woman in trance, Rusalja - photo by S.Trojanovic (1901)

ANCIENT WITCHCRAFT IN THE BALKANS

Try to imagine a small village in ancient Serbia. While you slowly walk along a steep path, you see dilapidated houses, built of mud with wooden roofs, scattered on the mountainous hillsides. A full moon illuminates the whole region, and you have the impression that everything that surrounds you shines with a silvery light. You clearly see pastures and forests; you hear the roar of a stream, the fluttering of leaves, the hooting of owls and in the distance, the howling of wolves. In the village, you hear the barking of dogs and you have the urge to hide. You see a small house with an open door and the twinkle of firelight on the hearth. You jump over a low fence that corrals a herd of sheep. You walk up to the entrance and see the interior of a house. In the middle of the room, there is a small space encircled with rocks with a fire burning in the middle.

The space around that circle is paved with flagstones, and there are several small three-legged, backless chairs. Above the fire, a cauldron hangs on a big chain hung from the ceiling. The name of that chain is Verige and you are looking at Ognjiste, the most sacred ritual area of the ancient Serbs. On the walls hang bouquets of various medicinal and holy herbs. Earthen and wooden pots are placed randomly around the room. In one corner, laid out on a piece of fabric, are roots of some herbs that irresistibly remind you of a human body.

You go out to look around the yard. You notice colorful fabrics tied to branches of adjacent trees. You have an impression that someone is watching you. You turn around, and you see the head of a black ram above the door, and on the right side of the threshold there is a birch broom. From the direction of the stream, a nude

13

old woman approaches you with a Hazel wood stick in her hand. Just then you realize that you have been in a Witch's house.

The question arises, what are Witches, and how did people see them in ancient Serbia and in the Balkans? The first definitions of "Witch" in Serbia start to show up in the early 19th century. The most meaningful are ones from the Vuk's dictionary and somewhat later, in ethnologic literature. It is a well-known fact that Vuk Stefanovic Karadzic was a reformer of the Serbian language. He collected many folktales, folk songs, popular proverbs, fairy tales, myths and numerous folk beliefs. He adapted and clearly defined grammar in the Serbian language. In addition to that, he published the first "Srpski rjecnik" (Serbian dictionary) in 1818, where one can find the term "Witch". Here, we provide an approximate definition of "Witch", from the Vuk's dictionary, with some changes that will help this text be understandable to all:

A "Witch" is a woman (in folklore) who has some kind of demonic spirit inside her that comes out at night and transforms into a butterfly, hen or turkey. She then she flies through houses eating people, especially small children. When she finds a sleeping man, she hits him with a stick over the left breast to open his chest, then removes his heart and eats it. After that, the chest heals. Some of those eaten people immediately die, and some of them live on until a time that the Witch determined when she ate the heart. Witches don't eat white garlic, and that's why many people, during the Christmas carnival, rub themselves with garlic on their chests, the soles of their feet and under their arms, because it is said that this is the time that the Witches eat people.

No one will tell a young and beautiful woman she is a witch, just old women. When a Witch reveals herself and confesses, she can no longer eat people and she becomes a healer and heals the ones she has eaten with herbs. When a Witch flies at night, she shines like a fire and goes to a threshing floor; it is said that when the

Witch wants to fly away from home, she applies some kind of ointment under the arm and she says: "Not on thorn, not on shrub but on smart threshing floor". It is said that a woman, who was not a Witch, applied this ointment on herself, and instead of saying "not on thorn, not on shrub" she accidentally said "On thorn, on shrub." Then she flew away and broke into several pieces.

In Srem (a region in Vojvodina) it is said that Witches gather above the Molovina village on some kind of walnut tree, and in Croatia they say that Witches gather on the mountain pine over Ogulin. They say that in Srem a man in bed, after seeing a Witch fly away from his house, found her pot with the ointment and applied it on himself. He said the words that she said, and transformed into something and flew away, following her. He came to one walnut tree above Molovina and found a number of Witches, seated at a golden table and drinking from the golden glasses. When he looked at them, he recognized many of them and crossed himself saying; "*anate vas mate bilo*". At that time, they all disappeared and he fell under the walnut tree as the man he used to be. The golden table disappeared as the Witches and their golden glasses became animal hooves.

When the spirit of a Witch leaves her, she will lie as if dead. If someone turns her body around so that her head lay on the place where her legs had been during that time, she would never wake up again. When people see a butterfly flying around the house, they think that is the Witch and then they catch it if they can, burn it on a candle a little bit and then they release it, saying: "Come tomorrow again I will give you some salt.". Then, if some woman came to ask for salt or for any other reason the next day, especially if she has been burned, then they think that she's the one who came the day before.

If a great number of children or people die in some village, and everybody says that a certain woman is a Witch and has eaten them all, they will tie her up and throw her in the water to see whether she would sink (because they say that a Witch cannot sink). If that woman sinks they drag her out and let her go, but if she cannot sink, they kill her because she is a Witch. This was the way of investigating Witches at Karadjordje's time in Serbia. In some villages at the time of the carnival, Verige is turned against the Witches. In some places they burn some horn because it is said that Witches run away from this bad odor. In other places they crush egg shells so the Witches couldn't sail on it across the water – Where the Witch will go than to her clan…"

Vuk continues with a small supplemental in which he says that in Zabari, a wife of Pavle Stanojevic was tied to a spit at Karadjordje's order, and was then barbecued between two fires and at the end, when she didn't admit to being a Witch, she was thrown into the fires. In addition, he mentions that Petar Jokic's stepmother was killed by a pistol shot and then dismembered with knives, because she was believed to be a Witch.

We could find many similar descriptions of Witches in the contemporary ethnological literature of the time. By the late 19th century, Nikola Begovic, in his book "Life of the Serbian Frontiersmen", describes beliefs of that time related to Witches by the Serbian population in the Vojvodina of that time. Among other things, he cited as Vuk did, that Witches are always ugly old women. That they have ointment that they keep near the flame, apply it under the arm and on their knees and recite a somewhat different incantation, "Not on log, not on block, not on tree not on rock, not on Todor's pear tree" and then they would fly away through the chimney hole on their brooms. He also cited a somehow different story about the husband who tried to follow his wife during her night outing, but he could not remember the incantation correctly, and that is why he ended up being beaten.

Ethnologist Dr.Veselin Cajkanovic sheds a little light on the subject in the first half of the 20th century. He published several books and articles on ancient Serbian religion and mythology. In his collection of articles, which were assimilated and published in the book "Ancient Serbian Religion and Mythology", he speaks of Witches, and claims that the former understanding of Witches, based on the combining of three types of different "beings" could be clearly separated by their nature and function. In the first group, we can put female demons that stay in the grave by day, and at night come out and feed on the people – female vampires. The second group consists of demonic women, who have supernatural capabilities by birth, or were taught by some older Witch and learned their trade well. The third group consists of women who do fortune-telling, spells and generally, they are not true Witches in the common sense of that word.

Regarding the other group, folk belief is that every person who was born in the placenta will have supernatural capabilities. Cajkanovic also mentions that, if we look at the word Witch, we will see that word is made of the word "know-craft" and according to that, it marks a woman with a lot of knowledge. Literally, she is a clever woman or man (Craft woman-man). You will notice that there is little mention of a male Witch. That is because Witch men are well known by other names. By the way, in the Serbian territory, as well as the Balkans, there is a lot of confusion on who is who, because of various terms can be used for the same persons, with the same supernatural capabilities and field of work, as well as the same term being used for quite different people or fields of. For example, anyone who goes out of the body is confused with incorporeal demons, which Serbian folks believe of which there are many. Because of that, for many years people taught that a Witch is the female equivalent of a vampire. In Serbia, a vampire is incorporeal from time immemorial, but he is solid enough to deliver a bite and to feed himself with blood, or to be precise, with energy while his physical body is in the grave. Theories like this would later be rejected by science. Only a small number of ethnologists were interested in studying Witches, so there is a lack of serious research in that field.

Before the Second World War, ethnologist Tihomir Djordjevic collected voluminous materials trying to thoroughly explain it, like other ethnologists with an evolutionary orientation. During the collection of that material, he added some folk beliefs concerning Witches, such as the ones that say a Witch has the power to knock a man down with a look, or even to kill. Likewise, he also cited Croatian belief that a child who was born during the last quarter of the Moon could became a Witch.

Vid Vuletid Vusakasavic cited, in his thorough study on Witches named "Witches in the South Slovenia", published in Karadzic journal in Aleksinac, October 1901, the belief that Witches used to gather (whether each Saturday or once per year), at which time their leader taught them and assigned them various tasks. It is very interesting that each of those present was prevailed upon not to do any harm to her family. A newly initiated Witch was given a bat wing that she would carry around and she must wear her hair free and wear a black robe. It is also believed that Witches, after admission in the society, would dance around a Witch's brew and then they would sign their name in the registration book.

However, one thing that is missing with the earlier ethnologists is fieldwork, and someone else did that. That person was Radovan N. Kazimirovic a civil rights professor and the first Serbian parapsychologist. He collected voluminous written materials on the paranormal, including materials on Witches while he was going out into the field and finding living Witches. This data collection lasted for 25 years and the whole project was crowned with the publication of his masterpiece book "Mysterious Phenomena of the Serbs", in 1941 in Belgrade. In the very beginning of the book, he states the medieval belief that Witches are in league with the

Devil and that they meet with him by night and are promiscuous. In return they receive the power to do bad things to others, coming from the Christian ascetic-scholastic view of woman as an inferior and unclean being. According to Kazimirovic's sources, when the Croatians used the term Witch, they meant women who have sexual intercourse with the Devil, slaughter their own children and use their little bodies to work their magic. They also believed that Witches were guilty of cattle pestilence and that they were responsible for hail clouds over the villages that destroyed crops. It was said that Witches apply some kind of ointment on themselves in order to be able to fly; that they practice sorceries by banging on small leather drums and that they are very familiar with herbs for making various poisons, which they sell for money. Bearing in mind the fact that between 1360 and 1758 several Witch trials were conducted in Croatia, some of the confessions gained were preserved and the following is based on them:

The male and female Witches gather in the circle. They come from all sides to surround the Devil, on the cross-roads, under the gallows. There is always a big celebration. They jump around and dance, drink and entertain themselves. One of them said that her late husband brought her there, because he was a Witch man. Others said that other Witches persuaded them to fall into the Devil's arms. When someone wants join Witches for the first time, others must beat her with live snakes… "

The most severe Witch persecution in Croatia was in the 18th century. A bad crop year, hail and frost destroyed all the efforts of the villagers and they looked for a scapegoat. In the Zagorska district, in the period from 1742 until 1743, eleven women were burned. Those trials were forbidden by an Imperial order in 1758.

Beside Kazimirovic, today we have more recent data collected from Croatia, in the region of Ivanec City and the Medvednica

Mountains. According to that information, those two zones are, if not the main gathering places of the Witches, at least centers of strong folk belief in Witchcraft. Ivan Kusteljeg and Cvjetko Sostaric collected all data from Ivanec. According to local beliefs, Witches or "coprnice", are women who have supernatural powers and can hurt people and cattle with the help of their magic, potions, and spells, and that they can cause drought and floods. Local people describe them as women with long and bent claws who wear gloves to hide them. They say that they are bold and wear wigs, have very big noses, that their eyes can change color and that they do not have toes. The place for their meetings is the top of Ivanscice Mountain.

In one of the stories from that region, three women dressed in silky clothing intercepted Jendras, the miner, who was returning home from work. It is said that they took him by his hand, spun him around three times and then took him somewhere. For almost the whole night they took him by Bistrica, and then they came to one place that is called Cernih mlaka. There he saw more Witches who were carrying beech boughs and they were sweeping floor with them instead of using brooms. In the morning they brought him back, alive and well, to the very place they took him from.

The second story from that region speaks of a meeting between a family and a Witch. One day the family set out to visit their native city, and because they had no means of transportation from Ivanec to Prigorac, they walked. Shortly before arriving at Prigorac, near an old mill, they sat down on the grass to rest. In that moment, the youngest son saw a woman, dressed in white, washing laundry in the stream. Everyone turned their heads to see the woman, but she disappeared. At that same moment, the family lost its ability to speak for several minutes. Then the same woman showed up in the stream, but this time wearing black. It is said that the woman was a Witch who was washing her sins in that stream. They could not remember anything else about the incident, just like everyone else who saw the Witch. In the south of Serbia, this Witch's capability is called "*omaja*", which means they drove the victim crazy, hypnotized him so that he could not remember anything.

Here is one more story from this region. Sometimes residents of Prigorsica take their cattle all the way to Ivanscica and leave them there to graze for a few days. They had been doing this for many years, then one day cows started to go missing. A man called Stief passed by Cernih mlaka and found a pile of bones there. It is said that Witches used to make sacrifices and conduct rituals at that spot. In addition, it is said that one of the cows came back, but she was half-black and half-white and that the spirit of a Witch had entered her. That cow gave a lot of milk until one day she disappeared once again and never came back.

From the region of Medvednice Mountain, we have more interesting stories. The first one is about a trial from 1699, of a woman whose name is Kata Tinodi, who admitted in desperation, that one day Witches (in the form of a whirlwind) on the crossroads near the city hospital, took her to the hill at the bottom of the Medvednica Mountain and received her into their group. After two years, she promised her soul to the Devil.

In the "History of The Jesuit's Order from Zagreb" written in 1652, the author cited that a woman was accused and burned under accusation that she was a Witch in Rakitju. On that occasion, she betrayed many of her companions with whom she feasted at the bottom of the Medvednica Mountain, during the well-known bad weather from 1652. The people obviously believed that the Witches were responsible for that bad weather.

Jaga Cestarka and Margareta Krznar in 1704 testified that women of Kavalerka, their chief, gave them Witch's grease for flying, and that they gathered on the Medvednica Mountain after applying that ointment, to make hail.

When we talk about the state of things in the other former republics according to Kazimirovic, the situation in Slovenia is similar to that in Croatia. In Slovenia people believe that the Witches gather by night, usually on the peak of a mountain, and they get there by flying on their brooms. They believe that Witches fly on Birch wood brooms to the maintains (Klerk, Slivnica, Grintavec, Rogaska) where they gather in hazel groves. They practice their magic after midnight, on the crossroads or inside a magical circle. It is also said that they dance under the influence of the Witches brew. They are known for stealing milk by magical means and other similar activities, and we can conclude that they are identical to other ideas of Witches in the Balkans. They leave a shining trace and when they gather around those places, they could be spotted from a distance by the gold or blue light. These Witches are described as physically attractive, much the same as in the rest of the Balkans.

From time immemorial, Bosnian Witches were considered to be connected to the Moon and they came together during various phases of the Moon. In that region, the ritual that women conduct when the new moon shows in the sky is still preserved. When the new moon showed itself in the sky, the women would point at him and say:

"Just as you grow and renew yourself in the sky, I encourage my own renewal."

This could be very interesting if we take into consideration that Russian Witches – "vedme", are also very connected with the Moon. They are described as women that age and grow younger with the Moon's waxing and waning. Those women are always accompanied by a yellow cat, which is also a symbol of the Moon. Let us now go back to Kazimirovic.

Kazimirovic said that the people of Serbia treated Witches differently . He cites the testimony of Joakim Vujic (a famous

22

writer), who claims that he took part in digging up of a woman near Novi Pazar, who was accused of being a Witch. It was said that she was stabbed by a Priest. Vuk Karadzic cited a similar incident, also at the beginning of 19th century, is that a known outlaw named Stojan killed an old woman, having accused her of being a Witch and of eating his child. During the first half of the 19th century, during the government of Karadjordje, a so-called "Investigation of Witches" was undertaken. This involved dunking suspects into water, because they believed that a Witch cannot sink. The case of a certain Duke Antonije Pljakic, (Karadjordje's son in law) is also well known. In the Nevadima village he murdered a woman that, allegedly, was a Witch. He also burned an old woman alive in the Knjazevac city square, roasting her between two fires after she denied that she was a Witch. This was mentioned when we were talking about Vuk's definition of Witch. During the reign of the Obrenovic family (in the middle and latter part of the 19th century), there were several cases of Witch hunting. The best known is the case that happened 1841 when the Black Plague was affecting children. At the persuasion of Priest Spasoje, the people burned the old woman, Stamena, because they saw her reciting an incantation. Kazimirovic says that there are a great number of cases like this.

I think we can conclude that the Serbian description of Witches was the result of mixing several elements. On one hand, it is wrong to link women and men who have the ability to leave their bodies and to commune with incorporeal demons. On the other hand, we have the Christian Ascetic-scholastic view of woman as an inferior and impure being, although it is good to be reminded of the status that women had in the family patriarchal community. There is also the belief that every other type of religious or sorcerous practice is considered to be the worship of a Devil. This means anything that is against religious teachings, a priori, is bad. This kind of thinking was not hard to impose on uneducated people in the strict patriarchal communities, in which woman already had a subordinate role. Kazimirovic continued to study the various names for Witches in his country and abroad. There are many names and some of them are *mora, moria, brkna, striga, malesnica, samodiva, coprnica,* etc. Because of the complexity of these names, that mainly represent neologisms, they will need supplemental explanations. We will bypass this part and just say that the basic term for a Witch used by Serbs is *vestica*. According to Kazimirovic, this term originated from the Slavic word *"vdeti"* which means knowledge-skill-craft. Mr. Cajkanovic, who we mentioned earlier, also agreed with this. It means persons that possess unusual skills or abilities, they could provoke good or bad in humans and it is normal that people will be afraid of them. Reading the work of Russian ethnographers who studied the people of Lapland in the extreme north of Europe, he spots several similarities to Balkan Witches, and he concludes that this kind of Witchcraft is probably a remnant of some old "original religion". I completely agree with this and I believe that shamanism is, as a type of religion with the people of Lapland, what leads Kazimirovic to this conclusion, because our domestic Witchcraft has more elements of shamanism than Paganism.

Here are some examples that he cited regarding real Witches discovered throughout the Serbia of that time. First he presents the ones whose "specialty" was the discovery of con men (murderers, thieves, etc.) with the help of incorporeal demons - "Unchristian forces in the service of well-being" as he called them in his book. Here we will describe one such ritual in its entirety, in the way that Kazimirovic noted. Let us start at the beginning.

In his first example, he mentioned a well-known old woman named Lalonja, from the village of Urovice whose greatest skill was the discovering of criminals. She would do something magical and criminals would surrender, or die. Kazimirovic whose mother and aunt were also involved in following case, testifies to the following event: On December 15, 1891, Nikola Marikic, a twelve-year-old boy was thrown down into a hole - *"velika cesma"* - by his own uncle, who wanted to get the boy's inheritance, because Nikola was an only child. Not knowing at the time why the boy was missing, Kazimirovic's mother and his aunt (to whom Nikola M. was a cousin) asked the old woman, Lalonja, to do something. She agreed and called on "unchristian forces" who required some sort of sacrifice in exchange for certain services. When the mother and aunt agreed, the old woman finished her ritual and everyone went home. They probably did the rite near some large body of water, because in that region of eastern Serbia people always ask for help from the Great Water Spirit, the King of the all water spirits, the Tartor. Kazimirovic didn't know who this was, and he called him the "Devil in the service of well-being". When they got home, their ox was dead – it had been healthy until then - and the perpetrator of the crime surrendered himself, offering his help to pull little Nikola out of the hole.

Grandmother Joana (undated)

25

This case involved one more Witch, Kazimirovic says, who could also call "unchristian forces", using a ritual called "skoace draci". But the woman's specialty was clairvoyance. Her name was Joana and she was from the village of Urovice. Kazimirovic said that he knew her for forty-five years, until 1935, when she passed away, and that she was an exceptionally good, and honest woman. The mother and aunt went to see her. She used horse beans in her ritual, and she told them that the child was not alive, but he had not been buried, and that they could go home because the murderer had been found.

It is very interesting that she frequently came to visit them at on Kazimirovic's father's invitation, remembering that he was high-level Orthodox Priest. She was very popular among the people, and in her old age she stopped invoking spirits because, as she said, she had lost her former bravery. She said that many of the women who did the same thing died a long time ago and that they would all disappear in time.

Kazimirovic cited another example of one more woman who performed the "skoace draci" ritual. He knew this woman personally, because she was the grandmother of his friend Radomir Radulovic, an architect from Zajecar. That woman was Stanka Radulovic, 1835-1921, who claimed that she was taught this skill by her aunt from the Valakonje village near Boljevac. Stanka tried to impart that knowledge to her daughter, Marija Dinulovic, but she was not successful, because she was always too busy with agriculture. Kazimirovic remembers the time when she said to him that if she did not do her spell precisely, it was better to stop learning them than to make mistakes. The author concluded that it is necessary to have strong nerves and to be courageous to perform this kind of ritual, because if something goes wrong, the Witch could be in big trouble, especially if things get out of control. Once all Stanka's cattle died because she forgot to tell them whose ox should be sacrificed.

Now we will see the ritual "*skoce draci*" in its' entirety : the way that ritual looks and how it has been applied, probably for hundreds of years if not more. The way of performing this ritual had been transferred solely by oral tradition. The first time it was written down was by Kazimirovic himself, who recorded it in its homeland (Eastern Serbia), as described by the old woman, Stanka. I think I do not have to emphasize that this letter is priceless today. This text will be cited word for word, but with certain explanations of some parts to make it easier to understand. I quote:

Ritual Skoace Draci - Artist Stasha (undated)

27

"Very late at night (for Serbian and other Balkan people, this is the time between 12p.m. to 2 a.m., although it could be extended to 5 a.m., when the third rooster's crow sounds for the last time before dawn. This is considered to be a holy time, because it is the time when two worlds and two dimensions intercept; the world of people and the world of supernatural beings; the Witching hour in England). Grandma Stanka would go to Timok (a river in Eastern Serbia), and there she would perform her magic in the nude, with the help of unchristian spirits… She would bring with her a zobnica "a handbag made of goat's hair", 9cm long. In that handbag she would put nine barley grains, nine wheat grains, nine silk yarns of different sorts and one silver coin.

Arriving at Timok (or some other running water), she would find some kind of stick that was in the water (because it fell in there by itself and was floating on the surface), and then she tied the handbag to the end of the stick. She would go up and down, not saying anything except for ritual words that she mumbled. Totally naked, she took the Hazel wood stick (Forgetting to mention that she had brought it with her from home) and dug away at the water with it upstream and downstream. Then in the Vlach dialect she would say, "I'm coming with the Hazel wood stick and with the good horse. I am coming with the handbag made of goat's hair 9 centimeters long; I have nine barley grains in my handbag, nine wheat grains, nine silk yarns of nine different sorts and one silver coin. The stick is made of Hazel wood and the horse is good, bridled with a silver rein. However many drops (of water) sprinkle, that many Devils begin to move, Devil man and Devil woman (here Kazimirovic makes a mistake in translation from the Vlach dialect, because in the original it sounds like tartar and tartarica, who are water spirits, servants of the Tartor, the greatest water spirit.) You shall move to one who has committed a theft (for example, of cattle or something else) and make him say that by the water mill or in the tavern, or some place where there are many people. Because I give you this Hazel wood stick, a good horse bridled with a silver rein and nine barley grains to feed a good horse, and to you I give nine breads; one chicken for supper, one colt for lunch, one ram for a snack (by this she means she is offering all the animals that exist as a sacrifice). Cross the nine boundaries and tell me so that I may feed you."

After this act the Witch returns home, not saying anything, and does not look back… If she does not succeed to set the unchristian forces in motion, then she will do the exact same thing two more times. The third time (the last one) she's always successful."

Kazimirovic said that one time her cattle were stolen too, and that same night she performed this ritual just once, and shortly after that, some bloke named Andreja Cokovic confessed his guilt and was sent to prison. Another time, after performing this for some other person, she dreamed of two dwarves with measles who took her into the house of someone called Nikola from Zajecar. She saw in her dream that those two dwarves gave him dirty pig hoofs to eat, and blood came out from his mouth and nose. In the morning she discovered that Nikola had bled from his mouth and nose for real and that he passed away two days later.

This ritual was not always performed the same way, nor does it follow the same course. We can see that from another case, related to the famous Stanka. It happened in Vrazogrnac village, when all the money had been stolen from the house of a farmer. Stanka was called. In the night, she went with that farmer under the mill wheel, carrying a wooden flask and pestle. Completely naked, she stood under the water and start banging against the wooden flask with the pestle. The farmer heard her talking and shouting. Then, he heard slapping over the water. When he walked up to the water, he saw dark beings with the Witch and noticed that the largest one was talking with her. She came out from water for a few seconds and asked the farmer if he was prepared to make a sacrifice, because without it they would not do the job. When he agreed, she returned to them and concluded the arrangement. Shortly after that, all of the cattle of the suspected man died for no apparent reason, causing him a big materiel loss.

Grandmother Stanka (undated)

Grandma Stanka passed all of her knowledge to Stanija, who lived in the Grljan village. The case of Stojna from Zajecar is also famous. She made a mistake during the invocation and suffered a nervous breakdown.

Let us pause here to explain the creatures that appear from this invocation. More about this will be provided in following pages. In contrast to Dr. Kazimirovic, these Witches knew exactly whom they were calling. It is about Tarator, the water spirit, who they call the Old Man. According to folktales from eastern Serbia, he is the master of all waters and he lives in palace made of glass on the river bed. His appearance is like a dwarf. The only difference is that he has pointed ears and a large beard. He has legs like a goat with one or two horns on his forehead. An appearance like this is not surprising at all, if we bear in mind the fact that "dwarves" belong to the underworld and the water is the symbol of that world. It is said that he has 99 servants and that his main attributes are the whip and drum. He is supposed to be very powerful and communicative. He accepts invitations and if he gets angry, the only one who could induce mercy in him is the Mountain Mother. For now, let us just say that S. Zecevic collected the most facts and published them in a book "Mythical Creatures in Serbian Tradition".

Let us go back to Kazimirovic's work. In his further presentation, he speaks of famous craftswomen and craftsmen who had some other specialties. One important one was healing people with epilepsy and mental breakdowns. Because his father suffered from epilepsy, Kazimirovic turned to help from Stanka Miljkovic, who ensured that his father never, ever experienced another seizure for the rest of his life by invoking the water spirits. That happened in 1886. It is possibly the reason why his father was kind to Witches. Although he was an Orthodox priest and he raised his son in the same spirit, we are grateful for such a book as the one he wrote.

His father told him a story that during his "treatment", it seemed to him that he saw a big, black eagle come out of his chest and fly away. At that moment, he realized that he was healed. He also said that grandma Stanka used to make amulets of worms that she took from dead snakes and gave those amulets to sick people to wear. Similar methods of treatment were used in the treatment of mental illness. The basis of this method was the conviction that the causes of those illnesses were demons who possessed a patient and those demons needed to be expelled. We now know that this is not true, but that method certainly was successful. This is why is not surprising the to find that western psychiatrists use a shamanistic method of healing mental patients. During these treatments, it was discovered that is easier to treat someone if we assign some appearance to the illness, because psychic illnesses are still too abstract in the eyes of the common person. The essence of these treatments is to bring a person into a hypnotic state, and then to point out that the illness looks like a black double in the body that has weight and density. When the patient starts to feel the physical presence of that double, they are scared to a certain limit and then, in one moment, the double is pulled out and dies because it has no more energy that it can feed on. If the patient experiences this event, emotionally and physically, the recovery is successful.

Trance, photo by G.A. Kuppers (1938)

Few abilities attributed to Witches from Eastern Serbia attracted as much attention as their ability to get into collective trance during the one holy day that they all take part in. The epicenter of this event was the village of Duboka, but this holy day was transferred to adjacent villages, most probably by marriage. Women who participated in these rituals were called "rusalje" or fallen women. Because of its attraction, its size, and the public performance, this ritual was the subject of study and writing by many domestic

32

and foreign authors. Kazimirovic, ethnologists M. Milicevic, D. Gligoric, T. Djordjevic and others wrote about it during the time when the ritual was performed in its original form, in the beginning of the 20th century.

Here is what happened: During the now Christian holiday "duhovi" that overlaps with the village's holiday, the people gathered in front of a deep cave at the source of the Dubocka river. Before gathering, rites dedicated to the dead were performed, and they walked to the "wooden cross" (most often an oak) where sacrifices were offered in the form of food and drink. By the way, this holy tree has many names in Serbia and the assumption is that it represented the former main Pagan god or god of vegetation. After gathering around the cave, people start to dance in "kolo" (A circle) with the deafening music.

That lasted until some of the dancers, most often women, started to fade, shivering, and falling to the ground with a piercing shriek. That condition represents entry into a trance. On the ground, those persons would clench muscles, scream, and sing or speak. As they were talking, the spirits of the dead would get into them and communicated with them, or they were pulled out of their bodies by fairies who took them away. They were brought back from the trance in several ways. Sometimes they were sprinkled with chewed Wormwood, garlic and vinegar, or sometimes they were sprinkled with the river water that was poured over a sabre. There were many variations. While a person was into a trance, three girls in dresses named "queens", three men with sabres named "kings" and a bagpiper would dance around them. This holy day was celebrated in the Balkan territory but the ritual trance was preserved only in this area.

Bearing in mind the fact that these girls and women only received this gift from their families, ethnologist Dusan Bandic in his book "Earthly Realm and Heavenly Realm" concludes that here was the idea of hereditary Witchcraft, in direct relation to Witches, which they in essence really were.

M.Milicevic wrote about the belief that the ability to fall into a trance was a prerequisite if someone wanted to perform magic. In his book "Principality of Serbia" from 1876, he cited the example of grandma Dokija, the former "rusalja" who contacted supernatural beings, fell into trance and with their help performed magical healing and other magical feats. Beside this, during this holiday Duboko and adjacent villages were engaged in orgies, so the scholars found a connection with similar traditions in Bulgaria, Romania and some regions in Greece, Thessally, Ipiros, and Thrace.

Various theories about the origin of these customs exist. Some theories link them with the Dionisius festival and some with the Mother of Gods cult. However, we think they are wrong. In my opinion the basic reason for this is the knowledge that the religious system of belief in eastern Serbia, with its Serbian and Vlach population, has barely changed shape since ancient times. A contribution to this is their belief in primary deities, especially in the Mountain mother. It is normal that this system reminiscent of others, from neighboring regions, but a priori that does not mean that it originate from there. If we realize that in Europe since the Paleolithic period, there has existed a reverence for the Goddess of fertility and nature, and the Horned God, protector of venison and cattle, still that does not mean that the early population had a tendency to migrate. The reasons for this must be explored in other ways.

You probably noticed that I have concentrated on the territory of Eastern Serbia. The reason for this is the level of preservation of the original cult of Witches there. We could say that in this territory the influence of Christianity was very weak, which is not the case with other parts of Serbia; especially those where only

Serbs live. The Church managed to tie the national identity of the Serbs to Orthodox Christianity. A crucial moment was the medieval reforming of Christianity, by Rastko Nemanjic (today's St. Sava), when the whole Serbian pantheon was united with Christianity or with the Saints of Christian history. Today, while reading myths related to certain saints, we can see that everything is about the Pagan deities, but their names were forgotten a long time ago. After Saint Sava's death, Pagan myths that were attributed to the supreme god of the Serbs (probably Dabog-Veles) were transferred to the saint. So today, we have stories of how Saint Sava taught the Serbs to plow, blacksmiths to forge, women to knead and he even gave them fire that he robbed from anathemas, a type of demon. He also cursed everyone who opposed him; bringing wolves with him, moving mountains, turning cities into lakes and guiding clouds. All this is certainly much different than his real life and even some myths that are related to him.All this is certainly much different than his real life and even some myths that are related to him.

However, the Witch's religion survived in these regions of Serbia, but in a slightly different form. For example, if we look at Southern Serbia we will see that, among women, the most respected is Saint Petka-Paraskeva, Saint Evdhokia or Mother of God-Maria, although less than with the catholic population in other parts of the Balkan region. Saint Petka takes the role of Great Mother. That is clearly shown in many rituals performed in her honor, and those rituals are different to other Christian ones. Let us just say that many calling for help with barren women and infertility, but also for all other diseases, are sending their prayers to her. Witches from other parts of Serbia, Montenegro and Herzegovina may not be as famous for controlling spirits, but they are known as very good healers, gatherers of herbs, fortune tellers and the ones who protect the village from storms and hail. In Serbia, but also in all of the Balkans, there is a belief that demon creatures bring storm clouds and that craftsmen and craftswomen rush to fight against them so that these creatures don't destroy crops.

Let us pause a moment to explain what a Witch is, and what makes them different from any fortune-teller, sorcerer or conjurer. As we said before, in the Balkan territory several different names exist for people, male or female, who perform magic. When we speak about women, we can say that there people that exist among them that are simply practicing Serbian or Balkan Traditional Witchcraft, but they have names like Sorceress, Fortune-teller, Clairvoyant, etc. In contrast to them, Witches use ritual tools like sticks, the broom and cauldron. They leave their bodies through trance or, as mentioned earlier, by applying some kind of ointment for flying. They use spirits of nature or other supernatural entities, communicate with deities, most often with some aspect of the Goddess and, more important, they pass through initiations. These few parameters are necessary to separate them from fortune-tellers and other persons who practice fortune telling, alternative medicine, magic, and similar things. Let us clarify the question "What is a Balkan Witch?" with a definition:

"By Witch we mean a woman who has gone through the initiation process by birth, by family inheritance or by intervention of "higher forces", although often several of these factors come together, imbuing the woman with supernatural capabilities, such as voluntary entry into a state of trance, communicating with incorporeal creatures, clairvoyance, healing, etc. All Witches use a similar method of operation, and the rituals have an almost identical structure. They use similar tools and the differences among them are only cultural in nature. This is superficial and noticeable only on an empirical level. Group work isn't compulsory, although in some areas Witches gather as agreed for the goal of joint ritual practice.

To be more precise, let's just say that a sorceress is a woman who has magical capabilities acquired by learning from some other sorceress and she uses that knowledge in accordance with her needs, and with the needs of the environment if she is affirmed as a sorceress, using her techniques which don't contain any kind of ritual trance. She could imitate a Witch, literally using the Witch's tools such as a stick or magical knife and she can try to communicate with supernatural beings, but if she did not pass through the initiation, she does not the abilities for that, and she could never be considered a Witch. She is more like a person who performs folk magic.

When we speak of Goddess belief in the rest of the Serbian areas, such as Montenegro and Herzegovina, it survived, albeit to a somewhat lesser extent, without merging with Saint Petka or Saint Evdhokia, as in the Christian religion. So here, we can meet the Goddess in her original shape, as a Goddess of fertility and protector of nature. To be more precise, she is encountered in Her bright aspect as the Forest Mother, or in Her dark aspect, as in the **chthonic** aspect as Baba or Baba Yaga. In Russia, Baba Yaga is considered the queen of all Witches and she is seen as riding a boar or riding a sphere, while around her the other Witches ride on brooms. However, she is much different than our Baba as we will see that later in this book, although that does not have to mean anything because she may have just been demonized.

The original names of the Great Mother, Forest Mother, or Baba in Serbia and other areas, are not preserved, as scientists assume, out of fear and respect for these powerful and supernatural beings. We will, however, publish some of those names in this book. The Horned God had much less luck because He was identified as the Christian Devil. We can conclude that this situation was more or less based on people's relationship with him. People say that the Devil isn't as black as he appears, and that he helps people. He may also require a candle to be lighted for him, because when Good doesn't help (in the Christian way) then you should turn to him. According to the way that people call him, (He is Daba, or Lame Daba, although today we know based on the work of academician Alexander Loma, that Lame Daba is the name of the

37

great water spirit), he is indeed Dabog among the Serbs and he is a well known master of underworld. Later in the book there will be more information about supernatural creatures and some different conclusions will be presented.

You probably noticed that until now male Witches are rarely mentioned. According to ethnologists, facts about them were not preserved except for the term itself. Judging by current practice, the reason is very clear. There were always fewer male Witches than female Witches and those men who were, kept it to themselves. You could conclude from my earlier presentation that male Witches existed in the territory of eastern Serbia, although in lesser numbers than the females, and the data for that still exists. However, in other parts of Serbia, Montenegro and Herzegovina, this term simply disappears, as does the meaning of what a male Witch actually is. If we took the same parameters that we applied earlier to clearly determine what a "Witch" is, we will see that this situation is favorable to us.

Then we could clearly see that certain people existed who were characterized by supernatural capabilities and who had certain skills and knowledge. Here we talk about the Dragon People or Wind People, or whatever they were called in the area from which they originate. What earlier discoveries have been collected, synthesized, and published by the famous Serbian ethnologist Slobodan Zecevic, in the book "Mythical Creatures in Serbian Tradition" in Belgrade 1981. Here is what he says:

"In Serbian tradition is a widespread belief that people exist who can protect their region from bad weather, and that they can drive away the evil forces which cause it. The essence of this belief is that when someone felt that bad weather was coming, that man would withdraw himself somewhere on the side and fell into a sleep in the place where the natural disaster found him. His soul would leave his body to fight with the dragon or other leader of that natural disaster. After he chases away the troubles, the man wakes up and become conscious, sweaty and tired from the struggle. During his sleep (trance), his companions protected him by waving some kind of blade over the sleepy body, because they did not want to let some evil spirit get inside of the body. Because they believed that the "*Vetrovnjak*" (dragon man) could provide protection from disasters, the people like to have him in their midst."

People with these capabilities in Western Serbia were called *vetrovnjaci* and in Eastern parts were called Dragon Men. In the Dinaric areas of Bosnia and Herzegovina, Montenegro and Sandzak, they were called *zduhaci* or *stuhe*".

Zecevic cited more examples of people believed to be dragons. A man called Zivko, a shepherd from Sljivovice village, (who lived over a hundred years) who just before a storm would fall into a trance and go away to struggle with the black bird that was leading the clouds. After the struggle he would rest, but he never told anyone what was going on during the struggle. One man from Razane village was to lead the clouds to exactly over the field of a man with whom he had a dispute. An interesting example is one man from Bogujevac village who always carried a knife that he used to stick right over his head whenever he left his body. One time, while he was in the army, he did not have his knife with him and the storm had already begun. He laid down, got out of his body, and never came back again. From this example, we can conclude that blade was not only to prevent a spirit from possessing the body, but was used in the struggle too, so that the *vetrovnjak* would not be injured. There is a belief that the souls of both Witches and some dragon people take the form of some animal, especially a bull, after leaving the body.

Luka Grdjic-Bjelokosic provided some very interesting facts from Herzegovina. He states the belief that if the *zduhac's* body turns over during the trance, his spirit could not find it again, because

39

the soul leaves the body through the mouth, and as a result the man would die. The same goes for the Witches. He also mentions that the most important weapon for them is a broom from the threshing floor, and if they lose it in the struggle, or someone takes it from them, they will lose crops in their area, or die. They also have a rod of Scotch Pine that was slightly burned on the both ends or was tapered like a spindle.

In the territories of Croatia, Slavonia, Istra and Slovenia, especially on the coast, people called them *Kresnici* or *Krsnici*. People believe that they got their capabilities at birth (chosen by higher powers) and that they have ability to go into a trance, while asleep or awake. In these moments, their spirit goes out through the mouth in the shape of black fly or something similar. Their main enemies were probably werewolves, who fought in the air or at cross-roads. People also believed that they flew over the sea and participated in the struggle in Venice over Saint Mark Square. During these struggles, they could change their appearance and take the shape of one of the animals. Of the highest importance were bulls, male goats, and horses. In the struggles, they mostly used their wooden rods, but animal horns and other items were also used. The same was also believed to be true for Albanian Stuves, Italian Benadante and Malandante, the evil versions of Benadant.

Kazimirovic published more information about these people in his book. He states that all Dragon People were clairvoyant and subsequently, were very good prophets. In Serbian history we find famous examples, such as Mato Glusac and Milos Tarabic.

Mato Glusac (1774-1870) was born in Korita, Herzegovina. People say that he was a tall, thin man with shaggy black hair and large moustache. It is known that he always carried a little pocketknife with him and engraved symbols and unknown letters with it on every maple tree that he could find. He also carried a cross-shaped stick made from the yew tree. He had a little bag where he kept all the necessary things to light a fire, as well as wax, incense, cotton, icons, medicinal herbs and other trinkets. He wore the clothes of a beggar, lived alone, and was always wandering. Everybody loved him and respected him; even the Turks, who occupied that area, during his time. His predictions and feats of healing were well known throughout the region. People used to say that he had the ability to disappear physically, whenever he wanted to. They also said that he healed mentally disturbed people by communicating with the Master of the spirits, that he was in a trance for two days to pick some kind of herb from the bottom of the Black sea to heal a man, and similar stories. Many stories about his life and work were collected, but we will not repeat them here, because they would be beyond the scope of this book.

Nowadays, Milos Tarabic (1809-1854) and his nephew Mitar Tarabic (1829-1899) are remembered as the greatest prophets in Serbia and the most well known of the Dragon Men. It is no exaggeration to say that almost every household in Serbia has at least one copy of the book "Kreman's Prophecy". It was created when Zarije, their friend and priest, wrote down the prophecies of Milos and Mitar. It is very interesting that Milos' son did not have any supernatural capabilities. It is said that Milos was the main prophet, although the two simultaneously predicted almost identical occurrences.

After the death of Milos, Mitar continued the work, although according to Mitar, the information came from his late uncle, who often appeared to him while he was awake. They were not on good terms with the Royal Family because they predicted the end of their reign. Let us just say that Milos predicted that world will use paper money and currency that shines like fish scales. He also predicted the existence of armored tanks with weapons and various other things. It is said that the local people died of laughter at hearing such stupidity. However, today's Kreman Prophecies are used for political purposes, because their influence on the spirit of the people is well known. I believe that the prophecies were

41

"edited" several times, based on the political situation of any given time, so it is almost impossible to determine what is true and in keeping with the original version.

Later ethnological studies show that the main traits of this group of people were not only leaving their bodies, but also healing, either using medicinal herbs or by magical means. They practice folk medicine to remove negative magic from the people who came under its influence, and they defended their community from different types of demons and other supernatural creatures. From stories about some of them, we can conclude that they were in close contact with some of those supernatural creatures and cooperated with some of them. They were said to be stronger and more intelligent, as well as happier, than normal people.

It is very difficult to verify their connection with ancient deities. People believed that they were chosen by higher forces, but the forces are not specified; a Dragon Man could be identified from the moment of his birth. A baby who was born in placenta, or with some kind of mark such lock of hair on the shoulders or hands, or a tail would be expected to become a Dragon Man. The same is said of Witches, with the exception of the lock of hair. Conversely, Luka Grdjic-Bjelokosic said that in Popovo Polje he met the men who told him that someone could become a *stuha* if they perform an appropriate ritual. I quote:

"When someone wants to became a *stuha* he must not wash himself for forty days and he must not to pray to God. After forty days, he must go to some clearing, make a circle around himself and sit down. After some time the Devil would show up and would ask him if the man wants to join his army and into what shape he wants to be transformed. He agreed, the Devil then made the transformation, and that's how he became a *stuha*".

We do not know whether this, extremely simplified ritual, should be taken seriously but it is possible that this is remnant from some more detailed ritual from earlier times. If we look at it closely and compare it with the things that we already know, the Devil could very easily became a horned God, the God of the Underworld who is identified with the Devil by the influence of Christianity. Then we have a male Witch in a magical circle who was initiated by a horned deity giving him an animal astral shape that he requests. It is a very well known fact that during trance some shamans assume the animal shape of their spirit protector, which they have from the birth or get him from some higher forces. Although Dragon Men were very popular among the people, the church ignored their existence. Maybe the reason for this is the strong patriarchal community that was much more mild with men that with women. It was said that a *zduhac* who died would became a werewolf or vampire, and if he did not want that, the only thing he had to do was to confess to a priest before his death.

From all of this it is very clear that role of the male Witch in Serbian tradition is that of the Dragon Men. They, like the Witch, can enter a trance state and leave body to perform various tasks. Their tools are the magical knife, the broom from the threshing floor, the rod, and similar items. Both perform healing with herbs or magic, communicate with supernatural creatures, and foretell the future. Of course there are some differences but they are most likely classified by polarity, in the magical sense, than anything else.

INITIATION

Anthropologist Van Gennep first marked initiation as a phenomenon in the year 1909. The word initiation itself originates from the Latin word "initiatio" which means introduce, lead, or canonize. Until modern times, this phenomenon was thoroughly studied and its model was applied in the translation of many social activities such as getting married, coming of age, birth, death, etc. Another name for the initiation is the rite of passage. Among primitive people the initiations marked specific development phases in the life of the individual, from birth until death. The marking of crucial life stages exists in modern culture as well. To primitive people every initiation has another facet, a parallel segment that the initiate gets during the initiation. In most cases, this was the acknowledgement of his part in the community, his place in universe, the myths of his tribe were revealed to him, and he was introduced into the Mysteries. In other words, the secrets of the tribe and life that he did already know were revealed to him.

Each initiation in primitive societies consisted of three phases. During the first stage, the initiate withdraws from the community for a specified time, which is spent in a way customary to the community. The second stage follows, which lasts for an unspecified period of time, and after that the ritual begins, and in most cases the initiate would pass through a ritual death, purification and rebirth, in this case a rebirth into a completely new person. That new person could be someone who has just come into the adult world (puberty initiations), or an adult who becomes a shaman, a sorcerer, or who could be an individual to whom the tribal Mysteries are revealed (Mystery initiations). The third phase marked a return to community and acknowledgement of the "newborn" by the community of his new status.

Initiation does always contain a ritual death. It could represent a ritual of passing on certain knowledge that reveals and bestows certain secrets, Mysteries, or some secret skill. With this act, the initiant transfers from one phase to another by performing its special spirit "upgrade". They will not be born here as totally new person, but one who has expanded their awareness, skills and knowledge. Still, they are not the same as before, despite the fact that they did not go through a ritual death. Once again, this person has new status that is accepted by the social community, or at least the small group of people who have travelled that path.

Almost all world religions, sects, cults, occult groups (public, secret and semi-secret), lodges, have some sort of initiation. Some are rites which the individual must go through only once in their life, while other initiations must be performed several times and mark a graduation of the initiate. Let us explain this.

In the case of shamans, only one initiation exists, through which an intitiant must pass if they want to become shamen. After that, remain a shamen for the rest of their lives. The situation is the same in Christianity, where a person must go through christening once, becomes a Christian, and there is no need to go through it again.

In contrast to these examples, some religious or magical organizations use more initiatations in their practice, depending on how many stages their system contains. That means that if there are ten stages, the individual will pass through all ten stages of initiation. This doesn't mean that the same initiation will be performed ten times. Rather, according to the level of knowledge, readiness or "time served", the initiate is inducted to a higher level where new secrets and skills will be revealed to them, because now they are prepared to take them, use them or it is simply that the time for it has come. Such a system represents the gradual spiritual progression that we just spoke of.

The same situation can be found in both modern and ancient Witchcraft. Most Wiccan covens use three rites and most Traditional covens use one rite of initiation. The one exception would be French Witchcraft, which contains four steps of initiation. Usually, if anyone wants to devote themselves to Witchcraft and to become a member of a coven, they must wait for at least a year before initiation into the first degree. During that time the rest of the coven members observe them, and then they decide whether that person is suitable to be initiated into their coven, that is, whether they fulfill the necessary criteria. Not to be too mysterious, let us just say that during that period, the members are looking for several things.

First, whether the candidate is mentally sound; second, whether they have any problems, such as a criminal background; and the third thing is to see if their desire is only temporary, or if their sincere intention is to dedicate their life to the practice of Witchcraft. Only then is the actual training given which will provide what is needed for the first stage of initiation. The candidate must pass through the last part of this period on their own. Modern Witchcraft took this system of introducing a candidate to the Mystery from other western magical lodges.

This period is called the "temptation" period and the person who must go through it is the "neophyte", or novice. The first degree of initiation is dedicated to the Goddess, and the initiant is introduced into the Mysteries of Goddess.

This stage represents the life; that is, accepting the holy secret of the Goddess, the secrets of making life, and creation in general. The waiting period between the first and second stage, depending on the coven, must be a period of one to three years.

The second degree usually represents death, that is introduction to the Mysteries of the God, and this is the period when the initiate goes through the ritual death that we previously mentioned. It is then they take mystery of death and resurrection, the Sun that sets and rises again.

After the appropriate period, if the individual is ready, the third stage of initiation is performed, the so called "Great Rite", which represents the essence of the Witch's Mystery. This rite is sex magic, and represents the unification of the Horned God and the Goddess. In most cases, this is the Wiccan model of initiation, and the Traditional Witches all over the world are against it. In Great Britain, for example, according to Michael Howard (the editor of "The Cauldron" magazine and author of esoteric literature), local Traditional Witches have just one initiation, and their whole system is very different from the Wiccan one. There will be more about World Traditional Witchcraft in my next book.

In Serbia and the Balkan region in general, there has probably never been any organized groups where these types of initiations were performed. Witches gathered, physically and astrally, on certain holidays. They became Witches not by their own will, but because they were selected by "higher forces". The same goes for the Craftsmen of Traditional Witchcraft. So that we understand, anyone who had the desire could learn magical acts and perform them, but that person was never considered to be a real Witch, but a magic user – a fortune teller, sorcerer, or something similar. This means that the person did not have all the necessary elements that would make them a Witch.

According to tradition, a person becomes a male or female Witch by being born in their placenta, or if their body has certain anomalies, like a tail or a lock of hair. But early and recent investigations have shown that this is not strictly true. Male and female Witches *were* going through various type of initiation, but mainly unwillingly because they were led by so-called "higher forces", or within their families, the process of learning and initiation was performed by some older relative who already belonged to the order. However, even then they waited for a sign from the "higher power", and it is believed that without this the training would give poor results.

On the other hand, sometimes a rite of initiation existed on a physical level, a story from Hercegovina that Luka Grdjic-Bjelokosic cited tells us, and that story we related in its entirety in the previous chapter, so there is no need repeat it here. The story that was published in the Herald of the National Museum in 1890, on page 416, is also very interesting. P. Kemp mentioned this story in the book "Balkan Cults" that was published in 2000 in Belgrade. It speaks about a man who was taken into a mountain by faerie folk. They healed his fever and initiated him into their coven. This story starts abruptly, without any introduction, and it talks about the man who was taken away one night - by twelve Witches and a thirteenth man with a yellow beard - to a mountain that "reaches the clouds", where Witches and spirits were gathering. They gathered greeted him, as if he was a fairy king, with the following words:

"You are precious to us, and useful to people. You will be a physician and a helper of man".

They taught him how to use medicinal herbs to prepare medicines, but they demanded from him that he never charge more than one coin (Of small denomination) for his services. The following night he was introduced to another group of spirits that gave him a rod made from a willow tree, teaching him how to use it if he runs out of medicinal herbs. All that he had to do was to take some ashes from his family hearth, stand in front of it and touch himself three times. The fairies would arrive and bring him all he needed. In the process they taught him to say this prayer to Saint Antun:

"Anto santo velepanto. Anto sigo preporigo. Ante mange cerepange. Anto silo soparilo. Anto tale

dividale. Anto lemi natilemi. Anto pana dilovana. Anto saki karasaki. Anto vanem ustiamem."

(Translators note: To my knowledge this is an antiquated form of the Serbo-Croatian tongue.)

Of course, they taught him many other things. On the third night the spirits separated themselves into two groups, undressed a child they brought with them and made him pass between their lines three times while they whipped him with a bough from a willow tree to drive out a fever from him. When the healing was over the initiate received a small stick that he used to dismiss the meeting. He swung the stick toward the four corners of the world, and the Witches and fairies dispersed all over the world to do damage to people that the initiate would then have to fix. After this, he spent the following three years in his bed, and although he was completely healthy he did not eat or drink any normal food or drink. Instead he consumed only what the spirits brought him by night.

This story is very old through the centuries, various additions were probably made, because it was passed on as an oral tradition. Over time, storytellers would forget to mention something, or would add something else. It is very clear that Witches were confused with the fairies that are a very common phenomenon in the Balkans. As we said before, Witches were also confused with various types of incorporeal demons. The initiate was then taught how to say a prayer to Saint Anton. The Christian Saint is not a logical addition, but was added later under the influence of Christianity. Those "Christian" prayers exist even today in Serbian Traditional Witchcraft. But if we carefully examine the story from the start and perform a deeper analysis, then compare it with the things that we already know, we will see that within it may hide the remnants of the former ritual of initiation for Traditional Witchcraft.

First, the initiate goes away to the mountain with an escort consisting of twelve Witches and one man with a yellow beard. We assume that the mountain hid some holy place where the initiations were performed. For example, it was a custom of the Serbs and other Balkan people that idols of deities must be placed at the top of the mountains or hills. Certain "sacred places" existed, and even holy mountains (Miroč, Romanija, Mosor, Perun, Radan, etc). From the number of Witches and the man we can assume that it was some kind of coven. If we assume that the yellow beard is Grand Magister then there were thirteen of them, and that is the most used number with covens.

There is a tradition in the west that every coven has twelve women, and one man whose main task is to take over the role of the horned God. This is not mandatory, but it is strongly encouraged that all covens have the same type of congregation. Put simply, the women represent the energy of the Goddess, and the man that of the God. However, in most existing Western Covens, the situation is considerably different from this ideal; there is no consideration to the number of people in a Coven, and some are exclusively male, while others are exclusively female.

Further, we can see that the chosen one receives initiation in three days in various ways, and then he is trained to complete various tasks. One of them is to invoke a spirit of nature who will supply him with needed items. From this, we can conclude that initiation lasts for three days and that after the third day he was given the honor to dismiss the meeting by waving his stick at "all corners of the world". It is well known that a great number of traditions exist that end such rituals, or dismiss the elemental spirits that were invoked during the ritual. Another interesting thing follows. After the third night, the initiate is healthy, but he lies down in bed and stays there for the following three years. He does not eat or drink anything but what the spirits bring him. This staying in bed can be recognized as a metaphor or some kind of coded message, if we remember that in some traditions the next stage of initiation of the individual occurs after a three year wait. The part about the food could simply mark the start of a new diet that is given to the initiate after the initiation. Some of them become vegetarians. The part about charging for the services does not need to be commented on, because that is the case throughout the Balkans. It is said that health must be bought, but people should only pay what they are able. Because of this there is no set rate, everyone gives as much money as they are able or there is no charge at all, because everyone will bring something, if they can. This goes for the "folk doctors" too, who proceed in this manner in respect to the higher forces that gave them either power or knowledge.

Almost all folk traditions from central and western Serbia, Bosnia and Herzegovina and Montenegro describe identical ways of receiving initiation. Basically, after the "higher forces" choose a man to receive initiation, he starts to behave differently from the other members of the community. First of all, he isolates himself, avoiding people and going out at night to wander through the woods, mumbling incoherently and eventually he is afflicted by public attacks of hysteria. It is clear to everyone that the fairies have adopted him.

Then, one night, he receives an initiation from the fairy queen whose name is Forest Mother (one aspect of the Goddess) and is taught various things. There is a belief that each fairy is the master of some skill so some of them taught him about sorcery, some of them taught him about magical and medical herbs, even the language of plants and animals. Finally, they form a circle and, completely nude, dance *kolo* and sing. The name of this *kolo* is the "*vrzino kolo*". An almost identical example is recorded by P. Kemp in his book "Balkan Cults". The original name of this book is "Healing Rituals", which is very interesting. The book was written in 1935, and from that we can conclude that the perspective was closer to previously-held folk beliefs.

Everyone who is somewhat familiar with shamanic initiations will conclude that the first part of this story is almost identical to the people who prepare the shaman calling, from Siberia all the way to North America. However, the second part looks like a classic Witches gathering. This is not at all surprising, because the ancient Witchcraft in these areas came from shamanism, and accordingly it retains some of the main traits of shamanism. It is enough to mention "the institution" known as ritual trance that every male or female Witch must be able to achieve at any time of the day or night.

In contrast to these old stories from the territory of eastern Serbia, we have more recent testimonies that were noted by ethnologists Paun Es Durlic and Jasna Jojic Pavlovski, published that in previously mentioned book "Marvels of Vlach Magic".

Mrs. Ruza from Crnjak village, born in 1907, told Paun how she became what she is. One day during a storm, she was looking for shelter under a big Rowan tree. At that moment she saw a smartly dressed man, who set a table and chairs under the tree. Suddenly, as if from nowhere, a group of young girls, women and old women appeared. When they were all seated on the chairs, a woman with a tuft on her head showed up. She was demonstrating various magical techniques while the others were copied her. Grandma Ruza claims that from the first day they forced her to learn along with them. She remembers that her mother would often find her under the Rowan tree in some kind of trance. In contrast to Ruza, she did not see or feel anything, the only thing she did notice was that the grass was stamped down as if many people had been there. This continued for about three weeks, until she learned everything that she needed to. With this kind of trance, in Eastern Serbia among the Vlach people, they say that the person was adopted by "*sojmane*" – meaning adopted by spirits - while in other parts of the country, where the population is mainly Serbian, people say that fairies adopted them, as we described earlier.

As Ruza said, her family did not believe in this story until something similar happened to her stepfather. One day he was gathering hay and he was adopted by *"sojmane"*. Bearing in mind that he was against that, he resisted them for three full years. During that time, he became weak and fell into trance often. When he gave in once and accepted the call to practice magic, everything stopped.

We have similar testimonies from the south of Serbia in Leskovacka valley. An old woman told me that when she was a little girl she had the honor to meet a man dressed in "a dress suit". His main characteristics were a big black hat and mantle. From the conversation with some people we discovered out that among these people exists a strong belief that the God wears big a hat so he could hide his horns.

The woman with the tuft, the one that grandma Ruza was talking about, is the Forest Mother of course, and that is very clear so we will not explain that again. We suppose that the other people at this meeting under the service tree were initiates who came in from different places.

Jasna Jojic, in her book, describes a few more examples of initiations that are similar in essence, although they seem different at first glance. We have the example of Janko Durlja, who was initiated by a woman in Serbian folk dress, and he claims that the woman was Saint Petka. Then there is Desanka Peric, to whom three girls appeared in a very realistic dream, all with the same name – Maria - and they taught her and took her on various astral planes to learn their Craft and how to help people.

It is very interesting that the "gifts" they received after the first stage of initiation were knowledge and the ability to heal people and cattle, or simply clairvoyance and fortune-telling. The second stage is a part of esoteric Witchcraft and we will not talk about that in this book.

We have to admit, for a long time we thought that there was only the one method of initiation, but as it turns out, we met several people who went through various types of initiation. From our conversations, we discovered information that was more correct, and the probable reason for the mistaken belief that only one stage of initiation existed was simply that they had not been recorded in this area before. Frankly speaking, in this region there are several methods that coincide to a greater or lesser extent with the first one, but we cannot currently support the idea that they have any association with it.

The basic source of the erroneous belief derives from two things. The first one, which is the cause of everything, is the fact that Witches were mainly women from the villages who had never even heard word "initiation", let alone understand that they had passed through one. They were always aware of how it all began and how they became what they are, but all subsequent events are interpreted as an integral part of their lives. Consequently, they did not make the distinction between the first initiation, and what followed after.

The Second thing was that the ethnologists asked the wrong questions interviewed improperly, focusing on how one person became what they became, then focused on healing techniques, divination, spells, etc. This resulted in missing the chance to encourage an informant to divulge information that he did not know he possessed. To correct this error it is necessary to broaden the education of ethnologists, in particular about the field of Witchcraft and similar systems, both new and old, from all around the world but especially from those regions that are at the same developmental level as our rural regions. Only then would it be possible for an ethnologist to prepare the right questions, in a timely manner, in order to get better and more complete answers.

The justification for this attitude can be seen the example of the correspondence that we had with one young girl, M, from Belgrade, who is of Vlajna origin and who fulfills all the necessary parameters to become a Witch. From what I gather, she received her initiation from her late grandmother, who was one of the greatest Witches in eastern Serbia in her time. Her grandmother's favorite practices were prophecy and finding thieves. Her last predictions were concerning her daughter, who had problems with pregnancy. This time when she got pregnant, the grandmother said, everything would be all right and that she would have a daughter. When she found out that she did indeed get a granddaughter, the grandmother died. If you think that the granddaughter did not get to meet her grandmother, you would be mistaken. The first nocturnal visits came when M. was seven years old. The intensity of those visits increased and the daughter passed through an initiation and was taught to do various things.

The one surprising thing at the very beginning of our correspondence was the knowledge that M was not aware that she had passed through the initiation. After we explained what initiation is, specifically concerning Balkan Witchcraft, we received the following answer. Part of that answer we give in its original form:

"... I have never thought of that act as an initiation, although now, when I think about that, it could have been some kind of initiation (in fact, it could be it in its literal meaning). The initiations that I went through consisted of some kind of test. It was never a literal test, but there was always a task set before me that I needed to complete. There were three of these incidents, and all of them were accompanied with some kind of reward and a continuation of grandma's chanting of unclear contents. When I mastered one thing, they taught me another. Each new phase brought completely new things to learn... Each time I passed through another phase, grandma let me ask a single question in addition to the things that were being taught to me."

We think that everything was so clear that no special comments or translations were necessary. It is obvious that this is a multi-stage system of initiation whose specific and original shape is in the spirit of Balkan Witchcraft.

As we can see from the above, all these initiations have some common traits. The first one is that people, whether they want it or not, are chosen by "higher forces" that initiate them. The second common trait is manner in which the initiation is conducted. Each person received initiation in dreams or through trance. When received in trance, the person is rarely aware of the trance, and then claims that they were physically in some other place, with certain "persons". Testimonials of others present say that the person seemed to be in the throes of an epileptic seizure, and accordingly we can conclude that this was some kind of "shamanic" trance, an out-of-body experience.

After research related to the first method of initiation, or dream initiation, I have to conclude that they were not dreams, but in fact, astral projections. They are much more difficult to confirm when the out-of body experience comes from a state of sleep. Often, after returning into the body, the person continues to dream, so when they wake up they have a feeling that they had strange, intense dreams throughout the night. This is very easy to understand if we know that those are mainly people from the village who do not know anything about incorporeal experiences. Because of this, we have a tendency to think that only one type of initiation exists, the initiation through trance. However, we will leave room for this possibility.

The third important thing related to initiations in the Balkans is that there is no tradition of one person initiating another, in other words, living people. All initiations were received from supernatural creatures, or at least incorporeal creatures of human origin. In most cases, these were spirits or fairies. If we carefully examine these stories, we will notice that the initiation is led by a supernatural being – their leader. This is the Horned God, Fairy Queen, Forest Mother, Samovila, Muma Padura, Saint Petka or Saint Evdhokia. Those are all known variations of the Great Mother; in some areas, we can see the presence of the Horned God, to a lesser extent - mostly in South Serbia, Montenegro, and Herzegovina. Beside this, the "spiritual leaders" could be deceased persons as well, who were male or female Witches when they were alive.

Although ethnologists like Bandic were not aware of it, our research shows that a pattern of hereditary initiations received from "higher forces" exists. This means that newly initiated people in a family had at least one other family member who had passed through the same initiation. It was most often her grandmother, sister, aunt, etc. It is particularly interesting that we know many people that went through these things, and afterwards they found out that they were not alone, and that similar things had happened to their grandmothers, great aunt, their aunt or mother, even some male family members. Accordingly, Balkan Traditional Witchcraft could be included in the group of Family Witchcraft, better known by the name "Hereditary Witchcraft". It should be said that in the Balkans, these currents are probably passed on by the maternal line, and that the first event usually happens around the age of puberty. This is logical considering that the viewpoint of modern parapsychology is that spontaneous astral projection or OOBE (Out Of Body Experience) can happen at that level of maturity.

There is one more interesting thing concerning Balkan traditional initiations. This is the fact that there is very little specificity, that no two initiations are the same. The basic structure is satisfied without much deviation, but they appear different. This could show us that their appearance is the product of individual or collective unconsciousness which shapes their visual form, influenced by the cultural environment of the people involved. Let us explain that. We experience our world that surrounds us through our five senses. When we need to observe subtle things, our unconsciousness - linked with the collective unconsciousness - helps us through our ego, shaping the "information" into a familiar form. For example, if we meet an elemental (not elementary), for example, the element of Earth, we cannot see it physically because it exists in a range of frequencies above the ones we inhabit, and so it has no physical characteristic.

Our mind, based on available information, creates an appropriate image and enables us to see it as gnome. That is the reason why two people who see the same elemental will give a different description of hat, boots, or beard but in the essence both will see a gnome. The situation is the same with initiations. In essence, the initiations mark the opening of new energetic channels for the initiates, raising their whole being to the next stage and providing them the ability to increase their level of receiving and translating energetic frequencies, absorbing them like an antenna. We could jokingly say that they are changing a radio station that they listened to up until that time, but to listen to the new channel they will need stronger "headphones" in the form of a stronger energetic body, and a new radio –the initiation - while the layout of the apparatus is provided by the collective unconscious.

Because all of this, we think that these initiations of ancient Witchcraft are authentic. Whether it is the collective unconsciousness, astral records, or real supernatural forces that actually perform the initiation, it is difficult to say. One thing is certain, and that is the fact that these skills have not been forgotten or lost. The source of this information will always find its way back into our reality. Today's education will give us a new translation of those contents, and make possible for, if not for all mankind, at least for individuals, to follow the path of spiritual evolution more safely.

Self-Initiation or Initiation

When we observe this nonspecific form of being initiated, the question arises how a person can be initiated into this system, based on their own wishes, not by being chosen by so-called "higher forces". Based on what other authors say, we can make the following conclusions.

There are two ways to obtain initiation, and we will talk about them later in the book, but before we can do that, we must mention some basic conditions that a person must fulfill if they want to be initiated.

Bearing in mind the fact that in this system there is only the astral form of initiation, the first and most basic condition that a person must satisfy is to possess the ability to leave their body at will. Without that, it is not possible to carry out the ritual of transition. We will discuss mastery of this ability later in this book.

The second important thing is that a person must prepare their body for accepting the initiation. By this, we mean mental and energetic preparation.

Mental preparation is carried out in by cleansing the mind of complexities, frustrations, insecurities, etc. This is done with ritual, or with the help of hypnosis, depending on the individual's desires. The whole the process is reminiscent of shamanic treatment of sick people, which modern psychoanalysts and psychiatrists are beginning to use.

The ritual form in itself involves, on a surface level, raising "demons" from the unconscious to the conscious part of the personality, complexes, frustrations, phobias, etc., and expelling them from the patient with the help of various herbs, energetically treated water and other things, depending on what is needed. The folk model used to consist of something like withdrawing from society, examining one's past deeds, and abandoning their old way of life.

Under the term "energetic preparation" we mean the strengthening of the energetic body of the individual, widening of the acupuncture channels, breaking through the barriers and the balancing of energetic centers.

Long ago in traditional Witchcraft, people did not know these terms, but in spite of that, some sort of energetic preparation existed. This preparation did not consist of complicated eastern-style exercises, but it rather the withdrawing of the person from public life, and it included going out into nature to a place where underground or above-ground energies were very potent. A long stay at these places was often enough. The energy emanated in great amounts, cleaned corporeal channels and stimulated the energy centers of the body. This is a something like an "Energy shower". In any case, this procedure represents some sort of energetic charging. Some may ask, "Why all this is necessary?". Imagine that you want to take a trip and drive a few thousand miles. To ensure that your car runs as it should without incident, you might have to change the oil or replace some part or another, and finally you must fill up with gas. The same thing goes for the body. It is important to mention that only a physically and mentally sound person should attempt an initiation..

Beside all this, it is necessary to develop the knowledge of that person, to instill in them the things that are expected of them, and to explain their purpose to them. It is also very good give them a good background in mythology and the occult..

Further, it is necessary that person has self-control, meaning that they are capable of raising the level of their concentration and visualization, because without this, many things are impossible. It is necessary to spend more time in nature and to feel and absorb the energies native to the forest. This may seem unnecessary, but it is still important. Ask a person who spent the night in the woods how their experience was, and how it felt. You can also ask a mountaineer how he feels when he climbs to the summit of the mountain, and it will be hard for him to find words to describe it.

In the end, a person must decide if this is what they sincerely want, based on their personal beliefs and lifestyle, or they simply want the power for a short time, whatever that power might be. If the answer is the second choice, I guarantee that "higher forces" will not allow initiation because they are all-knowing and they are constantly testing humanity. This can be seen in many interviews that we had with the people who went through the "folk" initiation.

The whole process usually lasts between several months and a year, depending on the person that is preparing for the initiation. Most often the hardest part is learning to enter into a trance voluntarily, and it takes the most time. This happens with those who want to initiate themselves. When the "higher forces" choose the person, ritual trance is dependent on the will of said forces, and thus represents the smallest problem.

After all that explanation, we think it is the time to share the process of initiation. This can be performed in one of two ways. The first one is for someone who is already initiated to lead you through the initiation, and the second is to start this process by yourself and to provoke the "higher forces" to initiate you. That would be a form of self-initiation. In first case, the initiated person does not perform the initiation but has the role of "protector"; that is, to inspire confidence and tranquility while the process is taking its' course. We are familiar with a previously mentioned case when a grandmother took her granddaughter through initiation.

What if you do not know anyone who could take you through the initiation process? In that case, the best thing is to resort to a type of self-initiation. A person who wants to do that must first complete all the preparations that we mentioned before, at a bare minimum to spend time in self-reflection, preparing the body's energies and learning to leave the physical body. This can be accomplished through dreams, especially lucid dreams. If you try to do it without these preparations, this attempt is bound to fail.

After preparation, a much harder task awaits, one that may be impossible for some; that is getting into contact with the "higher forces" and convincing them to initiate you. This may sound unlikely, but there are many examples that say differently. In the Balkans, there are people that were initiated just because they spent the night in certain places. Let's take a closer look at this.

It does not matter what part of the world you are in, your ancestors, or local natives, surely knew some "holy places". Many stories and legends are connected to those places. All these places are dedicated to supernatural creatures or deities. It is up to you to find out where they are, and how to make contact with the creatures or deities there. This means that you have to leave the comfort of your apartment or house and go out. Of course, you need to check out all places that could connected to the Goddess, Horned God, forest or mountain creatures, or water masters. Find out about special dates and be at the site then, and participate in sacred celebrations. Finally, go back to that place and try to get a feel for it. Close your eyes, empty your mind and try to communicate, radiating your thoughts and emotions all around you. You need to think of an appropriate phrase that rhymes and that can be repeated endlessly. For example:

> **"Great (Spirit or being, male or female)... manifest in front of me,**
> **Just as I appear myself before thee".**

Of course, we must repeat this to ourselves with closed eyes, keeping our minds clear of any other thoughts. If you want, you could do a ritual that will give you even more chances to success. In the end, you should try to spend the night on that place. Pay attention to your dreams, and who comes to you in them. If you are not successful for the first time, that does not mean anything, do it again. You must believe you will be successful but it will take time. When you make the connection, all you need to do is to surrender yourself, and you will be guided, calmed with notion that you have mentors that few others have.

With this we close the theme of initiation, and in the following chapter we will try to explain ritual trance and to give precise advice on how to get in and out of trance with no danger to your physical and mental health.

RITUAL TRANCE

It is time that we say something more about ritual trance, the basic ability of ancient Witches. According to the definition of eminent world anthropologist Eliade, trance represents an archaic technique of ecstasy. Almost undoubtedly, the ritual trance of the ancient Witch developed identically but independently from everywhere else in the world, so the question is, "How did it get to the Balkans?". The answer is extremely simple, if we accept that one of the first forms of religion was shamanism and that it once existed everywhere that people lived.

From this, we can conclude that the identical situation existed in Europe in ancient times. In its earlier stage, shamanism knew only the spirits of nature, but not the Gods. At some point in time when the Great Mother and Horned God came to be revered, our ancestors left shamanism and built a foundation that became the basis of ancient Witchcraft. Because of this, we support the opinion that Witchcraft is a derivative of shamanism, not its surrogate as some people claim.

In the following centuries, as human religion was progressing, techniques of leaving the body were developing as well. The first techniques were different forms of the shamanic techniques, but later they developed and used various aids, such as Witch's ointment for flying, spell mantras, calling on spirits of nature, using ritual items, etc.

Getting into trance with the help of dancing - kolo – represented an improvement of the original shamanic entrance into a state of trance with banging of drums – *klampanje* - and frantic dances that lasted for hours. Beside dancing, shamans would get into a state of trance with the help of various herbs, but with great certainty we can say that Witches improved on this knowledge.

One crucial difference between shamans and Witches must be pointed out when discussing the use of herbs. Shamans often used herbs, though not in all cases of course, which provoked hallucinations that are very hard to control, and what's more important, in that way that did not take them anywhere, but simply made them hallucinate. Within shamanism, herbs were taken orally, by sniffing, or smoking. Some of the most popular herbs for this purpose were:

Ajahuska (Banisteriopsis (Caapi)), Kolorini (Erythryna Americana (Naked Coral Tree)), Muhara (Amanita muscaria (A mushroom)), Pejote (Lophophora williamsii(Peyote)), Gvatiljo (Iochroma fuchsiodes (Nightshade)) . . .

In contrast to shamans, Witches used few herbs that provoke hallucinations, and even when they were used they weren't taken separately, but in combination with other herbs among which at least one was used to prevent unwanted effects, like hallucinations or respiratory paralysis. We also could say that Witches rarely used herbs orally and, as far as we know in the territory of Serbia and neighboring countries, never. Witches ointment became legendary for flying, not only in Europe, but also in the USA. We think that the function of these ointments is well known to everyone who knows anything about Witchcraft. Their purpose was to help the Witch to leave their body, not to fly in the common sense of that word, as people used to believe. A lot of silliness was stated related to their recipes, from the nonsense that ointment was made from the fat of unbaptized children, or of the fetus of a Witch who has conceived with the Devil, or the skin that is left after circumcision, to the nonsense that these ointments consisted of some human organs or blood. The truth is completely different.

In the Balkans, the grease was mainly from the black pig, and in that fact that we can find hidden symbolism. We know that grandma *Yaga* rode a black pig, that the pig is a symbol of the underworld and there are some indications, by some ethnologists, that the pig was a Serbian animal totem.

Later on certain herbs were added to the grease with the goal of putting the Witch into a state of trance. In all analyzed ointments (analyses were performed in Europe and some recipes were saved) there was hemp (cannabis sativa) as the main ingredient. Other herbs were used too, but in small quantities, and among them were henbane (Hyoscyamus niger), aconite (Aconitum...), conium (Conium maculatum), poppy seeds (Papaver somniferum), rue (Ruta graveolens), thorn apple (Datura), and belladonna (Atropa beladona).

After that, herbs with symbolic functions were added, like the basil (Ocimum basilicum), rosemary (Rosmarinus officinalis), or the seeds of corn, barley, grain, or sunflower etc.

Beside all these things, the ointment sometimes contained some other ingredients of animal origin, like scrapings of deer or sheephorn, the wings of a bat, or the skin of a toad.

Of course, each Witch added something of their own, such as a hair, a nail, or their own blood (menstrual or from laceration, not from another person), etc.

This specially-prepared ointment was rarely used, only on special occasions. The Witch rubbed it on their naked body, especially under the armpits and inside the thighs. After that, they laid down by the hearth where it was warmest, which sped up the process of the absorption of the ointment into the bloodstream, and eventually they flew out astrally through the chimney. This flying out through the chimney is not a myth but a true description of movement. Balkan Witches deliberately used this direction for exiting because they believed that he chimney is the conduit towards the Ancestors and other supernatural creatures. That is why many houses that did not desire these kind of "guests" put thorn of hawthorn in their chimney, because people believed that all supernatural creatures, including Witches, are afraid of hawthorn.

We should mention that after the Witch applied ointment on themselves and lay down by the hearth, they started to picture the desired destination and repeat a mantra, such as "Not on thorn, not on bush, but on smart threshing floor", helping themselves to fall into a state of trance. This method is very good because it increases concentration, blocks unwanted thoughts, and facilitates the sensory deprivation that is necessary to get into the trance state.

All the herbs that were in the ointment have the goal of placing the Witch in a state of hypnotic sleep, to numb the body and muscles, and to leads to mild intoxication and relaxation, which causes instability of the astral body to allow them to leave their bodies by their own will by using visualization and concentration. In ancient times, before broadcast media (TV, radio, etc.) and widespread literacy, the elders would sit by the hearth, tell stories, and talk about legends, and imagination and visualization weren't a problem at all. Hallucinations or any other effects that would disrupt the Witch's reasoning and concentration were very undesirable. This was because all these ointments were carefully prepared with great knowledge of herbal lore.

Because of that, we advise that no one try to get out of their body with the help of the ointment that they make themselves. We found one site that had a recipe for a Witches ointment that facilitated flight, and we were stunned. It contained thirteen different plants, each more poisonous than the last; to say the least, the finished product would have killed a horse, not to mention a person. You must realize that the role of the ointment is only to help you relax, not to cause astral projection. If you do not have good concentration and visualization, nothing will help you. Some of these ointments from our region were subjected to chemical analysis in Zagreb, and that analysis showed that they mainly consisted of pig fat, hemp, and ashes, probably from the hearth. As far as we know, these analyses were made before the Second World War, when chemistry was not so advanced, and it is possible that something else would show up with today's technology. The data of anthropologist P. Kemp, who studied Witchcraft in the Balkans before World War II, supports these findings.

As much as we talk about this, our findings tell us that in the past, leaving the body in the Balkans with the help of flying ointment was rare.

Bearing in mind that "higher forces" chose male and female Witches and that they receive their knowledge by initiation or by birth, it was normal and expected that they acquire this ability at that time. Very rarely, they were initiated with the help of dancing "*kolo*" and falling into a trance. That was mainly in the territory of eastern Serbia, where collective celebrations were customary.

Ethnological investigations show that all those who use techniques for leaving their bodies, without exception, recognize two types of ritual trance. The first one represents the state in which a person is aware of things that happens around them, while the second type is a total trance, in which the person doesn't feel any contact with their body or environment. Both types are equally valuable and both states were used for performing similar tasks, without any difference.

The first type of trance could look like common fantasy for many people, but in practice it is not that way. Modern hypnosis gives us the best explanation for this. All hypnotists think that several levels of hypnotic trance exist, however, they do not agree on how many. Some say three, some say five, and other say up to nine. It's not really important, especially since there are no clear, specified boundaries of defining each level. The fact of the matter is that levels of hypnotic trance do exist. For example, let us say there are three levels, and that they are equivalent to brainwaves. According to this, the beta waves would mark the state of awareness; the alpha waves would mark relaxation and entering into first level of trance, a sort of reverie, and theta waves would be a deeper level of this "reverie". I don't think that they include the first type of the trance, because that is where a person doesn't imagine anything, and pictures come as in a dream, while the person is still aware. Finally, there are delta waves, which represent the deepest state of trance, equivalent to deep sleep, where a person is completely unaware of their surroundings. This leads us to the conclusion that this level could represent another type of trance of the ancient Witches.

To make things even clearer, we will cite the following example. Imagine that you wanted to get out of your body. You are comfortable and relaxed. If you want to "get out" , you must to begin with the process of visualization that will bring you out of the body. Let us say that you imagine that you are flying through the clouds. If you are successful and you keep your concentration, after few minutes you will enter into the alpha state. You will feel very pleasant, but you are still aware of the environment and your body. If you continue with this visualization undisturbed, after ten or fifteen minutes you will enter the theta state, and you will notice that you feel less of your environment. Virtually everyone reaches this level. However, if you can still hold your concentration, in thirty or forty minutes your brainwaves change and you will fall into the delta state.

Now you are literally flying through the clouds and you are aware that your body is far away. It means that the trance started at the very beginning stage, and the only thing that has changed is your awareness of space and your physical body. It means that your senses were what needed to be "excluded". That is why you should not make quantitative differences between the first and the second type of trance with ancient Witches, because they themselves did not differentiate.

It is not difficult to achieve the trance, but seeing the "big picture" is. Our mind, in any level of trance, plays with us and allows our ego to interfere. Since we are in a dream-like state, we have the same possibilities as in a dream, so we can change the given "reality" and project pictures of our own. We see what we want to see. To avoid this we need to be impartial, and our mind needs to be completely focused, allowing no other thoughts as we travel toward our destination. That can be very difficult but you must realize, that like any kind of sports discipline, you must practice every day to realize your greatest potential.

Many of you who want to know more about this subject can find a large number of books by different authors, with widely differing opinions. This should not be surprising, as it is very hard to determine the absolute truth about this phenomenon. The first thing that causes differing opinions is a matter of terminology. Some call it by its ancient occult name, "astral projection", and some others use the anthropological term "trance", while modern parapsychology calls it OOBE (out of body experience). Further, there are many discussions on the different types of projection, levels of trance and the appearance of the astral body. Whether the chakras (the energetic centers through which the body absorbs and emits energy, according to Indian belief) exist or not, whether an "umbilical cord" (the silver thread that connects the physical and astral body) exists or not, and so on. All this is irrelevant, though, because if we look at what everyone agrees on, we will conclude that projection exists and that it is real and that is what is important to us. After practicing for an extended period of time, you will probably make some conclusions and form opinions of your own.

If we compile the opinions of many authors, and carefully read what they have to say, we will be in a position to construct a classification system that is related to some of the kinds of projection that people can experience. Because of the lack of better terms that may be used to describe a given state, we will use the existing ones and these are:

1. Mental projection
2. Astral projection
3. Etheric projection (Projection of one's essence)

Under mental projection, we mean the kind of projection that is initiated from the state of "lucid dream" or the waking state, when the conscious person is exploring their internal planes and does not leave the body. This form of projection uses a symbol or tarot card as a gateway.

Astral projection represents actually stepping out of the body, journeying to a parallel dimension or some other realm in the upper, lower, or middle Astral Plane. During this projection, the person may fly; pass through walls, but they can also check their credibility by seeing who is in the next room, checking the time, etc.

Etheric projection represents a relocation of the whole essence of the person. The etheric body has both weight and density. When projecting etherically, the person can neither fly nor pass through walls, although it is possible to move lighter things and for them to observe their energetic channels and chakras. The person in this form can be visible to others as well. It is very interesting that during this you can change your appearance at will, with the help of a technique of awakening energetic centers, or the manipulation of the contents of the subconscious, the Shadow etc. The etheric projection itself is very demanding and dangerous to your physical body. Every injury or energetic imbalance that happens to the etheric body is transferred to the physical body and can produce various ailments. In reality, the ethereal projection has no great value because your movement is limited, and you can do everything astrally in a much safer manner.

We started one other subject that we have not yet discussed in detail, and that is how many "bodies" a person has. Once again, many answers have been given, and we will try to simplify things and answer in a way that should represent what most authors agree with.

Let us first say that each person has a physical body that is material. Next, the etheric body, which consists of the acupuncture channels, energy centers etc. Then the astral body follows, which is even more intangible, which is in essence is the "glow" of the body's energy, something like an aura. Lastly, we find the mental body or mind. Some say that this is essentially the soul and that it is not material. To summarize, when you are projecting a mental body, you project only the mind, but when you project astrally, you take both your mind and an astral body with you. With this type of projection, your physical body falls into a stupor and that is the reason why this kind of projection is also dangerous. Some authors says that the human energetic body consists of several different layers whose number vary from author to author, but that is not the topic of this chapter, so we will skip it.

The experiences of many people trance should be simplified, and implemented then in the easiest and most straightforward way. Because of this I advise the old technique, with two levels of trance, which I hope I have explained satisfactorily. In essence this is the same "phenomenon", and the only difference is in the perception of the external environment.

Those who are less familiar with the subject of Witchcraft will probably will ask why Witches leave their bodies, and where they are going. The first thing that must be clarified is the understanding of the astral plane in ancient Witchcraft. Throughout the Balkan region the astral world is divided into upper, middle and lower planes. We will maintain this "folk" point of view because we do not want to translate the astral world through the formula of tetragrammatron or aethyrs, because this point of view satisfies today's criteria as well. We perceive the astral as an ocean of energy that flows everywhere. We will assume that it has varying densities, that its upper parts are lighter and the lower ones denser, and are accordingly closer to our material world. Some perceive its' inhabitants as real beings, and some as figments of our imagination.

We can say that both viewpoints are correct because our egos give form to the energy frequencies. We do not know how these frequencies originated. Some say that people made them, and some say they are creations of the Gods. They exist either way; some of them are self-aware which makes them beings, although incorporeal or with "bodies" with very little density. Modern parapsychology managed, with its most sensitive instruments, to detect some of these creatures and even record them. Some of them are residents of the world that we mentioned a bit ago, so can see better what they look like.

Tit is safe to say that the upper plane was never interesting to Balkan Witches, so we have little information about its residents, and it is uncertain whether they exist independently at all, or more precisely whether they are real independent entities. Some occultists perceive this realm as the home of archetypical forms and human abstract creations.

The middle plane represents a copy of our world, except that when you are in it you can see other inhabitants, such as the spirits of the deceased, spirits of nature, demons, deities, and other entities of a similar nature that are on different rungs of the spiritual evolution ladder. This means that Witches are not only able to contact these creatures, but to gather privately at a predetermined time at a predetermined place. This was the most visited realm. Some authors claim that the inhabitants of this world are mythical creatures that originate in folk tales that the astral "remembers" and reproduces them just like video tapes. This brings us back to the old dilemma of whether the Gods made people or the people made the Gods... In essence, the answer is irrelevant, and the most important thing is that everyone agrees that they exist and that most of them have their own independent consciousness, which mean that they are not just "holograms". It will be a long time before we discover how it all began.

For Witches, The lower realm is the home of aspects the Great Mother and the Horned God. The Great Mother is like Mother Earth when the vegetation falls dormant, the Goddess of Death, and the Horned God as the God of those who have died, in contrast to the aspects seen in the middle realm. It is also the home of dwarves, wise snakes, demons, spirits that guard spiritual and mineral wealth, and of course, the deceased. In other words, the underworld is always manifest as the home of the dead. It has so many different creatures, beings, and deities, that the realm is literally teeming with life.

Almost all nations of the world considered this to be the underworld, or Hell. It cannot be compared to the Christian Hell, however. To Witches, that world is not seen as a dark and dangerous place, but rather a beautiful realm where another Sun is always shines, the underworld Sun. We will talk about those creatures later in the book. We need to point out that the term "underworld" includes caves, holes, abandoned mining shafts, and all types of water, rivers, lakes, swamps, etc.

The three worlds represent three separate journeys. Each of them offers us something new, which one we choose depends on our personal affinities and the specific things that we want to do. I recommend that everyone begins their own experience with an investigation of the upper world, and they should stay there for some time until they learn the basic techniques of protection, moving without using physical muscles and projecting their own will onto the realm's environment. Let that world be some kind of "training ground". After all this is learned, you can pass on, journeying in the "middle world", where encounters with real beings is much more likely to happen. Some of them can have a hostile attitude, and you must not give up at the very beginning, because some of them actually have good intentions. After you become experienced, especially in the interaction with entities, you can go enter the "underworld" that will be full of life and will offer the highest amount of quality content.

Before we move on to the practical part, I will explain the terms that we mentioned before. The first one is protection. You should about this before leaving your body. Through the centuries, within the various magical systems known throughout the world, the basic means of protection has been the magical circle. There are various methods of creating the magical circle, but the best known are those of drawing it and "opening" it in a ritual way. We are going to discuss this, because it is not part of traditional Balkan Witchcraft. Balkan traditional Witchcraft knows many forms of protection circles, like those that we will see later in the book, but protecting your body while journeying out from it can be done in two ways.

If you practice leaving on your own without the presence of another person, the basic way is to place a blade over your head. If another is present, that person is usually charged with waving the knife or scythe over your body. Balkan Witchcraft is more oriented toward the individual, and therefore there is still a need for the Witch woman or Witch man to provide their own means of protection. That could be any knife or straight-razor, which, according to lore, should have a black handle. The best thing to use is a *"kustura"*, a specially made and specifically magical knife (We will describe this

75

process in thorough detail later.). Some Witches, before they leave their body, engrave a magical circle in the ground with their knife, then lie down inside because they want to be able to put the knife by their side. When in a house, they make the circle with the blade of their knife in the air, around the bed and then they put it next to them with the edge facing upwards. We had the opportunity to observe a male Witch as he drew up a magical circle around him with an ax, and then he left his physical body standing in the center of the circle. The scene was fascinating. His body trembled and his eyes simply went out (Rolled to the back of his head). He remained in that state until he returned around ten minutes later. The basic idea of this protection is that your body will be safe from various curious or hostile entities while you are not in it, and protected from anyone who would take advantage of that moment of weakness to enter your body or even physically hurt you. Some of our evidence shows that there are Witches who use something like familiars from western Witchcraft for protection. They are entities that look like animals, which they place on guard, so they can protect their body while they are not physically present. Beside those methods of protection, they use various types of amulets that they wear while leaving the body.

After you arrange your protection and leave your body, the first thing you experience is hindered movement. The reason for this is the fact that you are not in your physical body, and therefore you cannot use your physical muscles to walk. This problem can be solved very quickly, because the only thing you need to do is to get used to managing your movements with your thoughts, that is, by using your will. That means it is enough that if, for example, you want to stand, it simply happens. If you want to move your hand, you wish it, and the hand will move in the desired direction. You must understand that you are like a child learning how to walk. After a time you will perform those movements automatically, just as you do when you are in your physical body. You must remember that once you had to learn how to walk. With these actions are very vital skills that we addressed earlier, under the name "Projection of the will on the environment".

Bearing in mind that the astral plane is solely, judging by appearances, a blank canvas upon which our human thoughts are painted, it is obvious that we can use this knowledge for our own benefit. This means that when we find ourselves in this endless sea of energy, by the power of our will and our own energy, we can change the "reality" of the environment. This will be crucial if we want to perform a ritual, or we want to defend ourselves from a hostile entity.

This is the second level of protection, or specifically self-defense. This is how it works: The first thing that we must ascertain whether or not an entity has good intentions. If you think one can conclude this by observation, you are wrong. According to the unwritten rules, those who just want to hurt you usually look benevolent. What you should do is to test them with the help of some personal symbol of protection. You could draw a cross; pentagram, labrys, triscellion, swastika, or a symbol that is specifically important to you. Use your will to draw it, and it will imprint on the astral matrix, and what you drew with your mind will appear in the air, hanging like a neon light. If the entity does not run away or disappear, you can interact with it. However, if a struggle ensues, as a beginner you will probably get scared and in a few seconds go be drawn back to your body automatically.

Later you can counterattack by burning the attacker with fire or a ball of electricity, burning pentagrams, or simply with beams of pure energy. You will be doing this with your will alone. If you believe in something with conviction and clarity, the manifestation of that will come to pass. Do not forget that you are also in the astral, you can make a circle, a sphere or mirrored cube around you, inside of which you will be safe. With a little luck and willpower, all of this will come very easily to you. In reality, attacks on the astral are very rare, and the only thing you should be aware of are the other people you might meet. If you do not wish to enter a conflict, you only need to think of your body and you will return to it immediately.

Finally, let us just say that you should not relax too much or stay too long in the astral plane. In the beginning, you can stay a few minutes. With time you can increase that period, but try not to exceed twenty minutes. If you forget yourself, you will start to feel exhausted, apathetic, and your fatigue will be obvious.

Methods of Entering Into the Trance State

To get out of your physical body you must accomplish several things. The first thing that many authors mention is at least partial sensory-deprivation. That means you must find a quiet place, close your eyes, wear loose comfortable clothing, do not chew anything, and do not touch anything. You should find a very comfortable position in an armchair or on a bed, calm yourself, raise your level of concentration, and finally, try to relax. It is important that you should not over eat or imbibe too much alcohol before you try to enter the astral. There are those that facilitate this by taking a sedative or a glass of mild alcoholic drink. More than this is too much.

When this is done, begin relaxing every part of your body; free yourself of muscular tension or, to be precise, the feeling that you have a physical body. We recommend that you begin relaxing from the head and move towards the feet. You can help the process with rhythmic breathing, or simply by deep inhalation and exhalation. You can also try clenching the muscles in your body simultaneously, then relaxing them individually. One can accompany this process with visualization: Imagine that your body is empty inside, and that it is filled with molten metal. Then you can feel and imagine it leaking from your head, neck, chests, back, and feet. Notice how your "body" becomes lighter and lighter.

Once this is done we move onto the next stage, the visualization that directly affects removing yourself from your body. First, you must calm your mind and eschew distracting thoughts. This can be very hard, but with time and practice, the number of such distractions will decrease. When you are ready, you start to visualize your journey "outside". Some people visualize a tunnel through which they pass, or a duct that sucks them in, or jumping through an open door, but we recommend a technique that will help you to enter deepest trance state. It is necessary that your brain to be in the so-called alpha state to enter this trance, and that your heart rate must be approximately sixty beats per minute.

If you have done all the necessary preparations, you should start to imagine that you are flying among the clouds. Don't watch yourself looking from the outside in, rather, that you are looking through your own eyes. As this can be very difficult at first, we will employ an "assistant". Imagine some huge, wondrous bird in front of you. You watch it from behind and follow its' flight. That will focus your thoughts, and the added concentration needed to visualize this bird will prevent the constant intrusion of unwanted distractions.

Let the bird fly, up and down, left and right, and follow it. If you can do this successfully without letting it out of your sight, after about ten minutes you can enter into the first level of the trance, and if you continue to follow it, the second, then third, and finally the fourth level. In my experience, most people reach the final level after about forty minutes. This technique falls into the category of "direct entrance into the astral", which means from the state of wakened awareness. If we discard direct techniques that include the use of herbs or other medication, in modern times we have one more type of direct entrance into the astral, with the help of auto-hypnotic dreams. At first glance, it resembles the technique already we just illustrated, but the differences are obvious. Here is a technique of this type.

The easiest way to learn auto-hypnosis is to go and visit a hypnotist for several sessions and let him "program" you. It is necessary to explain what you expect from him, and ask him to use an appropriate text that you will use to induce your trance state; he will then take you into a hypnotic state and use that text and program you. We recommend that you have the following phrase in your text: "while your body sleeps, your mind is awake". Introduction to hypnosis needs to occur in the following way: When you say "one", your body will start to relax; when you say "two", your arms, legs, torso; your heart will slow and you will fall into a sleep… but your mind stays conscious. You can stagger the steps up to around five.

The conclusion needs to include a suggestion to forget the text and to remember only the numbers that you have heard, but also it should tell you what is needed to get yourself to get out of the state of autohypnosis. It is necessary to repeat this several times to obtain good results. After this, you can simply go home, lie down, relax for several minutes, simultaneously speaking and visualizing the numbers from one to five. When you get to the last number, you will realize that you no longer have control over your body, but you are totally aware of your surroundings. Additionally, it is possible to go directly into the dream state, but this time fully aware, and find yourself in a state that is identical to lucid dreaming. It is easy to pass to the astral from that state. It is enough to want it and to imagine something appropriate, then just fly away. It could be a door through which you will fly, a mountain from which you will jump, or whatever else you may decide. There are many books on autohypnosis that will give you a step-by-step to get into this state.

Beside the direct methods of entering the astral there are also indirect methods. They are very popular because they demand much less effort, but their shortcoming is that we cannot use them whenever we want. One of these methods is the technique of controlled dreaming, the basic idea of which is that while we sleep, we have the ability to become aware that we are in a dream state. If we do not have this ability naturally, it takes several days of testing our reality. For example, several times a day we must look around us, touch things, and say to ourselves "I am awake, and this is real.". After some time, often a few days, we transfer this newly acquired habit to our dreams and in that moment, when we finish testing and asking the question, we become aware that the "landscape" around us is not real and that we are actually dreaming. Because our body is in the dream state (decreased heart rate, our senses disconnected from the material world), the situation is ideal for leaving the body.

It is enough to symbolically jump through a wall, jump out of a tree, or simply to wish strongly enough leave your body, and you will. This method works with almost everyone. We have reason to believe that only energetically weak people cannot leave their bodies using this or other methods we have discussed previously. The cause of this could be illness, stress, or by any number of factors that we can eliminate by various methods, be it by visiting a doctor or by practicing some method of energetic rejuvenation.

We will share one more method of direct entry into the astral that is used by Witches. This is the method of flying with the help of a spirit assistant or magical item. Experienced Witches use this method, because this act greatly facilitates entrance into the astral. The basic reason for this is that spirits are real astral beings that are already in the astral, or very magical items that are already present in astral form on one side, because on the other they are filled up with certain energies. The Witch usually receives spiritual "assistants" as gifts from higher astral beings, or she selects one that she has from a previous trip. She can invoke them at will and use them whenever she wants. You've probably already heard or read that people observed ancient Witches riding a pig, goat, cat, dog, or some form of demon. Under the term "demon' we mean the anthropological category of lower supernatural creatures without the addition of the Christian interpretation thereof.

The same thing applies to magical items. They have an astral presence, and they are received as gifts after initiation or via communications with higher entities. Accordingly, they have greater value and they usually have magical traits that may be used in the astral. The tools used for this are primarily a broom, a forked stick or rod, a piece of wood, a cauldron, etc. The Russian grandmother *Yaga* was shown riding a pig, or flying in a cauldron or on a ball. When you have a spiritual assistant, all you need to do is to prepare yourself as we discussed earlier, then invoke him. He will literally "Uproot you from your body". The same applies when you want to use magical items. The techniques that we mentioned here have one common characteristic; the results depend on you. The harder you work and the more time you spend, the better your results will be. Your preparation period will decrease, and the speed with which you leave your body will increase.

Lastly, we will describe one more method. This is actually original method mental projection, which is often used today instead of astral projection. It is similar to the so-called "path working" that was mainly used by Kabbalists for their "journeys" on the paths of the Tree of Life. In a somewhat changed form, that method could be used like this…

Before you relax and prepare to leave the body, take a tape recorder or any other means to record yourself and dictate a previously prepared text that will tell you where to go and what to do. What you listen to needs to be accompanied by visualization. You do not concentrate on one aspect of your senses; use every touch, smell, and taste you can in order to make it as realistic as possible.

For example, you walk along a steep path, while a gentle breeze caresses your face. The forest surrounds you on both sides, and clouds move lazily through the sky. You hear your footsteps, your own breathing; you look down at your feet, at your hand. You pause and touch a tree, feeling the rough bark beneath your fingers, then you continue walking. You see a house in the distance and walk towards it. The forest opens into a meadow as you near the house, you see the clouds against the immense expanse of blue sky, feel the sun warm your skin and a warm, gentle wind on your face. You approach the house, and open the door. You see a picture on the wall, and you run and jump through it.

The text should last from twenty to forty minutes. Watching your hands or feet enables you to keep your focus, and not become distracted. The big finish is the jump into the picture or something of that nature. That is the moment when separation from the body actually occurs. Two people could perform this technique together, one person reading the text and the other "walking the path".

WITCH SUPPLIES AND ATTRIBUTES

In this chapter we will look at some of the most important tools of ancient Witches of the central Balkans. We intentionally use the term "central Balkans"; most of the information we provide comes from written and oral sources related to both male and female Witches from the territories of Serbia, Montenegro, a part of Bosnia, Herzegovina, and Croatia. We need to point out that in these areas the Witch supplies were different from one part of the country to another. Each Witch had their own tools that they would make independently based on need or by the order of higher forces. These tools were different from Witch to Witch. Each Witch, besides physical tools, had astral items that they acquired on some of their journeys.

Here we will just look at "universal" tools, the ones that almost every Witch from this area had. It is necessary to emphasize one difference between Witchcraft in Western Europe - especially the modern version - and ancient Balkan traditional Witchcraft, related to the treatment and preparation of these tools.

The basic difference is that in most cases, in the Balkan "school", there is no ritual item dedication. They are mainly tools that had some earlier significant function, and because of this they were placed in the service of a male or female Witch. Those that were not were so-called "virgin tools" that were new and had never been used. After their first magical usage, these tools were set aside for ritual use only. A third group would be items acquired in very special or unusual ways, like a whip - about which we will talk later – that would be prepared in a special way for a certain function. There is deep symbolism in the way these items are collected that finds its root in folk tales and myths. It is the fourth group that consists of tools that are in some way dedicated, but these are a rarity, were mainly connected with the practice of Witches in the rural parts of the Balkans.

Cauldron and Verige

As we mentioned before, for Serbian and other central Balkan people, the hearth is the most sacred ritual space. All ancient traditions related to the lives of members of the household were performed by the hearth. Deals were struck there, the myths were told, and people swore upon the hearth. Most rituals and magical acts were performed on or near the hearth. As Witches are an integral part of the people, it is quite normal that this is their "holy space". Why is that? To explain the holiness of this space first we must explain what exactly a hearth is.

The first thing that we see is a single-room building with an open door, with a fire burning inside. The fire itself represents very complicated symbolism, and because of that we will give a brief explanation. Fire most likely represented a living being for earlier Serbs. According to tradition, it was stolen from the Anathemas, mythical creatures with demonic characteristics. According to tradition, Saint Sava stole the fire by setting fire to his staff and when he saw the anathemas chasing him, he hid the fire in a rock, going back and collecting it later to give to the people.

From this it is easy to see that the myth is very old and Saint Sava replaced the role some old Serbian deity. The fire has a protective role, especially the "living fire" that was the result of rubbing two sticks together. People thought that this type of fire drove away evil and sickness. "The extraction" (Literal translation "Bringing it out") was a great and complicated ritual in which the entire community participated. Only twins (born on the same day) or innocent people, most often children, could bring out the fire. The ritual was performed at dusk, just before sundown. The fire was ignited by the archaic method of rubbing two pieces of wood together - in this case, oak and hazelnut. That fire was divided up, and everyone took a portion of fire home to light their hearth. The hearth fire was never extinguished, except for exceptional circumstances. Because the fire was considered holy, the place where the fire burned was also a holy place. Additionally, people thought that the souls of their ancestors lived in the hearth, which made it even more important.

Above the fire, there was the cauldron. It was used to prepare food for the whole family, and it represented the symbol of fertility. Ancient Witches prepared their magic in it. They mixed herbs, melted lead, extinguished embers. In most cases this was not the same cauldron from which they fed their families, but sometimes it was, because cauldrons were very expensive and there was very little spare money. You do not have to take this literally; many Witches used the first suitable receptacle, as economic ability dictated what sort of vessel used.

Verige, the chain on which the cauldron was hanging, was considered equally sacred for one reason. Once again, the reason is hidden in myth. According to tradition, chains once existed that hung from the sky and people would swear before them. If someone lied about something, the chains would pull back into the sky, exposing the liar. Once a great liar wanted to swear before them, but they broke, and no one has since. This story reveals that the *verige* was considered to be a link connecting the planes that separated gods and people. It is no surprise that they made sacrifices to the gods; to this day there is a custom in some places that the head of a black rooster, slaughtered on the threshold of the house, should be hung on the *verige*.

Some people would hang some part of livestock they owned, like hair or feathers. They were also wrapped with green yarn to bind the wolves, that is, to prevent them from killing their livestock. Because of this, the ethnologists conclude that they represent a link with a chthonic deity that rules over wolves. The black rooster origins are based there as well. Black and green are the colors of the Underworld. Verige do indeed have a connection with the Horned God, or at least one of His aspects. Because of this many magical acts are still performed with their help. They were used to destroy infectious disease and drive away clouds; people offered their sacrifices there, and there is where they prayed to God. It is very important to watch that no one placed any horn on the chain, because it was believed that it caused family quarrels. That is why *verige* are so much more important to Balkan Witches than the cauldron, because they represent a direct link with deities and other worlds.

The hearth as a sacred ritual space consists of one more important thing that is directly connected with the Witches, the chimney. Although we have already talked about it, it's a good idea to touch on it again briefly. First, there is the tradition that various demons live in it and pass through it. Through the chimney the Witch accepts visits from the ones that she called, but she also departs through, it riding on her broom, some animal, or a weaving beam. Second, the chimney itself is considered to be a link between two worlds, the world of people, and the world of spirits. Maybe this originates from the fact that its extension in some way represents the *verige*. In each case, all three things that make hearth represent the ritual space of the Witches but not the only one. We will take about other later in the book.

The Broom

The broom has always been one of the most famous tools of Witches, associated with Witchcraft not only in the Balkans, but most all of Europe. It is believed that brooms were used by Witches as a tool for flying, though some believe that instead of the broom,

Witches ride on the yoke of a loom, which looks like horse. Astral flight is not the only function of the broom, however. To explain this, we must understand how Witches acquired their brooms.

Witches used various types of brooms. The first type of broom is an astral broom that is a gift from higher forces. Its uniqueness is the fact that it is not physical and is used to a much lesser extent than the other types.

Another type of broom was made of the herb that is known as "field broom" (Lat. xeranthemum annuum), and it was gathered ritually on July 7. In modern times, thanks to Christians, this previously Pagan celebration has been transferred to Saint Jovan, who some people today also call "The broom-maker". Accordingly, we can assume that the broom was associated with some masculine deity whose magical attributes were transferred to Saint Jovan during the Christian era.

The ritual was performed at sunrise. Older women went to the fields completely nude with their hair unbraided to gather the field broom. They then bound it together with yarn, and dried it in the Sun until it took on a golden color. Once they were properly dried they were ready for use; they were not used as a regular broom, rather, for protection and driving away evil forces.

There is a custom that this type broom must be left standing upright near the door, or hanging over it to prevent any evil from entering the house. The broom itself has magical power and it does not require consecration. People would not hit a little child with it because, according to tradition, that child would stop growing or to hit an older girl or boy because they would never marry, etc. However, could be waved over a woman who is past term in her pregnancy to induce birth, to drive away disease, and to invoke the fairies. An old broom must never be taken into a new house, or be thrown into fire. A broom would be placed under a sick person so that he could recover, a mother would hang the broom over her child so that demons could not harm him while he was alone, and many other things of a similar nature.

The male Witch primarily used a third type of broom, the broom from the threshing floor. Earlier we mentioned the text of Luka G. Bjelokosic; he wrote that the basic weapon of the male Witch *"zduhac"* was the broom from the threshing floor. They used it in battle, and they must not lose it; if they did they would lose in the fight and probably their lives as well. When his enemy, who usually was a male Witch from another village, took the broom, he took the "fertility" of whole region.

It is easy to understand why the broom represented the symbol of fertility. This broom from the threshing floor, the place where the wheat was threshed and then collected with the very same broom. It was used solely for this task, and because of that it has magical powers, and holds the "fertility" of the entire community. Only one chosen by "higher forces" could hold it and use it.

Aside from these brooms, among the Serbian Witches two other types of broom were used. These are classical brooms made from birch wood, which young girls would wave in the air to persuade fairies to take them as sisters, and brooms made of oak, which ancient Witches used for the initiation of younger Witches. Regrettably, we do not know much about those oak brooms; the only source of information is the writings of Vuk Karadzic.

Finally, we should say something about the common broom bought at the market, or picked in the field without any special ritual, that was used in the home. This broom also had certain symbolism and was used by the people of the time for protection from evil. However, for male and female Witches, this type of broom was worthless.

Within Balkan Witchcraft, the broom usually represents a status symbol. Not all brooms are equally powerful, nor do they all have the same characteristics. Each Witch only uses their own broom, and if that broom was stolen or some other person tried to use it, the broom would lose its magical capabilities immediately. This rule applied to all magical items. As we saw before, the brooms are differentiated by their composition and place of origin. Many Witches had their own way of making brooms; some received instructions from the higher forces, while for others the "recipe" was passed on from generation to generation. The brooms acquired on the astral did not have a physical form but physical brooms had their astral counterpart.

Brooms play a crucial role in astral flight. By simply imagining that she was riding her broom, a Witch took this energetic-magical body and flew off through the chimney. We explained why the chimney was used. This way of moving was not just symbolic, but there were pragmatic reasons too. We discussed the symbolic reasons earlier, so now we will mention the pragmatic. The first reason was because Witches were in the deepest phase of trance while they were in the process of leaving the body, their projection was on the etheric level. In that state their bodies are material and visible, so it wasn't appropriate to go out through the windows or doors because someone might see them. The second reason was that they needed a small hole to leave, because as we said before, it is not possible to go through walls during the "dense" projection phase. Bearing in mind that the etheric body is very hard to separate from the ground they needed a means of transport, and that means was the broom. That is why brooms should be taken seriously.

Besides its basic function, the broom could also be used as a magical staff in various rituals. You could draw a circle with a broom, and you can cleanse its interior. When the broom was standing upright, it was a symbol of power. Negative forces could be pushed away with a broom, but they could also be destroyed; the mere sight of a broom was enough to instill fear in a demon. In other words, the power of the Witch's broom was so strong that it represented one of the most sacred items in Balkan Witchcraft, as well as all of Europe. That sentiment is as powerful today as it ever was.

The Knife - Kustura, Kostura

(**Translators note**: The word "Kostura" translates literally to the English word "Skeleton")

The magical knife is one of the well-known "ritual items" in ancient Balkan Witchcraft. Three different types of knives are used during various rituals. The first group are the knives we keep in the house for everyday use. The second group consists of knives that are bought for use in rituals, and the third group, the most important, are actual Witch's knives. They are among the rare items that must be consecrated.

The production of a magical knife required knowledge of certain laws that have been applied for centuries. First, the knife handle must be black, or the knife must not have handle, as is the case with the Witches in the territory of Montenegro, Eastern Serbia, and Herzegovina. The knife was called a "kostura". Using a black ram's right horn for the handle was highly encouraged. This is not surprising if we realize that the head of the black ram was considered one of the best protections from evil forces. This protective quality could apply to any other type of horn, including that of the stag beetle.

The blade did not have to be of certain shape but it was recommended that it be forged by a blacksmith specifically for use in ritual. The blacksmiths had a special role in ancient beliefs because they were connected with chthonic forces. They were seen as custodians of the secrets of the underworld and were therefore in direct contact with the God. In later times it was said that blacksmiths were wizards under the patronage of the Horned God, or, more simply, the God of the Underworld. They were also considered to have power over many different types of demons. Because of that, there are modern blacksmiths that make ritually forged fetishes, amulets, fertility belts, etc.

Because of this belief, it was very important that the blacksmith forged the blade of the magical knife. He did not do this in the usual way. Ritual forging was done on the night of the full Moon, after midnight, when the world of people and the world of "supernatural creatures" overlap. The blacksmith was completely naked while he was hammering, and during that process, and he dared not speak a single word. Sometimes nine blacksmiths performed this task, and just as with a single blacksmith, they were all naked and none of them spoke. During this process, women could not be with the blacksmiths or anywhere near where they were working. This process happened very rarely, so the Witches most often bought new knives, then removed the blade from its handle and gave it a new one made of horn.

After a Witch prepared the right horn of a black ram and obtained the blade, she assembled the knife and waited for the right time for the dedication. That time was the celebration of Saint Vratolom. On that day, people waited for night to come and the moon to go into eclipse.

Witches and many other women who wanted to have this type of knife would go outside and soak the knife in water, and then they would try to catch the moon's reflection on the knife while saying the following words three times:

"Just as Devils in the sky and Dragons cannot harm you Goddess Light-Carrier (The name given to the Moon), no disease can bring harm to she who carries this knife.

Empower it, Moon! (The folk name for this energy is power)
Strengthen it, Moon!
Consecrate it, Moon!"

This must be said three times while the Moon is in the sky. After this is done, women must cross themselves three times, than they must to take the knife from the water and carry it in the in their bosom the entire next day. The day after that, the knife could be removed and placed on their belt, and used their entire life. This consecrated knife should not change owners, nor should anyone else touch it; if either happened the knife would lose its magical powers. This means that it is useless to any other potential users.

Here we can see that this ancient ritual suffered some changes under the influence of Christianity, but that its basic structure remained the same. You can also see that the words are mainly concerned with driving away illness, but these can vary, and changes can be made according to what is necessary.

The original basis of this ritual is catching the Moon's reflection during the eclipse. The reason for this is that its struggle with the forces that want to "eat it", and its victory over them. In that moment of struggle, the Moon is the strongest and it proves that no one can harm it, hence, that is the best time to catch its power. The words from the chant do not say much. "Moon, give it energy, make it stronger and consecrate it."; from this we can clearly see that the knife belongs to the Moon, and that it acquired power from the Moon during the course of the ritual.

The custom that women must cross themselves three times after this ritual was probably added later, under the influence of Christianity, and therefore is not very interesting to us. However, the fact that the knife was kept tucked in the bosom for a whole day is. In fact, it represents the linking of the moon's energy with the energy of the knife's owner. Naked breasts are indeed a symbol of fertility, but realistically are also the place to raise the most precious feminine energies. This act established a lifetime connection between these two energies that manifests through use of the knife.

Knives created in this way were never used in the household or for cutting. Besides their basic ritual purposes, they were used as a means of protection during astral flight by both sexes. For the most part, men had knives that were not consecrated, but had magical capabilities due to black handles or handles made of the horns of some sacred animal; this was to prevent a demon from taking over their body while their spirit was in the astral. They placed the blade upright on the threshold, on the windowsill, or at the end of the bed. This prevented demons from getting into the house and attacking someone during astral sleep. Knives were considered talismans of protection from evil, though each Witch decided in what manner it would be used. The truth is, Witches used them in different ways, depending on the area they came from and to which tradition they belonged.

The Copper Dish

The copper dish is a wide and flat, and was used by almost all Balkan Witches. As far as I know, this dish was not ritually consecrated; it was mainly used for consecration and divination, and as an auxiliary tool during other magical rituals. Because we have explained the process of consecration, we will look at divination.

The basic function of the copper dish in divination was something like the "magic mirror" or crystal ball in western Witchcraft, and using it was very simple. Most often, it was used outside at night so that one could see the reflection of the moon in it. The Witch filled the dish with "untouched water", water that was fresh form a well or had not been used for anything else during the day. Then the

Witch would turn the dish to an appropriate angle, so as to see the smooth surface reflecting the light of the moon, but not the moon itself. After a short period of watching, or rather staring, into the dish, the desired images would begin to manifest themselves to the user. Later, when photographs were invented, they were placed into the copper pan during the divination to show something that is related to the picture. Of course, it could be something other than a picture. Other personal things could be used as well, such as hair, nails, saliva, sperm, etc.. These are items that represent means by which someone could be identified.

The copper pan could be used to heal someone as well; in that case, after the catching the reflection of the moon and putting a personal effect from the sick person in the water, medical herbs were added with appropriate conjurations. Of course, it was not necessary to use the herbs. Rocks could be used instead, parts of animals, teeth, claws, feathers, or some other symbolic item. In addition to Moon energy, star energy was captured in the dish as well, and that energy was called "*vedrina*" (clarity or serenity). Frequently the herbs were left soaking in the water outside over night to accumulate astral energy. The copper dish was occasionally used during the course of other types of magic, but its main function was divination.

It is important to add one more thing. The copper pan was always filled with water, but in most cases it was not ordinary water. For this purpose, "untouched" or "living water" was used, as people in Serbia call it. This is water fresh from a well, or natural spring water taken from where it rises from the ground. This is running water - it flows, and on its journey it did not pass through any pipes, especially metal ones. In many places where that water rises, fairies and other "spirits of nature" gather. Some of the springs are even dedicated to the Goddess (today's Saint Petka represents her) so the water from such places has additional value.

The Wand

(**Translators note**: This can also be a cane, a rod, or a staff, depending on context; they are all straight sticks made of wood.)

The magical wand belongs to a group of Witch's tools that does not require consecration in a ritual way, but it is necessary to be careful of its' origin and the means by which it was acquired. With the majority of those in the central Balkans, the their use and composition are the same.

Wands made of Yew and Black Hawthorn were mainly used for protection and chasing away evil demons.

Wands made of Dogwood were used in healing rituals. It is well-known that children were whipped with these sticks to drive away sickness and disease, because people thought that they were evil forces that entered a person. If there was no Dogwood they would substitute Willow, although Willow was mainly used to drive away fever.

Any wand that had a shed snakeskin in or on it became magical and brought great material benefits. The snake was the symbol of the earth, and people believed that they were custodians of buried treasure and reincarnated souls of the ancestors.

The wand with which a frog was taken from the mouth of a snake was used to help in various situations in life that were going very slowly or were very difficult to endure. For example, people used them when the cow had a difficult birthing. They waved the wand in the air over the cow and say to the calf, "as the frog separates itself from the snake, so shall you separate yourself from the cow."

One of the most powerful magical wands was that which a snake was killed before May 6. The original date probably was May 1, but it was moved to be connected with Saint George; the moment it was killed, it's power was transferred to the wand. The reason for this is the ancient belief that the snake is representative of the vegetation spirits who become stronger in the spring.

People believed that the greatest wand belonged to the Devil. It was long and black, and one who steals it from him becomes a great wizard. It is also believed that Witches always have a wand of red or black, though of course that is not true.

Probably the one of the most well-known wands, and the most valued, at least for Witches, was the Hazel wood wand. Among the Balkan people, the wood from the Hazel tree is sacred. "Live coal" was derived from it, many diseases were healed with it, and it protected people from evil forces. Serbian ethnologists connected it to the old Pagan Slavic deity Perun, or rather his sister, because she is well known by that name. This is debatable because the accepted view among ethnologists is that the Pagan pantheon never existed among the Slavic peoples of this region. In other words, Slovenians diverged from the southern Slavic peoples very early, and came to the Balkan Peninsula with a developed demonology but without polytheism. They accepted Christianity early on, so they never achieved the level of the Russian Slavs or those from the Baltic. This fact is confirmed by the absence of any related archeological evidence. No idols were found, nor were they mentioned anywhere in written documents.

The magical wand always must be made from a one-year-old hazelnut tree that has not been pruned. Male or female Witches would pick it after midnight, completely nude and silently. The cutting must be done in one movement, so that the wood is not tortured, and thereby lose its magical capabilities. In the territory of Eastern Serbia the Witches used Hazel wood wands to invoke Tartor, or other similar water spirits, and to control the weather.

On the other hand, the people from the south and southwest Balkans were famous for their pine wands, a piece of pine that is slightly burned on each end. According to tradition, they used these wands for fighting between individuals. Pine is known as "Soul Wood" (sen is the Slovenian word for "soul"), as the Balkan people says that this wood has particular capabilities.

Lastly, we come to Oaken wands. Oak is probably the most sacred tree among the Serbian people. It represents the God and His temple. Accounts of Oaken wands are very rare; the reason for this is the respect given to this tree, as well as the fact that almost all ancient oak trees are taboo. However, on Christmas day, one oak branch is broken off, and in the evening that branch must be burned. With this act, the body of the dead God is burnt so he could resurrect as a young man.

In addition, the wand could be an "astral" one, without a physical counterpart, and as such could be put into any physical wand made of the appropriate wood. *Zduhac* probably did not carry physical pine wands with when they went into astral battle. The situation with these wands is very similar to the one that associated with astral brooms. Most often, they were gifts that the Witch received in the course of a trance.

The Whip

There is no written rule concerning the whip, but to be considered to be a magical tool it was necessary to obtain it in a special ritual way. In most cases, it was extremely complicated.

First, it is necessary to find hemp seeds (cannabis sativa), because the magical whip must be made from this plant. Then a snake must be killed in the Spring preferably in the forest or countryside, and its head must be cut off with a silver coin. Then the hemp seeds must be placed in the snake's head buried in the ground. After some time, a hemp tree will sprout from the head. The hemp must be collected and processed, and finally a whip was woven that would only be used only for magical purposes.

A whip made like this was used for acquiring material benefits, because whoever was whipped with it would receive money. Negative forces were expelled with this whip, but it was also used for driving away the clouds, especially hail clouds.

Maybe for some this way of acquiring the magical whip seems cruel, but that is how it was done for centuries in the Balkans. Hemp has always been considered a sacred herb, and we can deduce this from the taboos that are connected to it. We will not touch on the subject of snakes at this point; their importance in the region is well known, and it would be impossible to discuss them properly and in detail without taking a significant amount of time. The silver coin is a symbol of material wealth and it was sacred to the Moon. The snake is also a lunar symbol. The basic idea was that the plant grows, feeding itself on the snake's juices. The whip that is made from that plant is not a whip any more, but the snake itself, and as such, it has all the powers that the archetype of the snake has among the people. Sacred hemp serves as the body of materialization of the snake's spirit and power.

Rope and Yarn

Among Balkan Witches, rope was rarely used, but in contrast, yarn was obligatory.

As a rule, they would use any kind of yarn; the only thing that mattered was its color. White, red, black, and sometimes gold colors were used.

White yarn was used exclusively in healing rituals. After a bundle of necessary items for the sick person was prepared, Witches wrapped it three times with white yarn, then it was tied with three knots while they chanted an appropriate incantation. Repeating the incantation while tying each knot. The bundle usually consisted of a piece of white canvas, a personal effect of the sick person, or a few hairs, or an herb that was used to treat the sickness at hand. Sometimes just a lock of hair was bound with white yarn, and while the knots were tied, the incantation was repeated.

Red yarn used for everyday situations. It was most used in love magic, first for "binding" a couple, then for material benefits, but also for protection from any evil. The method of performing the ritual is identical to the previous one, meaning that while the knots were being tied, the appropriate incantation was repeated for each knot.

Black yarn was used exclusively for black magic, with the methodology as in the previous examples. It is well known that black yarn is used in Vlach "binding", and according to that, we can conclude that this type of love magic is black magic.

The Axe

I think that is virtually impossible to find a Witch, sorcerer, or conjurer in the territory of *Sumadija* (The region in the very center of Serbia) who does not have an axe among their tools. In contrast to other ritual objects, the magical axe has wide use among the common people, that is, the people who do not perform magic directly. The axe certainly has all the hallmarks of a fetish, and many ethnologists agree with this conclusion.

Like all other blades, the axe has a primary role of protection. People used it to drive away demons, defend themselves from black magic, and block evil forces; hail clouds were dispersed with it, and the axe was used in sorcery as well.

Of special interest is the amulet made in the shape of an axe that parents gave to newborn children to protect them from evil forces and diseases. This tiny axe was forged in the ritual way and both parents participated in its creation. The axe was forged in the very early hours of a Friday from a horseshoe taken from a dead horse. This is the only ritual forging where women and men take part together. The process was performed totally naked, being mindful that they must maintain complete silence according to tradition.

In conclusion, it is a good idea to mention the opinion of ethnologist Veselin Cajanovic, who asserts that the axe was sometimes one of the basic attributes of Dabog, the ancient Pagan deity of the Underworld, and that this is where the role of this fetish originates in the Serbian culture. As a proof of this assertion, he cites the custom connected to modern Christmas of putting an axe under the straw strewn over the floor. We will mention more about this later.

The Mirror

Professor Dusan Bandic probably made the best case study on magical mirrors, which published in his book "Kingdom of Earth and Kingdom of Sky". This brief study summarizes all that has ever been written on this subject, and from it, he drew certain conclusions.

The mirror has always had a magical role with our culture, which we can conclude if we take a quick look at our folk songs and epic poetry. From them we can clearly see that mirrors were mainly used to predict the destiny of the person who looks in the mirror.

A ritual from Bosnia performed by unmarried women demonstrates this. The ritual is performed very late at night, after a girl cleans the adjacent rooms and gathers trash in the center of her room. On this pile she must place a mirror and light four wax candles. After that, she calms herself and stares fixedly in the mirror until the image of the man that she will marry appears.

A Similar ritual using mirrors was performed on St. George's day or on St. Vitus' Day, the only difference being that the mirror was placed under the pillow to help the girl to see her future spouse in her dreams.

As we have mentioned Kazimirovic cites an interesting example of the magical use of mirrors in the territory of eastern Serbia. He writes about the girls who undertook detailed preparations for the ritual that they wanted to perform. Among other things, he says that they abstained every Friday, and they would embroider the canvas that they later used as a ritual item. The process itself was performed at night under the influence of the New Moon. A girl of marriageable age must bring a boy younger than twelve years old, or a young girl who has not started to menstruate. After tying the previously prepared canvas around the child's neck, she places a mirror in their hand. The child must stare in the mirror and tell her what they see.

Based on what we have seen, it is easy to conclude that mirrors have many uses among the people as well as the Witches. There is one ritual that is associated with mirrors, and we will explain it in the section on divination. All these mirrors never were ritually consecrated, which means that everyday mirrors were used. We must not forget that the copper dish with water could also be used as a mirror. Frequently, in the time when mirrors were a rarity, people would use any smooth surface that could provide a reflection. In some areas, people used the method of foretelling with the help of melted butter or honey in their copper dish.

Little-Known Witch's Tools

The Bell – How the metal bell appeared along with Christian churches, we will not discuss, but we will mention the *"klepetusa"* a wooden gadget that has a similar function to bells in western magic. The role of the *"klepetusa"* was twofold; it was used to invoke deities as well as to "cleanse" spaces of evil forces and demons. Today we use small metal bells that are very easy to procure. Of course, among the people, the *"klepetusa"* had a wide role that was primarily about inviting people to gather at a meeting place, or to sound a warning alarm for approaching enemies.

The Bag - All Witches since time immemorial have had a bag in which they kept their magical tools when they had to use them away from home. It is common knowledge that Witches from eastern Serbia used a bag made of goat's hair that was nine units long of some measure. In other areas, the bag was mainly made of sheep's wool but there was no special ritual associated with it. It is safe to say that today's Witches mainly use store-bought bags. Eastern Serbia is the exception because mainly Vlach people live there, although the situation there has changed in recent years..

The Sickle – Usually this tool was taken from the wheat fields after the harvest. Back then, they believed that it absorbed the energy of the wheat it was used to cut. It was used for prediction (divination); it was thrown in the direction of the sun, and predictions were based on the direction it faced when it landed. People also used it for defending against evil forces and demons, as with other blades.

The Drum – According to Kazimirovic, Croatian Witches used the drum to get into trance states. However, there is very little information regarding this, and most which is written about the subject is pure speculation..

The author and a male witch at a sacred place - the Rock Gate

STRUCTURE AND TYPES OF RITUAL

When we talk about magic rituals in the Balkans, it becomes obvious that we could hardly call them by that name, especially if we compare them with those from western ceremonial magic. Nevertheless, when we look closely at their structure, we can see that it is possible to draw parallels between them.

There are a couple of basic differences. Above all is the use of ritual trance, although it is not necessary in all cases, is less demanding, simpler, and finally the level of relaxation during the trances.

If we start from the beginning, we will see that there is some extensive physical and mental preparation, and in occasional emergency situations, it is necessary to procure some item, herb, or candles.

Opening a circle, invoking deities or elementals in ritual form, or demanding their presence during the ritual is also unknown except in some rare cases. Deities and spirits of nature were invoked only when they were asked for something directly. The magical circle is well-known in the Balkans, and it was widely used, though not during the average magic ritual, when the Witch was armed only with personal protection – an amulet or totem she carried with her. Only when she felted endangered would she cast the circle and start expelling the source of the danger.

Rituals were always very simple. The witch laid her necessary things in front of her; her altar was the hearth, or in later times a common kitchen table, upon which there were no pentacles, goblets, sword, or any such magical tools.

While she was performing her ritual, the Witch repeated the appropriate incantation, focusing herself, visualizing, and slowly getting into the state of trance that helps her to free her psychic

105

powers. Experienced people needed just a few minutes to get in and out. The comfort that we mentioned before relates to the fact that during the ritual there was no great thoughtfulness or mysticism. She is what she is, everyone in her vicinity knows her, and sees her simply as a person who has a special ability, so she does not need all that "pomp and circumstance" that all "white spells" bring with them. If she was doing a ritual for someone, the ancient Witch would often pause and talk with them about mundane everyday things. She was only silent in the moment when she was casting a spell, or getting into a trance. If you think that this reduces efficiency, you are mistaken. A group of scientists consisting mainly of ethnologists and psychiatrists studied the effectiveness of this "matter-of-fact" attitude, especially in the areas of eastern Serbia.

In addition to this "comfortable" way of working, there is a second type of ritual, which is performed with great seriousness, with ritual nudity, at a specified place and at a certain time of the day. The majority of these are rituals in which deities are invoked, or major and minor nature spirits. Only one such entity would be called on in each ritual. Let us continue.

Ritual Spaces

Under the term of ritual spaces, we mean the places where the majority of Witches practiced their rituals. There were exceptions of course, but in essence the places that we are going to discuss here represented the basic form of the spaces inside which almost all techniques of ancient Balkan Witchcraft were carried out.

The hearth was the most traditional place where Witches performed rituals. We explained why in a previous chapter. As modern houses and apartments do not always have a hearth, as a they use the space around the stove or fireplace, in the kitchen or living room.

Using sacred places as a ritual space comes immediately behind the hearth, or in modern times, behind the kitchen. The kitchen was used as little as possible, because the rituals that were performed there were mainly celebrations or the invocation of deities, spirits of nature and similar creatures that were disturbed only when serious problems existed.

These sacred places were in nature, and most often they were forest groves, lakes, certain parts of rivers, springs, or specific parts of a mountain. For a better understanding of this, we must first explain something. In ancient Balkan Witchcraft, there was no general understanding of deities, fairies, dwarves, and other similar beings as spiritual and elemental phenomena that eternal and omnipresent. They were simply a part of their reality. Deities are ubiquitous, but if, for example, you want to want to contact one, you cannot do that in your home; you must to go to the holy place where it lives. For example, if you want to contact a water fairy, you must go to a specific place where they gather, such as a lake or a spring. Dwarves were usually found in caves or abandoned mines.

When people saw these creatures several times in the same place, people considered those places sacred, and they became cult places. The diversity of entities that reside in sacred places was huge. Besides the deities, fairies and dwarves, there were dragons, custodians of some reliquary, spirits of animals, mysterious unnamed forces, etc..

Other sacred places could be a wooden cross (a big oak tree with a cross carved in its bark – a former temple substitution), a pyramid of stones (from the areas where there are no big trees) and crossroads. People assume that at those places the worlds (Physical and astral) cross as well. Crossroads were probably sometimes used as graveyards as graveyards for people and animals. A great number of rituals are still performed in these places today. It is the custom that a rock or a coin wrapped in the clothing of a sick or dead person was thrown on the crossroads, and the sickness or disease of that person would be transferred to what was wrapped in the article of clothing. People also believe that demons could be found there, literally, especially after midnight.

One other existed, however, there is little information about it, possibly because of fear of condemnation; that is the graveyard. Witches often performed rituals in graveyards, although this practice is characterized as the worst. The Church contributes to this, whose surprised priests would find naked women there in the middle of the night, practicing magic. One can imagine the types of stories that resulted. However, the actual situation was completely different. For the most part, rituals performed in the graveyard were not related to black magic, rather, they prayed to the souls of their ancestors for needed help. The night is the best time for performing these rituals, because the worlds of the living and the dead overlap. Usually, assistance is asked from the most recently departed cousin. People took them presents, usually food or drink that the deceased enjoyed in life. This kind of magic is related to the ancestral cult that is particularly developed among the Serbian and Vlach people.

In addition to the sacred places used for performing certain rituals, so-called "Unclean places" were used. People believed these were the meeting places of various demons. Some of them are dry wells, abandoned water mills, bridges, trash piles, old graveyards, ruins, etc. These were considered taboo by the community, and such places were not supposed to be visited.

One typical sacred place, called *Prerast*, is located in eastern Serbia. It is a place where the water flows through huge, circular rocks. The water from that place is considered magical, and is used in rituals. It is the object of many rituals of folk religion, especially for the cult of the dead, but is otherwise considered taboo.

Once a year, people from many different countries who practice magic come to this place to take some water. Before they do, they must go to the mouth of rivers *Ravna* and *Saska* (Pronounced Shashka). There is an ancient tree there, in which lives a powerful demoness named *Danica* (Pronounced Danitsa). The name of that female demon is derived from the ancient name for Venus, who represented Lucifer to the Vlach people. Bearing in mind the fact that this is the place where mainly Vlach Witches gather, can assume that the demon in the tree is Lucifer, or *Lusjafur* as they call it.

Water taken without the permission of that spirit has no magical properties. It is said that first he asks someone to do something for him, usually something dangerous ,in order to get permission to take water with magical power. He could only be approached once yearly, and that is the duration of the magical properties of the water.

We shall not describe the Astral plane as a separate ritual space. It is used often, but it is mainly used by initiates who desire a safe and simple way get to the sacred place, and to see its' "residents" more easily. It is not surprising that entities could be seen outside of the Astral Plane, because there are those that have the ability of "second" sight (An example is people that can see auras.), or that the energy of that place is so thick at certain times that its residents become visible to everyone. Therefore, the astral plane represents a conduit, a realm through which we must pass en route to sacred ritual places already known to us.

Time of Day

There is an ongoing question as to what the best time is for performing rituals, casting spells, and invoking various entities. When we think this through, we see that this usually depends on the situation, and what you want to achieve.

The majority of all rituals were probably performed in the "no time", or very late at night. This is actually the period from midnight until the third rooster's crow. Let us explain this.

In many folk tales, it is said that demons, spirits, vampires, and other creatures come out late at night, then return to their lairs upon hearing the third rooster's crow. This rule could be applied to anything "mystical" or bewitched, such as feminine demons who were involved with humans Witches, but not necessarily. The first time the rooster starts to crow is between midnight and one hour after midnight, and this tells people that it is very late. The second time they crow is around three a.m., and the third is just before sunrise. Therefore, when the rooster crows for the third time, all supernatural beings go back to their lairs so they will not be killed by the sun.

Very late at night is the period when the worlds of people supernatural beings overlap. Consequently, many rituals were performed during this time; it was believed that this was the best time for Witches to make contact with the spirits. This was the time to invoke *Tartor*, as we saw in the second chapter, and the Forest Mother, fairies, nature spirits, and similar entities.

Everyday rituals were performed at any time of day. These were mainly rituals for healing, fertility, wealth, etc.

Certain rituals existed that required a specific time of day, a special day of the week, or some meteorological or astronomical phenomenon. The time could be very late at night, or sunrise (picking of the brooms), when rain falls (fertility), Lunar eclipse (dedication of the magical knife), etc. However, this was very rare. The majority of rituals were performed during the day or a few minutes after midnight.

Silence

Magical work can be performed in two ways. Incantations must be chanted inside the head, while magical words must be mumbled quietly and incoherently, so that a person near the Witch could not understand what is being said.

The best and most important rituals were always performed quietly. This applied to folk rituals as well. The Witches' circle was danced quietly, the amulets that would be used for life must be made quietly, the spirits of nature were invoked quietly, as were many other rituals and procedures.

Why quietly? The reason is simple; in those moments human speech is unnecessary and meaningless. These are mainly rituals in which it is necessary to communicate with the "other side". Supernatural beings are not from the world of people, and the rules of this world do not apply. It is possible to communicate with higher forces through ritual actions, gestures, or with some specific entities telepathically, because they do not speak and because they have no physical structure, they don't have vocal cords. Silence is a sign of respect that the Witch gives these forces.

Among the people who practice occultism there is a theory a ritual can be performed in any one of four ways. The first one is the simplest, when the person who performs it makes certain movements and recites the incantation out loud. In the second way, the person moves, but recites in their head. The third way encompasses a physical state of stillness and silence, reciting the incantation only in their head, and the entire ritual is performed through visualization on the mental level. The last one, the fourth level, involves performing rituals in the astral, outside of the body, in sacred places or astral temples that people themselves build there. This fourth level is considered to the highest achievable, and it can be considered equal to magical gestures, the simple and short moves by which some entity could be invoked. Each time we progress from one method to the next, more advanced one, we shorten the line of communication between our individual unconsciousness and the collective unconsciousness, each time increasing our effectiveness and attaining our goals more quickly..

We can say that when we pronounce the words internally, they have different meanings for us, and our level of concentration is higher so that we can respond to greater demands. Speech and vocal cords are our means of communication, the only thing that our mind taught us, and that we are accustomed to; we must unlearn that as our only means of communication.

Nudity

Balkan Witches have never wore any special vestments while performing rituals. With the greatest of certainty, we can claim that their "ritual vestment" was either the naked body or everyday clothing.

With mundane, everyday rituals, the Witch did attach any importance to what they wore; there was no religious institution with an established hierarchy to support them, and they saw no reason to dress themselves differently than other people. In other words, the only thing above them was the Higher Force, which was not interested in this kind of triviality.

Still, when important rituals were performed, when it was necessary to make contact with higher forces, whether it was with deities, fairies, and some other creatures, it was desirable to be naked, or to be precise, obligatory. Why?

By removing one's clothes, a person goes back to their original state. That could be considered their birth, but it actually refers to the nudity of the earliest humans that wandered the world, living unrestricted with no secrets or subterfuge, especially from the Higher Powers. By being naked, the person is relieved of the burdens of everyday life. It also shows the Higher Powers that they have nothing to hide, and people become more receptive to outside influences.

As we said before, ritual nudity was primarily used when connecting with supernatural creatures. For example, the invocation of *Tartor* was performed without clothes and this was obligatory, even when other people participated. The most sacred amulets were made with the obligatory nakedness of several people. For example, to create the shirt that heals all illness, nine naked old women sew it, nine naked blacksmiths make the amulet for protection, etc. Beside these examples, we need to mention the dancing of the Witch's circle; the entire community danced completely in the nude..

With all these rituals, beside the nudity silence was also necessary, as we will see later in the book when we cite examples of other rituals.

The Magical Circle

The role of the magical circle in Balkan Witchcraft is not very different from its role in western Witchcraft. The basic function of the magical circle was to protect those inside from evil forces, demons, spirits, and other supernatural creatures. These creatures could try to hurt someone for no reason and when they least expect it, or at the moment when they invoke. In both cases, it is necessary to make a magical circle.

In the Balkans, a circle was never opened ritually. The process itself was not as important as the symbolism of the circle itself. A circle could be made in many ways, here are some of them.

a. By fumigation (with hemp, sage, incense, etc.).
b. Enclosure (with rocks, sand, wood, etc)
c. With a ring of flexible plants (willow, birch wood, etc.)
d. With colors (coloring the ground with lime, paint, tar, etc.)
e. By binding (with fabric, leather, etc.)
f. With a rope (usually white or red rope that must be knotted and put on the ground in the form of a circle).
g. By digging (The circle must be drawn with a magical knife or some other ritual item stabbed into the ground)
h. Connecting both ends of *"verige"* or some other chain (you can use a padlock and lock; it as a supplemental magical action that symbolizes security)
i. Movement (moving in a circle around the place where the ritual will be performed)

These are some of the ways, it is very difficult to count them all: different methods were applied depending on the situation and, of course, the tradition of the area. Sometimes several methods were applied simultaneously.

Bearing in mind the fact that no one cared how the circle was going to be opened, the items from which the circle was created were emphasized. The rocks had to be smooth and white from a river or stream. The flour that is used must be the made from the first wheat of the first harvest and ground on a millstone. Candles that have been burned in graveyards were used, or the circle could be made with the sickle or the magical knife or the blade of a plow.

The circle was rarely made of salt, because at that time salt was very expensive. After making a circle there was no need to invoke any guardians; the desired ritual would have been performed

114

immediately, because it was believed that the higher creatures being invoked had no hidden intentions, so they had no desire to hurt the ones with which they make contact. The circle was not used in everyday practice, only when the Witch felt unsafe or unsure, or for some other important reason, which was not often.

Kolo (Dance)

Kolo is a folk dance in which all participants stand next to each other. They hold hands, or on rare occasions, they hold each other by their belts or shoulders, making a closed or semi-closed circle. Kolo was primarily for entertainment, and people danced the kolo at all sorts of celebrations, gatherings, during holidays, etc.

However, several types of *kolo* existed, different ways of dancing and functions that one kolo could have. The word "*kolo*" is in its origin Slavic, and literally means circle or ring. From ancient times, dancing in a ring represented a special type of ritual, with which all kinds of important dates were celebrated, the goal being to provide progress, good crops, health, and so on.

Kolo was always danced clockwise, except when it was danced to show respect to a deceased person. Then the direction was reversed, from the right to the left, and it was used to try to connect with the deceased to ensure their favor.

A special type of the *kolo* was the magical "*vrzino kolo*" (witches circle). In Serbia this term is used today as a phrase when someone wants to say that something is very complicated and that no one can figure it out. *Vrzino kolo* is the *kolo* that Witches, fairies, and other supernatural creatures dance. It was believed that non-Witches should only dance the *vrzino kolo* in exceptional circumstances, such as when great evil was threatening the whole community.

115

A similar example was recorded by Svetislav Prvanovic and published in his 1961 work "Our Ancient Superstitions and Customs" in Zaječar (Pronounced Zayechar). However, we could not find a copy of this book, so we will give a shortened version that we found in the "Dictionary of Serbian Mythology".

This event occurred in 1908 in the village of *Veliki Izvor*. There was a severe drought, and the local residents believed that a dragon that lived in the area was the cause. They thought the dragon visited their village each night to meet with some of the women; because of its flights the clouds could not assemble over the village, and that is the reason why there was no rainfall. Because of this, some of the farmers suggested that *vrzino kolo* must be danced to drive away the dragon, because for such a powerful creature, it is necessary to perform one of the most powerful rituals. Everyone agreed.

The ritual was performed late in the night of the 21st of July. Around fifty villagers gathered in the graveyard and lit a big fire. They elected a leader for the procession; the so-called "Czar" and he took off his clothes first, then the other people followed suit. They then joined hands and begin to dance around the fire. This frantic dance lasted until the people were not quite completely exhausted, and some of them started to fall into a trance (This is our conclusion), as that is the essence of the *vrzino kolo*.

While they danced, it was forbidden to speak, and if someone wanted to say something, they would express it by miming or mumbling. When it was determined that there had been enough dancing, the villagers ran through the village ringing bells, *klepetusa*, pans, etc. When they run through the entire village, they started to chase the dragon towards the graveyard, towards the big fire. When they drove the imaginary dragon into the fire, they joined their hands once more, and began dancing around the fire again. This lasted until the "Czar" said it was enough.

From this account it is clear that this complied completely with the structure of the most sacred Witches rituals. It happened very late at night, speech was forbidden, participants were naked, they danced in a circle around the fire, and there was possibly a symbol of purification and expulsion (maybe the fire was built from hazelnut or oak tree, but that was not written down). Besides that, it happened in the graveyard, the sacred place that meant that they were asking for help from the dead or other supernatural being with whom they could make contact in the trance state that they entered after the long and exhausting dance.

Prvanovich recorded more events like this, in 1935 and 1946, and he said the name of this ritual was "mugajale".

As we can see, the common peoples danced a *vrzino kolo* when necessary. However, the Witches did have a set of rules that must be obeyed. We have seen most of the rules in the previous example; they were concerned with time of day, nudity, silence, etc. We need to mention that Witches usually used their own gathering place, and according to tradition these were abandoned threshing floors, where they danced the Witch's brew, and their number was limited to no more than twelve. Many people have asked why twelve?

A basic mistake is that a false conclusion was made that the actual number was thirteen, and that is not the case. There were twelve Witches, and the thirteenth individual was the Horned God whom they invoked. Remember the story about twelve Witches and the man with the beard? There is always another present, the one that the Witches are waiting for, invoking, or the one they trained.

One more interesting story in this topic was given to us by Vuk S. Karadzich. I saw it for the first time in the "Dictionary of Serbian Mythology", and I cite this passage from there:

117

"Vuk Karadzic says that twelve students, when they graduated, wanted to perform the Witch's Brew together to improve their knowledge and to take an oath.

While reading some special book on the Witch's circle, one of the twelve students disappeared, "demons or fairies took him away". Those who remained could not find the one who is missing. From then on, these students were called '*grabancijasi*' and they consort with demons and fairies, and lead clouds during thunderstorms and hail."

A male witch performs a ritual - photo by author

This is a very interesting story in many aspects, although it has many negative undertones. If we reject the negative part, we have story that leads us to very interesting findings. First, this story is perhaps one of the rare indications that there once existed a so-called "book of shadows" in this area, and it could be supposed that they read the book on the threshing floor.

Here we assume that the Witch's circle is the threshing floor, or the gathering place. We can also see that beside that fact there were twelve people; the higher forces mentioned represent number thirteen. Though it is mentioned more than once, it does not have to be true because it is a retelling of the story that someone once heard. In the end, we can see that they keep "socializing" with demons and fairies, and accordingly we can conclude that this is all about the male Witch and the act of invocation itself, and that taking an oath could represent some kind of initiation.

In addition, we need to say that the Witch's circle is the basic kolo of all supernatural creatures, or creatures with supernatural capabilities. It is the basic "ritual" of fairies, demons, and spirits; when people want something special to be done, something that exceeds their capabilities, they joined forces by forming the largest Witch's possible so they were not individually dealing directly with those forces.

The Vrzino kolo has other name, the vilino kolo. Many locations across ancient Yugoslavia used this to mark the places where fairies traditionally danced a kolo. Those names were usually assigned to places where circles or semicircles of stamped-down grass were found, especially in the mountains or woods, or near a spring. This name was given to these places by witnesses who secretly watched the faerie dance wildly during the full moon.

Looking Back

Finally, let us say that all large and important rituals, as you will see, were terminated by going out of the place where the ritual was performed without looking back. Looking behind you, or turning back in the direction of the place where a ritual was just performed is forbidden in the Balkans. The reason for this is threefold.

First, there is a belief that by looking back, the link that exists between the two worlds will not be broken, which means that after everything is finished the ritual continues. This endangers the person who initiated the ritual, because the supernatural creatures that are "summoned" to this plane stay here and follow the one who performed the ritual. Suddenly turning around after the end of the ritual and leaving quickly represents some kind of "theater curtain" that falls down and marks the end of the performance. I do not think it is necessary that I repeat how important this is. We said something about it in the first chapter when we spoke of the necessity of a clear demarcation of the beginning and end of the ritual so that the barrier between conscious and unconscious parts of our character could be brought back to normal, because at the beginning it was temporarily weakened, if not removed altogether.

The second thing that is equally important is the belief that by looking back, the things that were achieved with the ritual could be reversed to the previous condition, to the state that existed before the ritual was performed. Primarily this is particular to rituals during which illness is healed or spells are cast. That means that if the person from whom illness was taken looks back, their illness will return, or so it is according to folklore.

The third thing is related to the belief that is mainly concerned with people who usually do not practice magic; meaning that they are not Witches, and for them it is strongly forbidden to see creatures from the "other world" that were summoned on their behalf. For example, the girl who carries the "wolf's dinner" on Christmas day runs and does not look back to the crossroads, because she doesn't want to see the creatures from the underworld who came to accept the sacrifice. It is the same with a man who makes an amulet from the Hazelnut tree, then afterwards runs away from the place where he worked without looking back, because he doesn't want to see the creatures that gathered there during the ritual. We will talk about these examples later in the book. All this could remind us of the myth of Orpheus and Eurydice when he ignored the rule about looking back, and because of that lost Eurydice forever.

Magic and Rituals

In old Balkan Witchcraft there is no differentiation between black and white magic. These terms were later added with the appearance a people who claimed to be "White magi", that were rivals of the so-called "Black magi"; and this was mainly due to competition within the market. The Christian church, looking at things from their point of view, claimed that all magic is black, and all this is the Devil's work. Real Witches, both male and female, did not care much for these claims, and they continued to use the magical abilities that the received either through higher forces or from family inheritance.

The magic was never black or white, but the people who used it described it in simple terms, neither bad nor good. The practitioners decide for themselves what they need or want to do, and take the consequences. However, the reality is that there are many self-taught people who use magic for their own personal interests. On the one hand, there is magic for the healing of the sick, and on the other, magic exists that is used to cause someone to fall ill. This means that negative rituals do exist, though they are not contained in a logical system that could be called black magic, but rather it is the decision of certain rare individuals to practice these techniques and rituals, which can be found in almost all systems. It is very difficult for us to decide what is "Black" and what is "White"; what we must remember is that different communities and cultures had varying ideas of what was considered moral or immoral. The question of morality is endless, and it is not one that we will discuss in this book. Each person must come to their own conclusions about the path that they wish to follow.

Witchcraft is not a classical religious system, and therefore does not regulate the norms of behavior the way that other religions do. Modern western systems developed a codes of conduct, but they do not originate from earlier times. There is an old Latin proverb that roughly translated reads, "What is allowed to Jupiter it is not allowed to an ox". In a crude way, it says that all people are not equals.

Some people think that influencing any man against his will is black magic; what about a father who influences his son to stop taking drugs? Is he a black magus? What if a group of people tries to assassinate a ruler who wants to kill half of humanity, are their actions evil or wrong? All this is debatable and the discussion could last forever, as people's opinions will vary greatly. We therefore leave this question to the individuals themselves to solve according to their own morals and ethics. Those who are spiritually advanced will know the answers for themselves, but they cannot answer for others. Each must take responsibility for his or her own actions, and believe it or not, this can be the harshest judgment of all. Jung once said that if a mentally sound man kills another he judges himself for the rest of his life, and therefore needs no prison; the greatest punishment is the torment he inflicts on himself. From the occult point of view, everything that we do is imprinted on our psyche. One part of today's modern Wicca incorporates the Indian philosophy of karma, while some other parts work with ethical standards, and even whole systems based on belief in the human soul and its journey to the afterlife after death, to either a good or bad place. At a first glance, this could remind us of the Christian story about heaven and hell, but it is in essence quite different, and we will not explore it here.

Now that we have established that ancient Balkan tradition had no differentiation between black and white magic, we will now see that people used another kind of differentiation. This is by function or the thing that the "magic" serves, that is, to whom or what the ritual is dedicated. Because of that, we have love magic, agricultural magic, defense magic, healing magic, magic for wealth, criminal magic, and many other types.

Below you will find some of these rituals in their original form. It should be said that most of these rituals were used by common people from village communities, not by Witches. If they were unsuccessful, they usually went to a Witch to ask for help, but these rituals are general and belong in the classification of folk magic.

The origin of these rituals is twofold.. The first is oral tradition, though some of it was written down in documents, from generation to generation through time. The other consisted of rituals that were obtained by the Witch in dreams or astral journeys, during which they were instructed by higher forces or the spirits of the dead. It is very common that a long-dead Witch will contact Witches and pass rituals on to them through dreams, or while they are in a trance.

Some Witches have small books with written rituals, but these are certainly not "books of shadow". In essence, they are mainly transcripts from the "Ancients". These are huge, ancient (medieval) books, handwritten by monks in the monasteries. Inside these books are various heresies from the church's point of view, such as the methods of divination, evocation, prayers for various things, and astrology, etc.

Healing rituals

Healing rituals used many components, such as incantations, the use of herbs and other things from nature that were believed to help heal a sick person. Sacred herbs (the ones that heal and have magical capabilities) we mention here only briefly, as a integral part of the ritual; we will address them thoroughly in the chapter dedicated to herbs. These rituals were mainly performed when the Moon was setting so that the illness would "fall down" too, or when the Sun goes down, so the illnesses would go away with the Sun, or by running water, so it would carry the sickness away, etc. The usual day for performing almost all kinds of rituals was Tuesday, though some other days could be considered.

If someone has an illness that is potentially fatal, the most radical methods will be used, even if they involve what is considered a necessary evil. These are techniques of transferring illness to another living entity, because the illness is too strong to be destroyed with other methods.

More often than not, the sickness was transferred to a tree or animal. There are some extreme examples where they tried to transfer the illness to another person, but this is considered to be an exceptionally immoral and unnecessary act, so accounts of these cases are very rare. People are still very cautious, avoiding anything that they find at a crossroads, especially bank notes, which people think have someone's illness transferred to them. This is especially true in rural areas,

Here is how it is done. One way is to take the clothes of the sick person and place them on a sapling tree; this tree becomes that person' duplicate. The illness is transferred from the person to the tree through visualization and an appropriate incantation. Usually it rhymes, although that is not essential. It could be written by anyone, not necessarily a Witch. For example:

"As the Moon crosses the sky, so the illness of (The afflicted) transfers to this tree" or "As the wind carries the white clouds through the sky, so my incantation transfers the illness of (The afflicted) to this tree".

While the Witch does this, she visualizes the illness in the shape of a black cloud leaving the sick man and entering into the tree. Usually the incantation must be recited three times, but in extreme cases nine times are required. It must be three or nine, no more and no less, that is a strict rule. On the following days, if the tree starts to die we have reason to be happy, because it means that the "operation" was successful.

The process is similar for an animal. Usually it is necessary to take a part of the body of the sick person, such as a nail, a lock of hair, or blood, and mix it in with animal's food, and give it to the animal to eat. During the transference of illness to the animal, the Witch visualizes and chants an appropriate incantation. If the animal dies or get sick, that is the sign that the sick person will get well. This may look very cruel, but imagine that this is your only way to save a loved one, what would you do? The women from the village never had a problem with "sacrificing" a hen or a pig that will finish it's life on the dinner table either way.

When the illness is not likely to be fatal, other methods are used. For example, in most cases you can use the setting Moon in following way. You must prepare a copper dish, fill it with living water, then add a photograph or some personal item of the sick person. Then go outside and catch the Moon's reflection in the dish. This is so you can connect energy of the Moon with the energy of the sick person You must then add an appropriate herb to the water, and while you do that you must chant an incantation (written for this specific occasion) three times. For example:

"Oh Moon that shines in the sky, help me and this herb to heal (The afflicted) from the illness that he has encountered. As you set, so shall the illness go away, as the herb falls down into the water, so the health grows. Cure him Moon, cure him herb, cure him water, chase illness away". Finally the Witch must "cut the water" three or nine times with her magical knife and then spill it on the ground, at a crossroads, or into running water, which perpetuates what was done by the Moon. By the way, the herb that was soaked in the water can be worn as an amulet against all illnesses. You can find suitable herbs in any book about medical herbs, even in this book, covered in the chapter about magical herbs.

A male witch performs a ritual - photo by author

One method of magical healing is by transferring the illness to a stone. For this purpose, you can use the smooth white stones found in clear streams and rivers. It is necessary to get three or nine pieces of white quartz and bring them home. The ritual itself must be performed late at night during the time of the waning Moon. The sick person must be in a prone position, and the stones are placed over the part of the body that is unwell.

An incantation is recited once for each separate stone. This means that if we have three stones, we must recite the incantation three times, and if we have nine stones, the same incantation must be recited nine times. While reciting the incantation on each stone that we put on the body, we must turn the stone counter-clockwise in a spiral, from the right to the left, finishing in the center of the spiral. Each placement a stone on the afflicted person needs to coincide with finishing the incantation, which needs to sound as if you are talking to the stone as a living being or force that can absorb illness. For example:

> **"Oh powerful stone, take this illness into you because it can't harm you; take it, absorb it, and it into stone!"**

Pay attention to the last word in the incantation. It means that the illness is transferred, but is "stoned" or petrified, which means closed and trapped, so that it cannot transfer to the Witch that performs the ritual and handles the stones. After the transfer process is complete, the stones must be returned to they were taken from, and you must throw them in back in the water, one by one, accompanying each with an appropriate incantation. It The incantation should be something like this:

> **"Oh water that carries the stones, take them and the illness far, far away, so that none see it, none step on them, no one falls ill, while the waning moon weakens**

them until they disappear... take them water... take... take...".

The stone is not a stone but the illness itself, and the water is the medium that carries it while the waning moon makes the sickness weaken and disappear.

We can say that for the classic form of ritual healing, rituals were performed using cloth and yarn. One of them is following: take piece of white fabric from natural materials (cotton, flax, linen, etc.) one decimeter square and spread in front of you. On that piece of fabric, you must put the things that we consider not only necessary but the most appropriate ones for this ritual. Everything must be first washed in running water, so as to be clean and ready to accept their new power. By these things we mean photograph of the sick person, lock of hair, a nail, or something to that effect.

After that the appropriate herb for the illness is added, or an herb that is considered a talisman against all illnesses, and a mountain crystal to improve the effectiveness of the spell. In the Balkans, that is usually a piece of white quartz from a stream or river. After that, you make a small bag that you tie up with the white yarn. After you wrap the top several times, you start tying knots. You always tie three or nine knots, and for each knot you recite a separate incantation, and as you do that, you must visualize the sick man getting better. The incantation should sound something like this:

"I'm not tying the yarn, I'm tying you (Afflicted person). I am tying you to feel better, I am tying you to get out of the bed, I am tying you to bring you back your strength, and I am tying you so you can run, to work, to enjoy life... I'm tying you to get well!"

While the Witch does this, she visualizes him getting out of bed, imagines him happy and healthy. After this, the healing bag must be given to the sick person or it needs to be taken a sacred place where

128

such things are put. Usually it must be taken away to some big tree where will be tied in its branches or buried among its roots.

Love rituals

The structure of these rituals is very similar to that of the other types of rituals. However, with love magic, as with all others types, the question of morality and justification exists. I must first say that in the territories of Serbia and all of the Balkans, these are considered to be Black magic, and based on that, it is extremely difficult to find a real Witch that wants to perform such rituals. People that do are usually Witches who perform the rituals for financial gain, or are mere hobbyists. Of course, not all rituals related to love are Black ones, but those that directly influence the will of an individual are considered, at the very least, immoral. The most famous ritual of love magic is most likely the "binding" ritual that is common in east Serbia. At the very beginning of the reading of this ritual you will notice that black yarn is used for which we earlier say that is used exclusively for black magic rituals. However, it still widely used, and we will discuss it in more detail. Since these rituals vary from Witch to Witch, here we only can express the basic structure, which is very simple and consists of very few elements.

It is necessary to provide a photograph of the person, their sperm, or menstrual blood and a length of black yarn for the process of ritual binding. You must wait until nightfall, and for the person for whom you wish to perform this magic to fall asleep, as to be more vulnerable to the external influence imposed by this ritual.

This is how it works. You must to sit opposite to the picture of the person and then you must soak the yarn in sperm or menstrual blood. After that you must stare at the picture, never taking your eyes from it during the ritual. After holding the yarn in your hand for awhile, the picture "comes to life", and you tie the nine knots. You only need to recite the incantation once, and to be careful to end it exactly when you tie the ninth knot. The incantation should look like this:

"I am not binding this yarn, I am binding (The subject of the spell). I'm binding his head, his hands, I'm binding his legs; I'm binding his veins, his heart, his stomach, binding his power and his essence. I bind all of him, I bind him to belong to me and to me only; to love only me, and to listen to me only."

You must keep this yarn, because as long as the knots are tied, the person is bound as well.

To remove such a spell, a Witch must perform the ritual of unbinding in a sacred place, in the presence of higher forces and with their help he perform the ritual. She does that following way; After midnight the Witch takes the person to the holy place. She then removed her clothes, and silently invoked the Goddess. The Forest Mother specifically, because she is known to be competent in love magic. She would then symbolically "bind" the person, then recite an incantation similar to the one for binding, but with the exact opposite meaning. The incantation should look something like this:

"I'm not unbinding yarn, I'm unbinding (The subject of the spell); unbinding his head, unbinding his hands, unbinding his legs... to give him back his power, to give him back his strength... I'm unbinding him now."

 The end of the final incantation should happen at the same time that the last of the yarn is removed from the symbolically "Bound" person. If the person feels better, the problem is solved, but if there were no progress, the piece of knotted yarn must be found, untied, and then burned

Not all love rituals are necessarily "black". A great number of them are exceptionally beautiful and romantic. In such rituals Witch tries to get the attention of a man in a neutral manner, not focusing on a specific individual when she asked the Goddess to grant her luck in love.

The first type of ritual looks like this: The Witch prepares piece of red fabric, of silk if possible, a length red yarn, a lock of her hair, and several herbs that have the powers necessary to assist completing the ritual. The most used herbs are Navala ferns (aspidium filix mas), Sanicle (Sanicula europaea), sunflower (helianthus annuus) and Immortelle (helichrysum arenarium) but the choice of herbs could differ, based on the wishes of the Witch performing the ritual. Choice for many herbs depends on the origin of the Witch because the same herbs do not grow in different areas.

When the Witch had everything that she needed, she spread the red fabric in front herself, held the lock of her hair in her hand and then started putting herbs onto the fabric. She would then begin the incantation.

"(The Witches' name) adds the Navala so that men will desire me, Sanicle so that men will notice me; I add sunflower so that turn to look at me, just as the Sunflower turns to follow the sun, and I add Immortelle in the hope that my Faerie sisters help me."

By the way, the Immortelle is considered to the fairy's flower, and only unmarried girls have right to wear it; it is said that flower itself attract boys, and that is not appropriate for married women.
After she made a bouquet from herbs and hair, the Witch took the red yarn and wrapped it thrice around the bouquet, saying:

"I'm not binding herbs but myself and the herbs".

At the end, she puts the bouquet on the fabric and makes a bag of it. This bag must be left at a place where Fairies gather, or it could be worn as an amulet.

We need to say that these incantations are arbitrary. They differ from Witch to Witch, but their essence is the same. Some of them were passed down from generation to generation, but the vast majority were composed on an impromptu basis, depending on what was needed at the time. It is simply impossible to find two Witches with same incantations. In literature, one can find those people that assert that all incantations should be uniform, and recited perfectly each time, but overwhelmingly, that is not the case.

If you want to compose your own incantations you should pay close attention to rhyme and rhythm, they should be short and precise, and have a direct connection with the subject of your efforts.

Here is a typical Witch's ritual that is performed with the broom and the nature spirits. All you need is the broom, a shovel, and some sort of "offering". The offering is necessary to attract the nature spirits, or elementals, however you choose to refer to them. We should immediately say that this type of ritual should only be performed by an experienced witch that has complete control over her surroundings and the process itself.

The correct time for performing rituals of this type is the night of the full Moon, because all manner fairies, dwarves, and other creatures gather at that time and are visible to the Witches eye, especially after the midnight. The Witch goes to a sacred place, which means a place where she expects the supernatural beings to appear. She then removes her clothes and sets out an offering. This usually consists of nine grains of corn, nine grains of wheat, some salt, etc. If the offering is of some sort of grain, there must be nine kernels. After she showed her offer, she starts to call those creatures to her with the following words:

"Come and see what I brought to you… I brought nine grains of corn, nine grains of wheat, some salt… I feed you well… listen to me well…"

After she pronounced this incantation either three or nine times, she takes broom and shovel and starts to collect the creatures that have gathered. When she feels that there are enough she turns in direction of the person for whom she is performing the ritual. She then tosses the contents of the shovel into the air and continues her incantation with the words:

"… go to (The person for whom the spell is intended) don't let him eat, don't let him sleep, don't let him work… until (name of the girl) comes, let him think only of her, let him dream only of her… I feed you well; you listen to me well".

This incantation must be recited only once in the moment the contents are tossed from the shovel. Of course, different variations of this ritual exist and one of its renditions involves the invocation of *Tartor*. We discussed this in the second chapter, and the only difference is the manner of the incantation.

We can see the huge variations in the types of love rituals from the fact that Witch from eastern Serbia would prepare a small love bag and used a hunting rifle to fire the bag in the direction of the person for whom it was intended.

One of the popular love rituals that is performed in current times takes place on St. George's Day. The greatest number of love rituals are performed in the Springtime which is consistent with the concept of harmony and renewal in nature.

The ritual begins on May 5 at midnight. It is necessary to take nine coffee beans three separate times, put them into a copper dish, then fill the dish with hot water. After a time, the beans must be removed from the water and placed on three small pieces of red fabric, nine beans on each. Next, it is necessary to salt the grains on the following way: with three fingers, a person pinches some salt and puts a bit on each pile, just one time.

Then the pieces are wrapped into bags. During that action, following incantation must be recited for each bundle, either inside your mind or in a murmur:

"I'm not binding these beans, I'm binding these (The person for whom the ritual is intended)".

The bundles must be tied under the belt with red yarn, with the following incantation recited thrice, once for each bundle:
"I'm not binding up these beans for me, I'm binding (The person for whom the ritual is intended) so that his love for me grows just like this bean grows around my waist".

After this, the person performing the spell approaches the hearth or some other type of fire, untying the bundles one by one and throwing them in. Before throwing them in, the person blows on it, then recites:

"Just as these beans crack, the heart of (The person for whom the spell is intended) beats for me."

This must be repeated three times and after that, the ritual is over.

Rituals for Defense

Under this classification of ritual, we mean all rituals that function to protect either a Witch or a person for whom the ritual is to be performed. They consist not only of several types of defenses, but also ways of giving magic back to the caster. In addition, this kind of ritual has defensive capabilities from supernatural beings such as demons, vampires, spirits, evil entities, etc.
A large number of these rituals can hardly be called rituals because they consist of just one or two actions, but we will mention them anyway.

When a Witch suspects that she is endangered, that some other Witch plots against her life, she puts water in a pot or kettle,, then places it on the fire until it comes to a boil. A few minutes before it actually does, she adds Mugwort (tanacetum vulgare), then waits for it to boil. That moment it does, she takes the kettle to the open front door of the house, pours the contents out over the threshold and recites the following words::

"I don't track, I give it back" or in the original form, "ne praćam neg vraćam". This must be recited just once. If, at the moment the water and herb hit the ground, one hears something like firecrackers, it means that the Witch has right and that the opposing magic has been reversed.

If she thinks that her opponent is very strong and that his black magic is exceptionally powerful, she will ask help from the Goddess. Specifically, very late at night, the Witch goes to a sacred place where Goddess lives, removes her clothes, then silently recites the invocation. It is in the form of an incantation, something like this:

"I turn to you, because if anything can be done, you can... to you who can create anything, you who can

135

destroy everything, you who has the power to give and the power to take away… take from me that thing that was sent to me and return it to the sender. Wherever she is let it find her, wherever she goes let it follow her, whatever she wants done to me, give it back to her in turn."

This must be pronounced three times, then she puts on her clothes and leaves the place without looking back.

There is a very interesting ritual with many variations, but in essence, it consists following. It is necessary to make a doll from beeswax, rag, or corn husk. After the doll is made, it must named after a person whom you think plots against your life. You may also assign it to that person by adding a personal effect of the individual to the doll during its' creation. After that, it is necessary to cut off the top and remove the seeds. When the pumpkin is cleaned, you fill the pumpkin with water and the doll must be soaked inside. It is then necessary to add some ingredients and herbs that have protective properties, such as salt, bell pepper, garlic, valerian (valeriana officinalis) etc. Then the Witch takes her magical knife, plunges the blade into the water and cuts it in different directions while reciting the incantation:

"Everything you sent me I salted, everything you threw at me I seasoned strongly, from all the ill you meant for me, I defended myself...there is nothing you can do to me, and there will never be".

After that, pumpkin must be sealed and taken on some cold place so it would remain fresh for a long time. With this act, you become protected from the evil intentions of the person that wants to hurt you, and at the same time, you brought no harm to that person. This protection lasts until the pumpkin is spoiled.

The other type of ritual for protection that is based on several similar characteristics. If there is a suspicion that vampire is coming into a house by night and feeding itself with the energy of the members of the household or disturbing them in some other way, it is necessary to fumigate a house with combination of hemp (cannabis sativa) and sage (salvia officinalis). Protection could be assured by placing a head of black ram over the entrance, leaving the broom standing upright, or by placing a magical knife beside the bed or under the pillow. Somewhat more drastic measures involve placing a protective circle of Hawthorn branches (crataegus oxyacantha) around the whole house.

We need to mention that in the Balkans, the vampire is not considered a physical being, but rather a spirit that feeds itself with the energies of the living. The easiest way to determine if someone is vampire is by digging up the grave of the suspected individual. If inside the coffin you find a fresh body that hasn't begun to decompose, regardless of the time since their death, that person is a vampire. It means that physical body does not rise from the grave, but the ethereal body still walks, maintaining life by feeding itself with energy of people while they sleep.

In these less complicated rituals of protection and defense, we include wearing of special types of amulets acquired in various ways.

For the end of this section on defensive rituals, we will discuss defense from the most famous ritual, the egg that evil Witches and sorcerers use to kill their opponents. We never actually learned the complete ritual as neither of women who serve us as informants want to tell us, for obvious reasons. Still, it is not difficult to find out how to defend oneself from it. This ritual probably exists in several variations but its structure is the same. The only thing that is necessary to know is that here the egg is used for evil intentions, similar to a voodoo doll. The egg is the symbol of life it and is considered a living thing; the characteristics of the individual you wish to hurt must be imprinted on it, then the egg becomes that person. Such an egg must be hidden, or buried in the backyard of the intended target. If someone accidentally finds it, this is what must be done: (It is preferable for a "qualified" Witch or sorcerer to do it.)

Before they go to bed, the person who finds the egg must put it in a dish with water place it on the fire until the water boils. While water boils, it is necessary to cut the water three times with the magical knife and to recite the following incantation:

"I don't cook water, I don't cook egg, but the evil souls, evil Witches, evil sorcerers, evil demons, and all the enemies that came to my house to do us harm… my foes, my enemies."

After the incantation is recited, you must use three fingers to throw in some kitchen salt. The water must then be spilled over the threshold, and following incantation must be recited:

"I cooked all my enemies, those that plot against my life, that sent me evil thoughts and mean for me the things that are not ordained by (**The God**). I cast water in the backyard to protect us from all evil. I am cleansed, cleansed with the glorious power of the ones destined by fate, for the well-being of all of us. So be it." Then the Witch crosses herself three times, reciting "amen, amen, amen".

After that, the egg must be wrapped in a textile of natural canvas (most often cotton or wool) and must be put in a container and covered with earth. It can be a dish, a flowerpot, or something similar. The dish must be placed in front of the house and the egg must be taken out at sunrise and observed, egg must be taken out and observed. You must pay attention to any special marks that might reveal the identity of the person that performed the black magic. According to tradition, there are usually letters, initials or some other marking or symbol.

Lastly, the egg must be taken to the river or stream (It must be running water) and thrown away, while reciting the following words:

> **"To the rocks and stones you go, and in the end you turn to sand, to endlessly count and never finish counting."**

This text is almost universal and is used in almost every ritual of healing or removing evil magic, especial on the east and south of Serbia.

Finally, the place where the egg is thrown must be abandoned quickly and without looking back, and the house must be consecrated, that is, purified with incense (the new method) or with sage (the old, original method). A candle must be lit; a Slava cake (A Serbian family delicacy for its patron saint) cake must be prepared, and sacrificial feast must be organized. Fresh eggs should be placed in the central areas of the house.

From all of this, we can clearly see this is not an usual ritual for removing black magic, but a demanding one, that calls for the help of demons of fate, "sudjenice". These supernatural creatures belong to a group of supernatural beings from ancient religion and although they do not belong to Christianity, they are referred to as "Holy *sudjenice*". According to folk beliefs, the *Sudjenice* or *sudjaje* are supernatural beings that manage the fate of man. They are respected in the territories of eastern and southern Serbia. People imagine them as three young women who determine destiny of a newborn child. In the north, Usud joins them and assumes the role of their master. Each interference with in life was considered the work of the sudjenica. That is why it is not surprising that they are summoned in this ritual. Candles must be lit for them, cake must be prepared, and it must conclude with a sacrificial banquet. Because of all that, we can conclude that Christian elements in this ancient ritual probably emerged sometime later.

Ritual production of amulets

Here we will mention some of the many ways of making amulets. It is very difficult to get to the basis of the structure of these rituals, as they are very different from one another and they are almost endless in variety. Some of them are very cruel, which isn't surprising at all if we understand that some of them are very old and resemble "recipes" from medieval grimoires. However, because of the fact that they still exist and are probably being performed, we have no intention of hiding them and we will show them here in their proper form. To be precise, we will describe a ritual in which the only difference is the type of animal used.

At night somewhere, around eleven o'clock the Witch goes to a crossroads that isn't often, so that she is alone. She carries with her a cauldron, nine liters of water, a mirror, and lastly a black cat or rooster.

After she lights big fire under the cauldron, she adds the water and waits for it to boil. She removes her clothes and lets her hair down in complete silence, as a single spoken word could nullify the entire ritual At exactly one minute past midnight (12+1=13), she puts a live black cat or black rooster into the cauldron. She waits until the meat has completely boiled of the animal's bones; she then pours out the water and collects the bones. She then takes up the mirror in one hand, and with the other, puts each bone, one by one, to her mouth. She watches each bone touch her lower lip through the mirror the entire time. It is absolutely necessary to do this with each bone. When she brings the particular bone to her mouth that she "seeks", her reflection disappears. She keeps that bone for the rest of her life, because it represents one of the most powerful amulets in existence. The amulet that is produced in this manner serves for protection, happiness, money… in essence, everything. After all, she leaves in silence and, of course, does not look back.

A special group of amulets are the so called "animal" and "herbal" amulets. Among the animal amulets are the eagle's claw, wolf's tooth, wild boar's tooth, piece of the ram's horn, a piece of goat, bull, or deer horn, bear and wolf hair, the shed skin of a snake, etc. These amulets does not have to be dedicated, neither any special ritual must be performed because those are considered powerful themselves.

Herbal amulets are consisted of parts of an herb, such as branches, leaves or roots. It could be herbs that we use every day, such as garlic or bell pepper, but the other herbs that were known to be used were rare and often grew in inaccessible areas. For the amulet, the most used part of the herb is the root, whose shape can remind us of the human form, to a hand, to sexual organs, etc
.

Beside those mentioned above, there are metal amulets that are very common. These amulets are made by either one or nine blacksmiths. They must be made on the night of the full moon, after midnight, they must also be naked and completely silent, as we mentioned before. If several amulets must be produced then nine naked blacksmiths must work in the same manner, using the same technique. There is a belief that he or they come into contact with the horned God, master of the underworld and protector of their craft, and therefore the presence of the women is forbidden. These amulets usually take the shape of the Sun, snakes, horns, knives, axes, etc.

So if you want, for example, a metal pentagram that you want to wear that is more than just a fashion statement, you can hammer it yourself if you follow these rules.

Applying the same rules, nine naked old women sew a magic shirt from one thread of yarn. They begin just after the stroke of midnight, work in complete silence, and they must finish before sunrise. The men are forbidden, because during that time they come in contact with Goddess, their protector. This magical shirt protects from all illnesses and misfortunes. This does not mean that men have no contact with the Goddess or women with the horned God, but there are some rituals to which this rule applies.

A special type of amulet are the ones made of umbilical cord or placenta. They are considered very powerful and sacred, but only to the one whom it belonged. As we mentioned before, there is a belief in the Balkans that male and female Witches were born in a blue or bloody placenta, the lucky people were born in white placenta, murderers in red, etc. There is a rule that the placenta must be dried, then sealed with beeswax. Later that placenta must be given to the child, or must be sewn into their clothes to protect them from harm.

An umbilical cord also must be dried and sealed with beeswax, but red yarn and herbs that symbolize health, prosperity, and protection could be added as well; some women add lock of child's hair from their first haircut, which according to Serbian tradition, must happen a year to the day after the birth of the child. In this case, the mother is the custodian of the amulet, not the child, as the mother is the most capable of protecting her children.

One of the most famous herbal amulets from the Balkans traces its origin to eastern Serbia and is called "*jarba fjeruluj*" or "Iron Grass". The complete method for preparing this amulet was documented by ethnologist Paun Es Durlich during field research near the

Porecka River and nearby villages. He published his findings on his website.

According to him, this is one of the rare amulets that was made and solely used by men who were decent and honest. The ritual of making this amulet was performed on Saint George's day, but the preparation started few days earlier. Here what it looked like.

Several days before celebration, the person who wanted to make an amulet for himself would go into the forest to find an appropriate Hazelnut tree and collect it's flowers from underneath it's canopy. After he has collected the flowers, he must dip a piece of white sheet in beeswax and a piece of Rowan wood. After that, from the Rowan, he makes small container with a lid or cork. After that, the container must be submerged for three days and three nights in water that is brought from three monasteries. When this period is over, the case is pulled out, dried, and sealed with wax. With this act, preparation period is completed and during that time, this person must not have sexual relations.

The night before Saint George's day, he must return to the hazelnut tree shaven, bathed, and wearing clean clothes. He removes his clothes; turns to east under the selected branch and spreads out the sheet with his hands.

Bearing in mind the fact that people in those areas believe that the Hazelnut tree has both male and female flowers, red and pink respectively, he remains in that position waiting until after midnight for one of the two types of flower to fall from the tree onto the sheet. He then folds up the sheet and dresses himself, all the while holding the bundled sheet in his hand so that it does not touch the ground (it could lead to losing the energy given by the flower, rendering the ritual worthless). After that, he must cross himself three times, and then go home. During his return home, the flower turns into the figure of a child; a boy if the flower is red, and girl if the flower is pink.

With the bundle in his hand, man does not enter in the home but goes under a tree, and by moonlight or some other means he checks the "sex" of the fallen flower. If a "girl" is in the bundle, the figure is given away to a barren woman in the immediate family, and if it is a "boy", it must be placed into the container, and the man will carry it with him for the rest of his life. People think that case has magical powers but in extreme situations it opens in the direction from which trouble comes. People also believe that this amulet lose its power if it was not taken off during sexual relations, or if it is worn while committing a crime. Borrowed or stolen amulets of this type have no power.

At the end of his life, the owner of this amulet gives it to some younger male family member in a ritual manner. The custom is that person must declare to whom is going to give that amulet during some celebration's lunch. The celebration during which the transfer will be performed must be predetermined. When that day comes, both men must wear clean dress clothes, and early in the morning they go to a previously determined place, most often a Hazelnut tree or a spring.

While he crosses himself, the older man gives the young man piece of wax to rub in his right hand, in which he will take the amulet. After that, he offers a piece of waxed sheet and places the amulet on it with an appropriate speech. It usually spoke of how the amulet would protect him from the knife, the rifle, and any other misfortune, but if he wants the amulet's power to work for him, he must be a decent and honest man. The young man swears to that, and signs with his finger on the sheet. After that, the young man takes the amulet and they return home for the celebration lunch. During the trip, the elder explains, in the form of stories, what it is, what it can and cannot do, how it is very important to keep quiet about it, and why. People believe that one who talks about the amulet will meet with an unfortunate accident and that the amulet itself will lose its powers. Because of the nature of this amulet, I think that Durlich the performed an amazing feat collecting this data.

For this area, eastern Serbia one more very important amulet is related that is also made with the help of the Hazelnut tree. Everything that is related to this amulet was also collected and published on the website by Paun Es Durlic.

This amulet is known as "*Aluna vojnjičaske*" or "Military Hazelnut" although its function is identical to that of the "Iron Grass". In contrast to "iron grass" that must be prepared on Saint George's day, the "military hazelnut" must be prepared on the Transfiguration. According to Durlic, there are three ways of making this amulet, the basic difference are their contents and who creates them.

In essence, only a male that plans to wear it could make it (this amulet is also usable by men only), a mother of wife could make it, or if the man asks a Witch, she could make it for him. The first of those three ways is considered the oldest, the best and the most original. The man must make it on his own in that moment when the need arises, such as when he must go to war, or on a trip where his life will be in harm's way. Here what it looks like.

The night before Ascension Day, between midnight and the crow of the first rooster, he goes to a previously selected Hazelnut tree, cleanly shaven and dressed in clean clothes. He then disrobes, and turns to the east with a previously chosen branch behind him. Throwing back his hands, he takes a branch and bends it down, trying to pick one, or better, three flowers from the tree with his buttocks. When he accomplishes that, he continues naked until the first fern bush he finds and tries to pick one flower with his buttocks. After that, he puts his clothes on and returns home.

145

The next morning, he sat on his threshold and picked up a healthy Hazelnut, drilled a hole in it and removed it's insides. After that, he put a little mercury, incense, marble, a piece of duck's feather, a piece of grass that was not cut during the harvest, a piece of gold, a clipping of the fingernail of an illegitimate child, a small bone of the wren, and finally, the flowers that he picked with his buttocks. After that, still on the threshold he waxed the hazelnut and recited the following incantation three times:

"Just as no one can catch mercury, as the scythe couldn't cut this grass, as the water didn't wet this feather, as the rust cannot harm gold, the bullet cannot harm me.... let it go to blooming ferns... just as the marble is strong, and cannot be harmed by the knife, let me be so strong. Just as incense chases away evil, let it stay away from me.

Just as the bastard is born happy, so I want to be lucky. Let me stay alive, clean, and sacred like the stars in the sky and the morning dew."

After this, the amulet is usually sewn into clothes, hat, or he can carry it wrapped in something in his pocket or his wallet.

Magical rituals for acquiring money

As the name says, the only function of those short rituals we will mention here have is to provide more money for the person who performs them. I must to warn readers that no one ever expected money to "Fall from Heaven" or that it was only necessary to perform the ritual and money would appear without any other effort. These rituals were intended to help a person to have more luck, to make a good deal, or buy or sell something, to be in the right place at the right time, etc.

146

Almost all people performed such rituals, therefore, they doubted in their success and their ability put them into effect, so they asked Witches for help.

The simplest ritual, if we can call it that, is a whipping with a magical whip. The ritual is so simple that all that is needed to do is to whip a human or animal, but creating the right whip is very difficult. As we discussed before, it is the whip made of hemp that grows in a snake head with a silver coin. It means that if someone wants to conclude a deal he needs to be whipped with this whip, or if we want to sell something, we need to whip that object or animal etc.

In this category of simple rituals, we include rituals that were performed in the night of the new Moon. The simplest is the one for which is necessary to prepare handful of coins, silver ones if possible, and if not, any metal money will do, jingling it in your hand a few times and showing it to the new Moon. People think that while the Moon is waxing, the quantity of the money of the person who performed this ritual grew as well. In earlier times a lot of the available currency consisted of silver coins, which was ideal because the silver is Moon's metal. Later on, other metals replaced silver in coinage, so people started to use them in rituals. The only rule is not to use paper money, because it is worthless in magical rituals. We think that the situation is similar in western Witchcraft.

In of the most famous Witch's disciplines is included control of spiritual assistants, whether they were elementals, familiars, or other entities. That is the situation in Balkan Witchcraft; it is not strange that they are used in rituals to help acquire money.

Now it is necessary to visit places in which the creatures that we want to contact live. In this case, those creatures are the dwarves that live in caves, abandoned mines, deep holes, etc.

The Witch brings an offering in the form of salt, quartz, or some other stone, then grain and spring water. In addition to that, she carries one metal coin that she will later take back. By night she goes to the pre-determined place, removes her clothes, and leaves her offering in an appropriate place. After midnight she he starts the invocation with an incantation that she recites silently, in her head. It is usually the following text:

"Come here my little ones, walk up to me little ones... to see what I brought to you... I gave you salt, I fed you grain, and I watered you ... I care about you... hear me well... help me to have the thing of which you have the most... that's why I leave you this silver coin to empower it, to multiply it... so that the silver will never be alone and will have many children, brothers, sisters.... do so and I will come to pick it up and bring you presents again... my little ones... my dear ones..."

This incantation must be repeated three times; the Witch dresses and walks away without looking back. After three days, she returns after midnight after and again offers the same presents. She can recite an appropriate incantation to herself, but it is not necessary. If she decides to recite the incantation, it has to be something like this:

> **"Here am I again my little ones, my dear ones... I came to give you presents and take the coin... thank you little ones, my dear ones... you take care of me and I will take care of you."**

After this Witch takes the coin, she gets dressed and goes away without looking back. This coin must be carried in the wallet and it must not leave it. That coin needs some real sources, contracts, or jobs to attract money to flow into your wallet. That means that it is to be used as a type of amulet.

Invocation of dwarves for wealth amulets is not a steadfast rule. Witches often contact the Forest Mother for this purpose, while male Witches usually contact other powerful creatures like Silver Tsar, *Troglav* (The Three-headed) or *Tartor*. All of them are residents of the underworld and are custodians of wealth and mineral wealth, and therefore live in abandoned mines and caves.

All these rituals resemble one another, their structures are similar, and it is not hard to perform them when the need arises. There are no special rules, except for basic structures and the logic behind them, and just as we mentioned before, they vary in detail from Witch to Witch.

Magic potions

Let us briefly discuss the magic potions that were made by Witches in the Balkans. The thing that makes them different from other type of drinks like juices and teas is their content and methods of preparation. In reference to content, they mainly have various herbs that have special magical abilities, but not healing ones, although these are not specifically excluded, then parts of animals, animal blood, herbal oils, fats, metals, crystals, and occasionally, mercury.

Preparation of those potions is always followed by certain ritual actions. Two very important things involve the origin and manner of acquisition of the component ingredients, and the choosing of an incantation that will recited during or immediately after the potion is prepared..
From this we can conclude that magical potions, by method of preparation and content do not significantly differ from the medieval potions that originated in west Europe.

Some of these recipes are very cruel and necessitate animal sacrifice. An example is a potion in which newborn mice must be soaked in oil for forty days, and then this potion was used to treat alcoholism by putting several drops of this oil in the drink of the afflicted person.

It is also well-known that if water in which newborn kittens are bathed was poured in someone's drink and after that, the person would be oblivious to his surroundings. One of the most morbid ones is the potion made from "dead man's water", which is the water in which a deceased person was bathed. As you can assume, the function of this potion is to kill someone, transferring the characteristics of a deceased person (Specifically, being dead) to a live person.

Aside from these potions, it is a well-known fact that healing potions were formulated and prepared as well. It is a generally known fact that the medicine for epilepsy must be made of raven's blood or from dried magpie's tongues that must added to a liquid and consumed during the waxing Moon. Beside this, it is very well known fact that the remedy for heart disease must be made of pigeon's heart, and that mercury potions are used for healing serious illnesses.

DIVINATION

Divination in the Balkans does not differ greatly from other systems all over the world. It was used by people that had no connection with existing religious systems, either seriously or for mere entertainment. The techniques for divination differed, determined primarily by the cultural environment. For example, if people drink tea in a country or area, they will divine using tea leaves, and if coffee is the favorite drink, coffee grounds will be used to tell the future. Peoples that live near an ocean will use shells or something sea-oriented to tell the future, according to their religious or traditional beliefs.

The main difference in the Balkans comes from that everyone uses the same technique, but the results differ. Here again we speak of qualifications; it is different when a random woman looks into the cup of coffee, as opposed to when a Witch or actual clairvoyant does the same.

A Witch is considered to be clairvoyant because she inherited her talent, by birth or after receiving her initiation. This is not correct. Not all Witches are equally clairvoyant, and some of them are not at all. There is a tradition that each of them has a specialty and, of course, you expect the best results from a Witch whose specific specialty is divination.

Techniques of foretelling within the group of Witches that practice this discipline can vary greatly, because the Witch herself determines the technique that is most suitable for her. That could a traditional method, but might be some newly created one that she created by her own affinities, or instructions that she got from higher forces during the ritual trance.

That means that the Witch is clairvoyant from the very beginning and the techniques that she uses serve only to clarify her focus additional for better concentration, and to better connect her to what she sees. For example, when a common person foretells the future through coffee grounds she observes shapes that are formed flowing down the walls of the upturned coffee cup and she interprets them one by one, exactly as it was taught to her from another person or from a suitable book. Unlike the common person, a Witch observes these shapes, but she also receives imagery in her mind, and it is very common for her to change her interpretation of events based on the additional information the imagery provide..

We need to say that Balkan Witches, no matter how long they have practiced, have never used crystal balls, Tarot cards, or astrology. It is almost impossible to say which methods were used and those that still are simply because of their individuality and diversity, but we will talk about a few of the methods that have survived the test of time.

If we look at it in this manner, we can see that there are three basic methods of fortune-telling, and these are:

1. Direct —either looking at the photograph or holding a personal item of the person whose fortune you want to predict.
2. Indirect – foretelling the future through coffee grounds, tea leaves, bones, etc.
3. Ritual – Using some form of ritual, such as using a copper dish, extinguishing live coals, the melting of lead, etc.

Direct foretelling
This is one of the most used forms of foretelling. In essence, this procedure is very simple, but to achieve success sometimes represents insurmountable difficulties for a beginner.

The method itself addresses the need of a person who not only wants to know your future, but your past as well. The person brings a Witch a photograph of the intended subject, and if that isn't available, the person must provide a personal such as a ring, a watch, a lock of hair, etc. This is not a steadfast rule, as it is enough for some Witches to look the person or just to talk to them patiently, and wait for mental pictures to appear. However, if the person who approaches the Witch wants to find out more detailed information about another person, it is necessary to bring some personal item belonging to that person, or at least their photograph.

If a photograph is used, it is necessary to put hand on it and to stare at specific area of the picture, most often the eyes of person in the picture. At very beginning of her endeavor, the Witch stops talking, trying to cease all thoughts. She is trying to "clear out" her mind. If she can maintain this state at least for thirty seconds, images will begin to manifest in a form similar to flashbacks, related to the person in the photograph. This procedure could be performed with eyes open, or after several minutes of observation of the picture, closed. When we close our eyes, it is necessary to clear the mind and try not to visualize anything, and the pictures will begin to appear spontaneously.

When using personal effects, the process is essentially the same. The only difference is that now we must hold that item in our hand, and it matters not whether eyes or open or closed, that is purely a matter of personal preference. The essence of the procedure is clearing the mind of thought for several minutes, allowing the images to manifest. This is not as difficult as it may first appear. It takes a measure of willpower and some practice, but I sincerely believe that anyone can master this method of divination with this method with a modicum of persistence.

In addition to these two well-known methods of direct foretelling, we can include the next method that is lesser known but it is equally effective. Its basic uniqueness is that the Witch in the moment of foretelling makes contact only with a specific fetish. That fetish could be a ring, stick, figurine, picture, crystal, etc. Through this method, a Witch only receives visions then when she is "in contact" with the fetish. Making contact could take on many forms and was based directly on the nature of the object. That means that if that is a crystal, a Witch will begin to get visions the moment she touches it. With a figurine of the Goddess, for example, she can talk to it, when it is a ring, she can turn it on her finger or put it on a specific finger that has special importance to her. For example, in eastern Serbia, it is believed that the little finger is dedicated to magic and that it has magical powers. It is difficult to enumerate all the variations of this method, because they vary greatly and differ from Witch to Witch. The choice of such a method can be very good for a Witch, because she can fully control her ability and negative results, such as unwanted, non-solicited chaotic and sudden visions that can be detrimental to her mental stability.

Indirect foretelling

As we have said, in this classification of divination, we mean group of methods in which a Witch divines by observing shapes, figures, patterns, etc. to achieve prophetic visions and draws her own conclusions from them. She can independently interpret symbols and numbers, for example, and according to those draws conclusions based on her previous "training" which can be learned based on tradition and lore, her family, or training from an older Witch, if she is not interested in obtaining "The vision". Both possibilities are equally viable, and that is probably why Witches often combine the two forms to make a whole. Here is an example.

The traditional method of preparing coffee in the Balkans does not include a coffee maker. The procedure of making coffee is very simple. All you need is very finely ground coffee (Much like an espresso grind), a kettle, and water. Put the kettle on the stove, and wait for the water to boil. The quantity of water depends on how any cups of coffee we want to make. One cup of coffee is about one deciliter of water. When it boils, we take the kettle off the stove and we add the coffee. Use approximately a teaspoon of coffee per deciliter of water; some use a bit more or a bit less, depending on personal taste. We then stir it a bit and pour into cups, continuing to stir so that the coffee grounds distribute equally. It is drunk while it is still hot, but if you want to use it for prophecy later on, you must not add sugar, cream, or milk. After you have finished your coffee, there will be a layer of coffee grounds remaining in the bottom of the cup. The cup must be swirled left and right, so that the coffee grounds are evenly distributed and flow easily. After that, turn the cup upside down on a small plate or piece of paper to dry.

It is necessary to wait approximately ten minutes because in that time the coffee grounds will flow down the walls, making various furrows, shapes, and figures. When an appropriate time has passed, the cup is turned upright and the reading can begin.

Some believe that coffee that is meant for reading must to spend the previous night under the pillow of the person who wants to know their future.

Notice the shapes of black, made of the coffee grounds, but notice the white shapes as well, which are the spaces between them. Brown shapes may also be present, made from the not yet dry coffee grounds.

Before the reading begins, it must be determined with which hand person was holding the cup. If it was right hand ,then the part of the cup starting from the handle to the middle of the cup is the present or near future, and the part from the middle back to the handle is the distant future. If a person was holding cup with its left hand, the direction of reading the coffee grounds is the opposite.

155

If the person wants to know something about its partner, then half of the cup where the handle is belongs to the person who drank the coffee and the other half to their partner.

The bottom of the cup represents the house, home, and family of the person who wants to know her future while the walls of the cup represent their "outside" social life.

If most of the coffee grounds settled on the bottom, it means that certain problems exist within the family and what they are it must be concluded from adjacent shapes.

If the most coffee grounds begin to move to the top of the cup, it is said that problems have left the house and become part of the past.

If small protrusions have formed on the bottom, like incompletely formed droplets, either the person or the family of the person whose grounds are being read will experience a significant financial gain.

A human likeness formed in the coffee grounds has various meanings depending on the person it resembles. It can represent the person for whom the coffee grounds were read, a relative, friend, or even an unknown person. Therefore, it is necessary to discern whether or not it represents the person for whom we read coffee grounds or someone else in their life.

After that is determined, we must ascertain whether the person is coming or going. If it's turned to the cup's handle, meaning in the direction where we start our reading, that person is coming, but if its back is to the handle, than that person is leaving. Adjacent shapes will tell where they are going.

If the person is standing on a thin black line, it means that person will take a trip and the length of the line will tell us the duration of the trip. If the line goes from the bottom to the top of the cup, then the journey is very long and the person will probably go abroad.

If we see something large, like a rock, above that figure, we know that person has something on his mind, or has a guilty conscience for something they have already done.

If the human figure is turned to the top of the cup, we say that they are going to be successful but if it is facing the bottom, there will be no success. The same thing applies if the figure is climbing uphill or going downhill.

We can interpret human figures according to body position in the following way:

Spread arms – lucky
Bowed head – shame
Turned head – possible illness
Kneeling – asking someone for something
Jumping – happy news or victory
Eyes covered with hands – doesn't want to see something
Ears covered with hands – doesn't want to hear something
Mouth covered with hands – doesn't want to tell someone something
Going nude towards somebody – sexual attraction to that person
Running away from somebody while nude– running away from unwanted sexual contact

Along with human figures, we can often notice animals that we can interpret together with the human figures or separately. We can interpret animal figures in the following way:

Bear – concern, problem
Fox – trick
Donkey – someone wants to make us look foolish
Rabbit – we will hear some news of little importance
Horse – we will receive good news very soon
Dog – fidelity
Cat – trick, manipulation
Deer – an honorable man
A black snake – health, wisdom; a white one – danger, illness; a coiled snake – patience
Bird – news or message, black bird – good message, white bird – bad message

If these animal figures stand next to the human figure, it usually indicates personal traits of that person or something that person brings with them.

In addition, shapes in the form of herbs, objects, letters, and numbers also must be interpreted. Here are some of the interpretations:

Bud – something new will happen
Flower – something nice awaits you
Tree – you will encounter something powerful
Weapon – aggressiveness, the need for protection, someone plans to harm you
Letters – Indicates the first letter of some person's name, especially if those letters are next to human figure.
Numbers – how many days will pass until you hear some news, or how many days, weeks, months will pass before something happens

.

After the reading of the coffee grounds is finished, you must not turn the cup upside down again, but return it to its normal position and wash it later. In recent times, new things have been added , such as the ability to manipulate ones' future. This is done by the person sitting in front of the cup, the one whose coffee grounds are being read. At the end of the reading, they formulate a wish or desire in their mind, at the same time presses on the bottom of the cup with a finger from the hand that was used to drink the coffee. This leaves a circular impression, and this can be interpreted by the same rules listed above. We can add only two things to above-mentioned rules for interpretation that are going to arise by dipping a finger into the coffee grounds. First, a full circle means that the wish will come true, and second rule is that interrupted or incomplete circle means that the wish will not come true.

Another, probably much older but equally popular method of indirect foretelling, especially among real Witches, is reading beans. What beans are used depends on the area and the plants that grow there. For this reason the most used were corn kernels, beans, peas, or some similar legume.

In almost the entire area of the former Yugoslavia, beans were used for divination, and there was one common rule, that the number of beans must be exactly forty-one. The origin of this number is very difficult to determine, as this is one of the oldest forms of divination in the Balkans.

When we talk about method itself, we can say that there are two basic techniques which are most often used.

The first one is very complicated and has many rules. It would take another entire book to explain it in detail, therefore we will not discuss it here.

The second, at first glance, is much simpler. Witches use it more often because not only are there no strict "game rules" but it also only requires a minimum of clairvoyant ability. The procedure looks like this:

It is necessary to take forty-one beans in your hand and bring them close to your mouth; is then necessary to recite an incantation whose end must be formulated as a question. Here is an example

"Forty one beans, forty one brothers and sisters, as you know to germinate, as you know to grow and to feed people, do you know when (The person in question) will marry?"

After this the beans are thrown on a flat surface such as a table or tray, and then the beans must be observed. In essence, the most important thing is the way the beans form groups. Multiple piles of three or four beans always mean a good result. Many solitary beans that do not touch adjacent ones represent negativity or that the wish will not come true. The same thing goes for piles of two beans. It is necessary to observe count the number of types of piles that have the most grains. This is general reading, but a Witch add her own dose of clairvoyance so that she could associate them in appropriate context to the things that she sees. Once more, in this kind of reading, the beans represent only the conduit that helps Witches see their visions.

At the end let us just say that according to our opinion, beans probably represent spirits of vegetation; that can be seen from the incantation that accompanies the process of foretelling. This is not surprising at all, if we know the fact that ancient man was fascinated with the fact that something as small as a bean, could have the power to grow and provide the food that fed the community. The fact that the spirits of vegetation were highly respected in previous times is apparent to us, based on the amount of folk traditions concerned with cultivation and harvest.

Still, the whole subject can be interpreted differently if we know two things. The first is related to the fact that the number of beans for the reading is actually forty and that one represents the person for whom the reading is performed. The second thing is the theory that in several ways Witches were linked with the Bogomils in the Balkans, and that the Bogomils themselves were accused of Witchcraft. What is interesting here is the Bogomil's myth of human genesis and medicinal herbs. Simplified, it looks something like this:

.

After God created man from the Earth, he left him to dry in the Sun, he left get a living spirit, with which to bring man to life. Seeing this, out of envy, the Devil poked forty-one holes in the earthen figure. When God returned and blew the living spirit into Adam's nostrils, it escaped through the holes. Seeing that, he took forty herbs and plugged forty holes, leaving one hole so the soul could slowly leave, so the man would eventually die and not be an immortal. Then God spoke to the man and told him that these herbs are very good for healing, and that each herb heals some part of the body.

I heard something similar to this from a Witch from southern Serbia while she was giving me some recipes. Namely, she insisted that the number of an herb must always be forty, otherwise the man will not be healed. So, if it was one herb, it was necessary to use forty leaves of that herb, or forty little bones, etc. On my joke and my question: "What will happen if I use thirty nine?" She answered: "Nothing, absolutely nothing." The same thing applies to using beans in foretelling.

Ritual foretelling

As the name says, this method of divination contains within itself some form of ritual which is applied in these methods to a greater or lesser extent. Bearing in mind that there are a great number of those techniques, we will present a few of them, specifically those that are directly related to Witches. Here we will discuss the Witch's most favorite forms of ritual divination.

The first one is the extinguishing of live coals. Live coals are red-hot pieces of wood that must be taken out of a fire with tongs, put it in the bowl with water and then carefully monitor their behavior. Let us start from the beginning.

For this purpose, the person who does the foretelling must provide a dish, usually of baked clay painted green. Today, mostly metal dishes are used, virgin, ones that have never been used for any other purpose, either purchased or made especially for this task and will never be used for anything else.

After that, in this dish must be poured water from a spring or well that no one drinks from or uses for some other purpose, it is so called "whole water".

Finally, a sacred item must be submerged in the water, one that has special meaning to the Witch. Those are often pieces of quartz but it can be another specific rock or crystal with unusual or unique natural origins. I witnessed them using pieces of red rock and even metallic nuggets, probably from an abandoned mine. Occasionally they use *"beleg"*, which is a personal effect of the person for whom the reading is performed.

After this Witch starts to mix water in the bowl with a sweet basil stalk (ocimum basilicum) and cuts it three times with the *kustura*, the magical knife that we mentioned earlier.

While she is doing this, she recites a pre-prepared incantation, either silently or in an unintelligible murmur. They are mainly questions concerning whether someone will marry, whether a sick person will get well, will business go well, etc.

162

In essence incantations are very similar, at least their first part that is related with invoking of the Sun, the Moon, and the stars in order to help a Witch see everything that is going to happen to a certain person. They sound something like this:

"Oh Sun, as you shine in the heavens and know all, Moon, as you sit high in the sky and see all... help me to see, to know, and to tell (The person in question) everything that is destined to be."

The prepared incantation must be recited three times, and then it is necessary to throw live coals into the water; some Witches take them out of the fire with their bare hands while others use tongs. A Witch always throws three, seven or nine pieces of live coal in the bowl, and those are usually coals of Oak.

Live coals are thrown in the water to the center of the bowl, one by one so that each of them represents a different question. When the red-hot piece of wood hits the water, several things must be observed simultaneously. The first is the sound it makes when it touches the water, the second is whether it floats or sinks to the bottom, and the third, if it is floating, which direction is it moving?

If the live coal sizzles for a long time, it means emphatic agreement, but it depends on the situation. If the question is related to the outcome of some event or undertaking, it means it will be successful, but not without a lot of effort. If it is related to another person or an emotion, such as "Does she like me?" it means that yes, she likes you very much.

A short, weak sizzling sound, as logic would dictate, has the opposite meaning.

The worst thing that could happen is for the live coal to sink. On the other hand, it is good if it floats; its direction of movement could then be observed. If it moves to the east or south it means a good result, if it floats to the west or north it means the opposite.

After the foretelling, both the coals and the water that was used are considered sacred, because they have magical power for the one in whose name this ritual was performed. Therefore, sick people could wash with it, those who are considered to be bewitched should drink it and blacken themselves with the coals that were extinguished in the bowl. The coals could even be kept and used as a sort of amulet.

A second technique that is almost as popular is pouring molten metal into water. Today people most often use lead because of its low melting point, though sometimes people use silver, copper, or even gold. Preparation is very similar to the previous method of extinguishing of live coals. It is necessary to prepare a "virgin" dish, a fireproof bowl, and whole water from the spring or well.

When the dish is ready it is necessary add the water and a forest crystal or some similar object. It is then necessary to stir it with a stalk of sweet basil, then cut the water three times with the *kustura* from top to bottom, and from the left side to the right. It is then necessary to recite the pre-prepared incantation three times, of course not out loud. Because it is almost identical to the incantation in the previous method, I see no reason to repeat it here.

First, the fireproof bowl must be placed on the fire, and it is necessary to wait until the metal is in a liquid state. When this happens, the Witch takes the bowl, and little by little, pours the molten metal in the dish with the whole water. She does it very slowly, observing each of the shapes as they are made as the metal cools and solidify. These newly created shapes often remind one of little clouds in the sky. What must be observed is their shape, the meaning of that shape, and its connection with the future-related question that is being asked. These shapes are interpreted in the same manner as coffee grounds, so I do not think that it is necessary to repeat that section.

After the foretelling is complete, one piece of metal with a specific shape set aside and given to the person. They will either wear it as an amulet or keep it hidden in a safe place somewhere in their house. It is very important that no one except the owner touches this piece of metal, and it is sometimes necessary to hide it from other's sight.

Still, as with the first one, this technique has many variations. To attempt to better explain how the ritual can be done, we will cite one more example, given by a living Witch, who is unfortunately, is very advanced in age.

The first thing that you notice when you visit this woman, it is the fact that she avoids any physical contact, nor does she greet you. The reason for this is her personal sensitivity to energies of other people, and according to her, energy exchange occurs with physical contact. When you enter the house, she seats you in a chair in the center of the room and she puts a white kerchief on you. She then stands behind you, and while holding a bowl with the whole water over your head, she recites her incantation. After a time her assistant gives her the little kettle with the molten lead, and she begins pouring the lead while continuing her incantations. She casts three figures, then shows them and interprets them. She throws away the ones that are negative, and recasts the positive ones so that she can use them for the following client.

If the person for whom the reading is performed is not physically present, it is necessary to provide a recent photograph with a full frontal view of that person. Over the photograph she places a red, unbordered cloth that is smaller than the picture. What is fascinating is that the part covered with the cloth shows up in the bowl.

165

Besides these two somewhat similar techniques among Witches, especially in eastern Serbia, a very common and often utilized technique is the method of ritual foretelling with the help of magical mirror.

That ritual is performing after the midnight while the young moon is visible in the sky. The Witch leaves her house and goes to her backyard or some sacred place. She disrobes her clothes, observing young moon for some time and then she starts to stare fixedly at her reflection in the mirror that she brought from home.

As she does that, she starts to twist slowly left and right, silently reciting an incantation to summon the Earth Mother. Although there is no special format to the incantation, it must be recited three times; the incantation will vary, based on the situation.
After several minutes, the Witch's image will disappear, and after a time the image of the Goddess herself will manifest.

The Witch then speaks to her, asking the Goddess to send her a vision, that is, to show future events that are of particular interest in the mirror. Then image of Goddess disappears, and the picture of an event shows up, much like a show on television.

It is a common rule that a Witch must not to misuse this opportunity to ask unimportant questions, and the ritual itself must be used only on special occasions so as to not anger the Goddess.

Besides the methods that we mentioned in this chapter, there are a great number of other methods of foretelling, whether direct, indirect, or by ritual. From this presentation, it is clear that to clearly differentiate and set boundaries between the different methods, because they overlap, much of it based on the personal preferences of the Witch performing them.

166

However, remember that we are not scientists, and that this book does not pretend to be a scientific work; it is necessary to understand that we introduced these classifications only to avoid confusion, and at the same time provide a clearer picture of divination techniques in the Balkans

Sultana Manojlovic-divination,
photo by Ranko Jovanovic before World War II

SUPERNATURAL BEINGS AND SACRED ANIMALS

As you already noticed in our earlier presentation, there is no way to avoid mention of supernatural beings, especially in the contexts of initiation and ritual. It is doubtful that simply mentioning them and explaining their respective roles would satisfy the curiosity of many of those who read this book, therefore we will tackle the topic in this chapter..

Because there are many supernatural beings in the mythology of the Balkan people, we'll try to give as precise a description as possible to those that have any connection with ancient Witchcraft in the Balkans , that is, those with whom Witches make contact.
We will apply the same criteria when we talk about sacred animals, so that we do not deviate much from the given topic. The reason for the huge variety of beings and animals stems not only from the diversity of peoples and ethnic communities that live in the Balkans, but also the immense cultural heritage that both natives and conquerors left behind.

The Goddess

Among Balkan Witches, in most cases the role of the Goddess is the Forest Mother. She is the oldest and most respected supernatural being in the region. It is interesting that the fact that she is equally respected and believed in by all those in the region, especially within Serbian and Vlach people. From this information, we can conclude that she belongs to a group of the oldest deities, and that she is a native of the Balkans. When we closely scrutinize the beliefs related to her, we can conclude that she is not deity, but simply said, a great and very powerful spirit of nature that rules

169

over many smaller, less powerful ones. This information only talks in favor of the supposition that her origin is very old, and probably originates from the period when human conscience did not know deities in the true sense of the word.

In different parts of the country, she has different yet similar names. The most famous are Forest Mother, Mountain Mother, *Muma Paduri* (translation from Vlach language for name Forest Mother), and similar names. From certain incantations that are primary directed to her, we can see that she often associated with fairies, and that she is the ruling fairy, their queen or empress.

As it is most often said, her home is somewhere in nature. It is said that she doesn't go to villages or towns, as she doesn't like crowds and noise. Because of that people must seek her out if they want to make contact with her. In contrast to classic deities, she is not omnipresent, but in nature, she is easy to find. To avoid wandering and endless searching, not only Witches but common people as well go to "sacred places", because it is well known that she frequents those places. These places get the epithet "sacred" because of this and they are considered an aspect of her home.

The Forest Mother always appears after midnight. She shows up as a middle-aged woman, nude with large breasts, long hair, and long nails. She sometimes wears transparent white dress. She has a loud, piercing voice that she uses when she wants to drive someone away, but at the same time, she can also sing a melody that will enchant listeners like the Sirens of legend. It is thought that her presence can be marked by a warm, pleasant-smelling breeze that follows her, and that trees bend toward the ground, bowing to her as she passes by.

When she does not want to be seen, she takes the shape of a haystack or she appears as an animal. The number of animals whose shape she takes is limited. She can show up as a turkey, cow, female dog, mare, goat, or a pig. Above all, she is protector of the forest and fields, wild animals, and nature, but she is also protector of fertility, pregnant women and women in general. Based on this, ethnologists conclude that she is very similar to Arthemida and Diana, although we will clearly see that she is probably the original Balkan Hecate who was preceded by a Slavic Goddess with similar characteristics, Morena – Mara

It is interesting that with Vlach people preserved a belief Diana that is recognized under slightly changed names of Djina or Dzina. This is a newer belief that came accompanied the Romans, so we can follow several religious layers related to Vlach people. The first, the ancient Balkan layer, consists of Muma Paduri and Tartor, the second one of Djina and Lushafur-Lucifer, and the third is a combination of Slavic Pantheon and Byzantine Christianity. It is very interesting that Vlach magic is identical to that of the area of Slovenia, while their religious rituals are related to Djina and Lushafur. However, let us get back to the Forest Mother.

As we mentioned before, she is the protector of women, but that does not mean that she dislikes men. She also considers her "pupils" under her protection, it is said that she is sexually promiscuous, and that often she has sexual relations with men that she finds in the woods at night, a mill, a hut, or some other deserted place.

In some places it is believed that she can appear in the shape of old, ugly woman who carries with her great magical staff. At that time, it is necessary to avoid her because she is in the bad mood and commits all manner of evil deeds.

It is interesting that on the other side of Danube River, in Romania, there are also beliefs related to *Muma Paduri*. According to local people, she is original Dacian deity of which several myths talks speak, as the one that describes her replacement from her previous position to the most potent one.

In fact, the Romanian *Muma Paduri* of ancient times was the protectress of the forest, along with the wild animals that lived there. She protected the forest from its enemies, who were mostly men. It is said that she protected people from wild animals as well, but she came to hate very quickly, and then she started killing any unexpected traveler that came into her domain. The Goddess Bendis heard this, and ordered that next man whom she kills must be revived and then he must marry her, even she refuses, and so it was. The first man that she killed was revived, and he married her. He became known as Paduroiul, which means "Sumnik". That is, the man of the forest.

The gods came to love him as a righteous and wise protector of the forest and wild animals; the gods gave him many different magical abilities and rose him to the status of a deity, the new Master of the forest. He retained a measure of his severity and continued to punish merciless destroyers of the nature, be them human, animal, or supernatural. He was eventually declared the Master of all magical creatures, and was given the status of the "voice of the gods". This means that anyone who wanted to talk with any deity must first summon him, so he became the fundamental deity for all who performs magic. According to myth, even the greatest Gods of Dacian's Pantheon listened to his advice. He sired a daughter, Fata Padurii, with Muma Paduri. This myth is possibly an illustration of the initiation mystery in which we can see the ritual death of a person who is revived by the will of higher forces, and then becomes deity himself.

One thing is obvious and that is the fact that Romanian Muma Paduri is very different from the Vlach one, although they have the same name. That does not necessarily pose a problem; the Vlach and Romanian languages are similar, and in both cases, her name means Forest Mother. The name Forest Mother could befound in most all of the Balkans, though it must be said that the Vlach rendition of the Forest Mother bears more resemblance to the Serbian one than the Slovenian.

That does not necessarily mean that she is the same Earth Mother as in the Dacian Pantheon, although we assume that she is much older, because she bears similarities to the great shamanistic spirits of nature. It is also interesting that Paduoriul does not exist among the Vlach; her partner is Tartor, the great water spirit

So we come to the second most important deity of Balkan Witches. As far as we are concerned, it is the same deity only in her other aspect. The previous text shows us that the Forest Mother has at least two aspects, and that she can appear as a strict, ugly old woman, perhaps a grandmother.

That is the name of the second deity, if it can be considered as such. There is probably an important reason for the fact that she has no specific name, which is out of respect and fear; the actual name was never recorded. Over time, what names there were have completely fallen into oblivion, so today we only have the substitutes, that is, their nicknames.

Baba (Grandmother) is an important deity who is memorialized by the Balkan people in the names of many places. Among them are Babino Selo, Babetino, Babajic, Babica etc. Many natural features were named after Baba, such as Babin Zub (Grandmother's tooth), Babina Gora (Grandmother's hill), Babino Polje (Grandmother's field), Babina glava (Grandmother's head) etc. These places are "sacred places" in the context that we have previously spoken.

In essence, the grandmother represents collective spirit of female ancestors. It is said that she was the first woman who died and went to underworld. That is why people think that she resides in all major caves and pits. She is dangerous, but she is also a wise old

173

woman the guardian of ancient knowledge; lucky is the one she chooses as a pupil.

In many fairy tales, the main character goes to see her and to obtain some magical object or animal that will help them to accomplish their mission. She then asks him a question or riddle; if he answers correctly, he will get everything he needs, but if not, she kills him or turns him to something, or even enslaves him and keeps him to be her servant.

It means that attempting to acquire her knowledge or assistance is a risky endeavour; in this way we can say that she is very similar to Hecate.

Her main animal is the frog, one called a Baburacha by the Serbian people; it primarily lives in pits and caves. It is strictly forbidden to kill this frog, because it is said that the mother of the person who kills the frog will die. It means that if you kill a frog, you kill your mother. This taboo clearly explains that the frog is the representative of collective female spirit ancestor, Baba. I don't think it's necessary to emphasize that the frog is the one of the most important attributes of Witches in the whole European territory. People imagined her as old woman with a black apron, and hands covered with flour.

As you can see, the Balkan Baba is quite different from Russian *Baba Yaga* because she is much less negative and evil, and quite possibly only way that the two are related is the fact that both of them are old women. However, if we know that people and Witches have different opinions of Forest Mother, we can assume that their opinions of Baba also differ. She is still the "ancestor" who helps her generations, and if she picks someone to be her pupil, they are not in danger because that person has passed all manner of tests that they were not even aware of. She only punishes selfish and

174

evil people who want magical knowledge solely for selfish goals or material profit.

The one who became her pupil was obligated to repay by helping their community or by performing charitable acts that she directed her pupil to perform. A reason for revealing knowledge always exists. A person who obtains this knowledge not only gets the ability or use it, but choice in the manner in which it is used. It is difficult to say who Baba actually is and which deity she represents. In the Balkans, many female demons and personifications of natural phenomenon exist that carry this name; we have Baba Yegu, Baba Rogu, Baba Rugu, Baba Martu , Baba Korizmu, Divija Baba (in Bosnia), and Baba Pethru (in Slovenia). Some people think that she is the ancient deity of fertility and death, just like the goddess Kibele, who can personify the Earth itself.

Let us form a conclusion. According to all the testimonies and interviews that we have, all Witches were initiated and led by the Goddess in the form of a young woma whom they say is the Forest Mother. There is also the old woman, or grandmother, who some say is Saint Petka . Ethnologists have tried to connect her with the Slovenian Mokosa, but we cannot agree because she is very similar to Morena, the Goddess or spirit of death, representative of the collective spirit of all deceased women. She is neither luminary nor solar; she is timeless and spaceless, and she greatly resembles the trinity of Stygian Witches with whom Perseus must cope in his myth.

Jozko Savli claims that Slovenian Baba Pethra is one of fundamental, ancient deities of death and regeneration. He links her not only with the Russian Baba Yaga but with Morena – Mara, the ancient Slovene deity of death as well.

One of the main Witches that is **celebrated** is Saint Evdhokia. She is also seen as an old woman. It is difficult for us to find any

175

real detail concerning whom she actually represents, but there are two myths that address her in neighboring Romania. There, she is known as Dokija - the Revered One.

More information about her can be found there. Namely, there are two myths, in which she is called Dokija, Grandma Dokia, or old Dokija who all personify the month of March. By all known facts, she represents the last gust of winter before spring.

According to the first myth, grandma Dokija has son named Dragomir of Dragobet and a daughter in law whom she cannot stand. At the end of February, she sends her daughter in law to bring her some berries from the wood. Then God appears to the girl in the form of an old man, and helps her to find some berries. When Dokia sees the berries, she thinks that spring has already come, she takes her son and their flock of goats, and they head for the mountains. She wears twelve kid (Young goat) leathers but when the rain begins, she takes them off, and when it started to freeze, she disappeared along with goats. Her son froze to death with the ice in its mouth because he was playing his flute the entire time.

This is a very interesting myth with strange symbolism, especially that related to the twelve kid leathers, and when the rain begins to fall she disappeared with goats and she probably became something else.

In the second myth she is daughter of Decebal, Dacian's king. After being conquering by the Roman Trajan, Dokia runs away to the Carpathian Mountains so she could avoid a forced marriage. She disguises herself as herdswoman, but again she takes off her leathers and freezes with her flock. She then transforms into a stream, and her animals into flowers.

While reading this it is not very hard to see that similar myths of grandmother's kids or goats exist, Babini ukovi and similar. According to the myth, a grandmother herded kids in the mountains around Blagovesti, but a cold wind was blowing from the north and snow was falling. The grandmother froze with the kids around her. According to ethnologist Spiro Kulisic, based on analog studies of similar myths with other peoples, the grandmother may be a lunar being and kids could represent lunar crescents, that is, the bright and dark Moon. Among many peoples, the transformation from bright Moon to dark is represented by petrification. This is very important to us. The Lunar Goddess of winter and death for the Slovenes was Goddess Mara-Morena, which is the secret name of Muma Padurii, the Forest Mother. It is not surprising that her holiday (March 1, by the Julian calendar) celebrates people who perform magic. It is very interesting that the name of the Moon Goddess with the Picts (England natives) is Marian, Miriam, and Mary and that she is revered in the so-called fairy tradition that is represented by Starhawk.

Finally, there are those who were initiated and taught by three identical Goddesses simultaneously. One example cited by Jasna Jojic Pavlovski in her book "Miracles of Vlach magic"; they were called the three Marys. This trinity is well known in the Balkans. They were sometimes respected Celt Mothers, Slavic Sudjenice, and similar deities we can find among the Greeks under the name Mojre, Parke the Roman, German Norne, etc. The thing that is very interesting is choosing the name "Three Maries". One of the biggest secrets of the Witch is the name of the Forest Mother. Her name is **Maria** but she is often called **Mara**. I think that this is the first rendition of her name. We need to say that the appearance of a trinity, especially with chthonic deities, is nothing new, as Cajkanovic claimed. Because all three girls have the same name, we can conclude that the female trinity does not represent three separate aspects (virgin, mother, and old woman) but triplication instead.

The God of Witches – The Horned God

In the Balkans, as in most European countries, main male deity of Witches was the horned God. For him, just like for Forest Mother, applies that he represents not only a deity but also the Great Spirit of Nature, which also confirms his ancient and archaic origins.

At first glance we can assume that his name is preserved only because people called him Lesnik in southern Serbia, but if we move north, he is referred to as Sumnik. Both names originate from the word "suma" (forest), with only difference that "Les" is an antiquated Slavic word; the name Lesnik means "creature of the forest" or "one in the forest".

His description reminds us of the Greek Pan, the Roman Sylvan, or Krampus. He is also represented as creature with a human upper body, while his lower body and ears are reminiscent of a goat. He usually has a beard, horns, and he is very hairy.

Serbian ritual mask from Bandic's book-Narodna religija Srba u 100 pojmova

178

It is said that he loves noise and music, he sings beautifully, plays instruments and dances. He is the protector of cattle, as well as wild animals. He is often followed by stags, wolves, wild boars, bears and other animals. Nevertheless, his main flock primarily consists of wolves, who consider him their master.

It is said that he socializes with fairies, with whom he often has children. He also likes milkmaids, whom he often takes to his hut, whose interior is covered with the fur of wild animals. It is said that he is well known for his insatiable sexual appetite, with both human and fairy females.

He is known to live in all major forests, and if you wish to make contact with him, those are the places you need to go. In contrast to the Forest Mother, he has a habit of appearing in broad daylight, though he does not like to be seen. We can safely say that he is the "God of the Hunt" because he controls the balance between domestic and wild animals; he could chase away a hunter, but he could also provide a catch. He announces his presence with a loud roar; after all, he is the biggest "beast" in the forest.

Up until the 1960s, during the Winter Solstice, a trio of men led a Christmas celebration in southern Serbia, near the town of Leskovac. Two of them wore sheepskins tied around their waists with a rope of bells, while holding a wooden sword and a staff of dogwood in their hands. They wore wooden masks with hair and beard made of wool. They called themselves "Lesnici". The third man dressed in women's clothes and walked with them while these two allegedly sexually harassed him. In that guise, they visited all the houses in the village. Their purpose was to provide fertility to these families and to their cattle as well. They were required to do something useful for every home they visited. For example, if they found a housewife preparing lunch they would help in the kitchen; if they found the head of household doing something, they would help him. When they left a home, the family gave them presents, sometimes even money. The entire time, they sang songs concluded with the following words: "As we leave this home, God enters!". From this text, we can see that they represent the former God of fertility, or at least one of his representatives. Because their names were Lesnici, we can conclude that God is Lesnik, which is obvious from their behavior; above all, not only does the exhibition of sexual desire represent their intention to bring fertility into the home but their physical appearance also, which is borne by their masks. If we make comparison with Russia, we see that it is actually the God Veles.

Slavic God Veles, drawing by Croatian artist Sandananda

Slovenians participated in a masked procession called the Koranti, and many of in the procession wore masks resembling a bull.. It is assumed that Koranti used to represent the God of winter and wild animals.

In Slovenia, there was a custom that involved the so-called horned "Plowman". He went from house to house, simulating rutting in each, to bring fertility to the fields. This is probably ancient ritual where the horned God with his plow (phallus) fertilized the Goddess (soil), and brought her fertility, which is symbolized by spring when everything is renewed.

In the territory of eastern Serbia, especially among Vlach people, one custom related to a horned God named Tartor is preserved. Unlike Lesnik, who lives in the forest, Tartor lives in rivers, lakes, and swamps which is normal because the majority of this population lives near the coast and directly depended on the catch that the master of the water gave them. Respect for the "watery" horned God is preserved in all for the territory of the former Yugoslavia, especially in Serbia, Vojvodina, Croatia, and Macedonia. In short, everywhere fishing was the basic economic activity.

He differs very little from Lesnika in his appearance, except for his height; it is said that he is about a meter tall. The upper part of his body is human; he has a large nose, goat's ears, wears a long beard, has either one or two horns on his head, and he wears a tattered red hat. Lower part of his body is animal, that is, he has the legs of a goat. In some parts of the country people claims that he appears naked and that he is very hairy, while in others it is said that he wears a green suit and red hat.

People in Smederevo described him as being identical to Lesnika, except that the water spirit had a reddish hue, and forest spirit is black.

In the territory of northeast Serbia, it is said that he has ninety-nine servants and that he is the hundredth, the oldest and most powerful. He lives at the bottom of large bodies of water in a great castle made of glass or crystal. He always carries a whip and golden chains to tie and choke disobedient people whose souls he brings to his castle to serve him. Like Lesnik, he also has great sexual appetite, and because of that, Witches cover their genitals when they enter water so they won't excite him unnecessarily. Still, he finds ways to engage in sexual congress, such as by assuming the form of a handsome man. He has power to take the form of a horse when he wants to go ashore. When he takes the form of a young, crying child, you must avoid him because his intentions are not good. He announces his presence by either splashing water, or beating a drum he carries with him.

According to Witches, contacting him is extremely easy, especially if a sacrifice of meat or poultry is made. However, if he gets mad, he can be very unpleasant. If he gets angry, Witches appeal to the Forest Mother to help them, because she is the only one who can induce mercy in him. The reason for this is the fact that she is his mistress, and above all, his friend. The two of them constitute ancient and divine couple, or if you prefer, a pair of great spirits of nature.

Out of respect and fear, Tartor's name is never spoken; he is simply called "old man". That name is preserved in many regions of the former Yugoslavia.

We can see the depth of respect for the "old man" in the residents of the town of Smederevo. During Communion, they held a piece of wafer if their mouth which they later they took to the Danube River and offered to him.

As Lesnik, the horned God cannot be called deity, above all he is a great spirit of nature or great water spirit, who origin is from ancient times when deities from various Pantheons weren't yet known in the Balkans. The Slavs brought their gods with them when they arrived in the area, and the assimilation of these gods into the collective consciousness brought about an entirely new religious dynamic. Although Witches had respect for these deities and they celebrated some of the holiday connected with them, they did not interact with many of them. That was the job of the Pagan priest, if one were even present. This form of religion is very different from ancient Witchcraft, and bears a much closer resemblance to shamanism. We will not cover those these deities now, because it exceeds the scope of this book and would detract from the flow of knowledge as I am trying to create it. We will cover them briefly in the chapter that is dedicated to Witch's holidays.

It is necessary to mention one very interesting phenomena. Within Serbian people, there is a custom to call noon "a horned noon". The reason for this is belief that noon is also time when supernatural beings appear, although in a somewhat different form than one that appears by night. Their leader is a horned creature that, by all accounts is identical to Lesnik. It is said that he is easily seen at noon under any big walnut tree. This is particularly interesting if we know that the walnut tree is closely associated is with Witches. When the Sun was in its noon prime, it was linked to the ancient horned God, and his daytime sun aspect. We can see from some Christmas customs that this deity can be solar as well; his essence represents the birth of the young Sun and the God who emerges from the underworld and announces arrival of longer intervals of Sunshine
.

Suppose again that the Vlach people believed in Lucifer, the "Light-carrier", who was associated with Danica, the planet Venus. His symbol is a piece of white quartz, which must be sewn into the clothes of deceased person so that his trip to the underworld would be illuminated. According to the Vlach, that is the one of his most important responsibilities the, role of a psychopomp. Ethnologist Paun Es Durlic first noticed the cult of the morning star, which is Lucifer, (Lusjafura, in Vlach language) near Majdanpek. He learned that a tree exists near Majdanpek, and that people believe that Lenka lives inside. However, as Paun says, Lenka is a nickname for Danica, which is Serbian name for Venus – the morning star.

The Lucifer tree from east Serbia-photo by author

With Vlach people, Venus is identified with Lucifer, who is not Christian in nature, rather an ancient that probably originates from the Romans. All local magi seek his permission before they undertake any magic.

We should say something about the Three-headed and the Silver Czar because that will help us to understand the remainder of this text.

Three-headed, as the name says, represents the three-headed deity of the underworld. Because he is the master of the underworld, all mines are in his jurisdiction, as well as all silver and gold. Because of this fact, some people contact him, although not as often as the Silver Czar, but there are some indications that these are actually the same deity.

There is no information on Three-headed but there is plenty of information about Silver Czar, so let look at him more closely.

We can put the Silver Czar or "spirit of underground" into the category of great spirits of nature. Miners who call him "Miner's Czar" were slightly afraid of him. They claimed that he is master of the ore and that he does not want to let any deposit be fully exploited, which means that it is was forbidden to completely deplete a mine, that something must be left behind.

His appearance is varied. Originally, he was represented as a human figure with a silver body or as an old man with silver beard. However, when he shows up to be visible to the human eye, he takes other forms. Those are mainly the forms of a little boy, a dwarf, a miner, or a miner supervisor. It is said that he carries a magical staff made of silver or hazelnut. It is also said that only good people or miners could see him, but everyone could hear him. When he speaks it is a good thing, but when he knocks against the walls of the mining shaft, you need to leave immediately because the shaft is about to collapse.

He is the lord of the dwarves who inhabit the underworld and dig ore for him. For that reason, it is not unusual that some people contact him when they want to perform a ritual for making money. They claim that he only goes out on the surface of the Earth at night, because he do not like Sun. In a word, he is something like a larger version of Goba, the lord of gnomes in western Witchcraft.

For a conclusion of this section related to the Witch's God, we should say something about what is the most important figure in all of Balkan Witchcraft. There is no known data in ethnological literature, with the possible exception of the ethnologist Cajkanovic, when he talks about the Lame Daba (Devil) and Dabog, God's opponent that originates from a dualistic heresy. Based on facts, we can conclude that is he is worth mention here. He is a mysterious nocturnal visitor, who above all is characterized by his external appearance. He shows up wearing a long, black mantle, and on his head he wears a black hat with a huge, wide brim that covers his face. It is interesting that almost all respondents agreed about his height, which is about 2.5 meters. He usually shows after midnight. Electrical appliances cease to run in his vicinity, as well as cars and other engines. His presence is very hard to withstand and "feeling in the air" is impossible to describe. You can meet him in both the physical and astral planes. They call him the "Man in black".

Who he is really is not difficult to tell. Based on current literature, we can conclude that he resembles Dabog, the master of the underworld, who the ethnologist Cajkanovic identified as a fundamental deity of our people in ancient times. Cajkanovic's, or we may say, the "folk" Dabog is very different from the Russian Dazhbog, primarily personified by the Sun. Primarily in the fact he takes the honorary place of the first deceased ancestor who went into underworld and imposed rule.

As chthonic deity, he wears a mantle, and a hat, and carries a magical staff and a hatchet. Wolves that represent reincarnated souls follow him, roosters warn of him, along with many other associated myths. Bearing in mind the fact that the hill were Silver Czar lived is named Dajbog, we can conclude that he is actually the Silver Czar. He was considered as the patron of blacksmiths and the inventor of blacksmithing, similar to the ancient British Tubal Cain, and the custodian of silver and gold. He was sometimes called "Czar of the Earth" who devours souls. It is assumed that

186

St. (Archangel) Michael acquired most of his traits, while national Saint Sava is described and portrayed as the leader of wolves.

Cajkanovic published his opinion in one of his works that was published in 1994, along with the works of others in a joint enterprise of "Srpska knjizevna zadruga", "Bigz", "Prosveta", and "Partenon" under the name "O vrhovnom Bogu u staroj srpskoj religiji" (Concerning the Supreme God in ancient Serbian religion). It is just one of five books that talks about folk religion, mythology, and folklore that are assembled based on Cajkanovic's documents. It is necessary to know that he collected and processed these facts before the Second World War.

Based on the analysis of available myths on Saint Sava, other saints, beliefs of the devil, fetishes, epithets, and attributes of Dabog, Tracian rider, Trojan and Black God, he concluded that the early Serbian supreme deity was Dabog.

Everything Cajkanovic says is correct, but based on currently available data, we can say that his only mistake is in the name with which he associated the deity; based on epithets like "God that gives", Daj Bog (God, give us) is shortened into "Dabog" , that was his conclusion . Everything that he says, especially citing a deity whose function and myths were acquired by St. Sava, is related to Veles. That name is simple his nickname that is preserved within our people. Cajkanovic's mistake could be that the being that he connected with Daba is actually a water spirit, possibly the former Dagon, whose cult existed in Danube River basin.

He also mixed it with Vija. Aleksandar Loma, in its text "Searching for Lame Daba" , clearly pointed out that Daba is a water spirit, but he made a mistake when he identified him with Vija. Daba is the same as the Vlach Tartor, and Dabog is the same as Veles.

Veles is very old and complex Slavic deity which some experts claim can be categorized as a deity of the proto-Indo-European Pantheon. The original Veles has been with the Slovenians since the time they were displaced and separated into three groups. According to tradition, he is the Lord of the Earth, water, and the underworld. He is represented as an old man with long beard and a robust figure, usually with bull's horns, although sometimes the horns of a ram or some other animal. He is sometimes depicted riding a bear or wild boar. In the underworld, he takes the shape of a large snake or dragon. Nevertheless, his main animal form is the bull. He was a popular folk deity, shamanistic in nature, and experts say that his main opponent was Perun, with whom he was always in conflict. One of the most important myths in Slovene mythology speaks of it.

At time when Vladimir the First came to the throne of Kiev, he erected statues of the most important gods. It is interesting that the statue of Veles was outside the temple on a hill near the market, which means that he was separated from other Gods, and that he was primarily a folk deity. Whether or not he is the central deity within Serbian people, it is not important to us, but it is very important to say that he is certainly the major male deity of Slavic Witchcraft.

Based on what we know today, we can safely say that he is the Sumnik or Lesnik, because that is his earthly aspect. Not only on land, but in the water as well, he can be bull or man with bull's horns. According to data and statistics from Russia, Christmas carols were sung in reverence to Veles, all incantations performed that day were addressed to him; he is the patron of magic and giver of magical knowledge. We also know that within Russian people Lesnik, or so-called Lesi, does not represent deity that resembles Pan , but is a spirit of the forest. We also know that Christmas Carols were not sung in his honor. Our Lesnik prefers to dance and to play instruments, and Veles was also the patron saint of music and musicians.

Veles is the protector of cattle, wildlife, music, magic, trickery, and health. He is also known for his generosity and magical powers. He was the one who bestowed magical knowledge concerning money, fertility, or anything else. He fought his battles in the form of a black dragon, a snake, or bull. This connects him with our dragon men and the zduhac who fight their astral battles in the form of a bull. He is also the great water bull in many stories from the Balkans. Because he is the greatest snake in the underworld, other snakes were considered the souls of the deceased, and that is why the cult of the snake exists in the Balkans. He can also take the form of a dragon, which we consider a positive and very beneficial attribute.

However, we cannot observe him as a Pan or Sylvan because is much more complex. To address all of his function from the Greek pantheon we would have to include Pan, Hermes, Hades, and Typhon. The only deity that he can be compared to is the Celtic Cernunnos, who like him is of shamanistic origin based on his function and his activities. However, we cannot take that for granted. By his appearance and function, he can be very easily connected with Hermes and Vodan. If we remember the testimonies of Witches that say that God shows appears wearing a black hat, we see that Hermes and Vodan appear in the same manner, that their functions are very similar, and that their main characteristic is that they are, in essence, shamanistic deities. His struggle with Perun is not just mythical struggle of natural forces, but a battle between the old and new God, between lunar and solar, between master of underworld and master of the sky. Let us just say that is the struggle between the ancient folk, shamanistic deity versus the new Pagan God represented by the clergy. That is the struggle between magical and religious points of view. Dragon men usually fight their battles in the form of the bull, which shows that they are aligned with Veles; because of their access to that form, they put themselves into the archetype of their God, from whom they get their strength. Interestingly enough, vampire hunters wore bull's leather as well.

With the advent of Christianity, the horned deity, the master of the underworld, the big snake and dragon, the master of the magic and demons, protector of cattle, wild animals and folk medicine was declared the Devil. In dualistic Christianity, he is represented as "Czar on Earth" who opposes the "Czar on the sky". It was during his demonization that the fact that souls of sinners go to him and that the souls of righteous men go to the Czar of the sky came about. By Cajkanovic's assumption, previously all souls went to him because he was master of underworld, the place where the souls of the deceased resided.

Fairies

Along with the Forest Mother and horned God, Fairies are among the oldest sprits of nature in the Balkans. They are not classified as separate group of supernatural creatures in relation to the gods or great spirits of nature, but they represent "lower" spirits who under the direct control of "higher" ones, the horned God, and above all, the Forest Mother.

As a rule, fairies are female, while elves were considered to be men, members of human race that have acquired supernatural abilities because of some good and unselfish acts. Fairies appear as beautiful young girls with light skin hue, and long blond, or reddish hair. They either wear white, transparent dresses, or they are naked. They have wings and large scarves that hold their power. If someone takes their scarf, they become ordinary human females.

190

Their power also lies in their long hair, so if somebody cuts it, they lose their power.

One very important thing that disrupts their appearance is their goat, donkey or horse's legs that they are usually successful at hiding. It is said that those legs do not have a pleasant smell, but it is never mentioned, as fairies are very vain and they usually punish people that offend them.

In essence, fairies are very nice and positive beings, and they love to sing and dance. They could be very helpful, but they could also be very detrimental if angered. Vanity is their main drawback. It is said that they get very angry if someone interrupts them while they work, while they dance in the *kolo*, or when they bathe naked in the moonlight. As a rule, they are very active by night, mostly during the full and new Moon.

They occasionally appear during the daytime, but in those cases, they take the form of a swan, snake, falcon, or some other animal. They also tend to ride deer, rabbits, birds, or other wild animals. They live in nature in places of astonishing beauty. You can usually find them near springs, waterfalls, and mountain lakes. Because of that, they take the names of the places where they appear. Therefore, we have lake fairies, river fairies, spring fairies, mountain fairies, etc.

According to Serbian tradition, many heroes originate from marriage between human and fairy, which gave them supernatural powers and ability to excel in battle. Those are the so-called dragonmen. Fairies have great sexual appetite, so they often seduce beautiful men that they meet in the woods and mountains. Those men must keep their relations with the fairies secret, or the fairies will become enraged and punish them. It is obvious that someone forbade the fairies to become involved in such relationships, most likely the Queen of the fairies, a.k.a. the Forest Mother.

According to ancient beliefs, fairies are born from dew or some special herb. Consequently, they have the greatest knowledge of how to heal illnesses with medicinal herbs. They are also known for their divination abilities, which can be seen in old folk poetry.

The names of famous fairies were preserved in this ancient folk poetry; I do not think there is a person in Serbia who has not heard of *Ravijojla*, the fairy. Other fairies are less well known, but their names are Angelina, *Andresila, Andjelija, Djudja, Janja, Janjojka, Jovanka, Jelka, Jerina, Jerisavlja, Nadanojla* and many others. It should be mentioned that Jerisavlja is mentioned as the leader of the fairies, and their queen.

We should mention another interesting fact; fairies could always nurse a baby. Milk from their breasts is miraculous and healing. If they nurse a human baby with their milk, that baby becomes a great hero or someone famous, and it will obtain special magical capabilities. The capabilities may be inherited, depending from case to case. The water in which they bathe has similar capabilities, hence the reason it is highly sought-after.

In conclusion, let us emphasize one more thing, the fact that fairies fall into the group of higher forces that decide who will be initiated. Because they are in close relation with Forest Mother and they themselves possess magical powers, it is no wonder that they bring their chosen men to their gathering places, test them, and put them through various forms of initiation. Even when the Forest Mother chooses a person and performs the initiation herself, the fairies are usually present. Just like the Goddess, they maintain contact with their protégé so he can call them when he needs to.

There is one more special subgroup of water fairies in the Balkans, theso called *Rusalke*. It is very hard to put them into the same group as fairies because they do not represent spirits of nature, rather spirits of young and often innocent girls who were intentionally drowned. By virtue of that, they are evil in contrast to real fairies, and as far as we know, no one tries to contact these creatures. Because of that, we will not mention them any more.

Dwarves

In contrast to fairies, there is very little information about dwarves. The information that exists is preserved mainly in folk songs, stories, and myths. However, although it is never specifically stated, it is very clear they are among the group of supernatural creatures in the Balkans. An excellent source of information concerning them can be found in folk' short stories.

Dwarves are also spirits of nature that are connected to the underground world. If someone wants to find them, it is necessary to look not only in caves, mines, and pits, but in bodies of water as well. As we said before, the dwarves are probably servants of the Silver Czar, who sometimes shows up as a dwarf; the only difference is that he is older and much powerful than the others, his servants. Tartor's servants are described as dwarves that resemble those from the Snow-white fairy tale, except that they have goat's legs, which is a normal phenomenon related to the spirits of nature, even the fairies as we saw before.

According to tradition, dwarves that live in water tend to transform into frogs. They are extremely powerful and they possess a variety of magical skills.

Although they are good-natured and they are not aggressive, few contact them because they are only the servants of a deity. People only invoke dwarves in special situations when they want to achieve some type of material gain, as they could be guardians of buried treasure or some form of knowledge or wisdom. People also believe that dwarves are very good blacksmiths because they know the secrets of creating special types of metals. Ethnologists believe that Saxon miners were responsible for bringing dwarves into the Balkans. This claim is disputable, because if we take into account folk beliefs in those places that never had Saxon miners, we see that they are no different from the areas that they inhabited.

Beside these two groups of dwarves, there are two more that are particularly associated to the Balkan Witches.

The first group consists of "plant" dwarves that are spirits of nature, and that in itself says enough about them. They are in the form of a plant called Raskovnik whose root has magical power, and if you find one in that form, he ceases being a plant and turns into a dwarf. According to some claims, you can find him at night; that is the time when the spirit of the dwarf, his astral double, walks among the plants and flowers. If someone finds one of these roots (Which are easily identifiable by their anthropomorphic shape), they should keep it. This root represents body of dwarf, without which he cannot exist, and that is the reason why the dwarf will serve the person who owns it. Goal of this action is above all to persuade a dwarf to divulge where buried treasure is located, which herbs are medicinal, and additionally, the dwarf can see if anything is endangering the Witch. We will talk more about this plant in the following chapter.

The last group consists of, so-called "house" dwarves or, as some refer to them, home spirits. This mention of the term "spirit-spirits" suggests that we should talk about creatures that occupy the astral plane, the astral world, which is a copy of our own. The moment of temporal overlap is after midnight, when these creatures became visible to some. But for now, let us get back to house dwarves. All of you have probably had the experience of losing something in your home and not being able to find it, regardless of how long and hard you search. After some time, that item in question appears, exactly in the place where it used to be. It is said that house dwarves are responsible. No one gets upset, however, as house dwarves are considered protectors of the house and family. Their existence was supposedly proven by an individual who spilled flour on the floor, then invoked the dwarves and asked for small gifts. The next morning, the gifts were there, as were paths through the spilled flour left by the tiny dwarfen feet. Just like Raskovnik, the house dwarf is considered to be a good helper with many magical abilities, and even acts as a special "alarm" when something is wrong.

There are other types of house spirits, the protectors, but they are not related directly to Witches, nor do they interact with them so we will just skip that.

Dragons

Dragons fall into a very interesting category of creatures in the Balkans, especially among Serbian and Vlach residents. The reasons for this are their rare appearance and the fact that in most cases they help people or the community.

Three basic groups of dragons exist in the Balkans. The first are the dragon-meteors that appear in the sky like flying fire, and set fire to everything around them. They are not evil, but if they stay too long in one place, they could cause drought. Then they must be chased away.

The second group consists of dragons that resemble those of Western Europe, which are in essence giant snakes with wings and legs.

The third group consists of human-dragons, and this is the most interesting one. Usually those are people whose astral body is not really human, and when they leave their body, it is possible to see their actual appearance. Descriptions of these dragons are different. They could be big winged snakes, big eagles, or men of huge proportions, with extremely hairy bodies, long hair, and beard. It is possible to determine if a person belongs to this type of dragons by testing their strength. As a rule, they have superhuman strength and powers. It is said that many folk heroes were dragons; this is evidenced in various folk stories and songs.

Other types of dragons can also take human form, and they could go and visit women by night. There is a myth that says they are great lovers and that women can hardly resist them. Children from those relationships are always human-dragons and by virtue of that, great heroes also. According to tradition, Witches often had such relationships with them, but they often chose young and beautiful girls. We need to say that female dragons also exist, and they also chose men for such activities.

Among both women and men, exhaustion and paleness were signs of such a relationship; maintaining relations with dragons is extremely tiring because it is very hard to "follow" the life rhythm of a creature with supernatural characteristics. If a drought occurs, it is usually said that a dragon has taken up that residence with a nearby Witch and his presence brought it about. Then house of that Witch must be found, and the dragon must be expelled in the way that we described earlier, when we talked about *vrzino kolo* (The witch's dance).

Some people connect these dragons to fallen angels, from the Book of Enoch, who occupied caves and trees after their fall. Because of that, their offspring are dragon men.

In conclusion, there is a belief that many animals, if they live long enough, could become dragons. Those animals are mainly carp, snakes, turkeys, geese, etc.

Sacred animals

Deer

In ancient times, the deer is probably was one of the most important sacred animals, not only in the Balkans, but in the whole of Europe as well. To our great sorrow, little information has survived. We can only conclude that fact from the frequent use of deer as a motif in handicrafts and folk art, and a small number of folk myths, stories, and fairy tales.

Every year on the 12th of July, in the village of Jablanica on Petrova Gora (Peter's Hill) in Serbia, a meeting that represents what remains of former Deer God's celebration is organized. A sacrificial altar still exists on Peter's hill where cattle were sacrificed to this God. According to the myth, deer with golden horns came to accept those sacrifices. One year people forgot to make sacrifice, and the deer ordered them to sacrifice themselves on the altar. As a memory to this sacred event, local people needed to cover the altar with the blood of a bull that is brought there adorned with flowers. This lovely myth tells us that sometimes deer represented the god of vegetation and wildlife. In Serbian territory, a monument to deer exists on which Diana the Goddess is represented, sitting on the back of a deer, holding it's horns in her hands..

Deer very often appear on tombstones, which is another bit of proof that the deer is a sacred animal. During the Christmas celebrations we spoke of earlier, persons would wear masks adorned with deer horns; these celebrations took place on Christmas and New Year. The deer is the key figure in the story of the origin of the Rowan tree (sorbus torminalis). According to the story, a girl was grazing cattle, and when she came to the river, she realized that she couldn't cross. A deer came and help her; it lifted her up in its horns and threw her across. The Rowan tree grew on the place where she landed.

Then we have the story of Croatian origin about a girl who frees a deer from a trap by magical means, hitting the trap three times with staff made from an apple tree, etc.

In the territory of eastern Serbia, many Witches claim that there are deer that walk erect, or that they saw a young man covered in deerskin with deer horns on his head. It is astounding to me that ethnologists did not record these stories. This only shows us how that many things have not been thoroughly documented.

In the Balkans, deer have multiple roles. He is a deity of the forest, a spirit of the underground world, the spirit of vegetation, and protector of cattle and wildlife. From this we can conclude that it could be the horned God that was followed to a greater or lesser extent in certain parts of country. The situation surrounding the goat is very similar, as we will see later in the book.

The male goat

For a long time people have thought that the male goat is the Devil's animal, and in some cases, even the Devil himself, because that is one of his favorite forms. It is obvious that this belief came with Christianity under the influence of Orthodox Church, or Heretical Christianity, specifically the Bogomils.

However, many folk customs show us that it has not always been so. The black male goat was slaughtered as a sacrifice to the construction of a new building. Last reaped sheaf of wheat was given to the male goat to start chewing, then the sheaf would be taken from the goat's mouth and kept as a universal medicine. A bag made of goat hair was not only a fundamental Witch's accessory, but also to other people who wished to practice magic. Young girls rode male goats to make cattle fertile. Men masked as goats chased women. All of these rituals originate from cult of fertility.

Remember that during Christmas celebrations young men wore Lesnik's mask, made from the skin and horns of a male goat. The male goat is the animal that simultaneously represents both the demon of underworld and fertility .

If we go back and pay attention to the fact that the Horned God was declared the Devil by Christianity, then we can take into consideration the fact that one of his animals is the male goat, or the image of the horned God himself. The appearance of Lesnik and Tartor who both have goat's horns, goat's ears and the lower body of a goat, speaks in favor of that.

In the southwestern Balkans, in the territory of Montenegro and Herzegovina, several myths are preserved in which a great male goat lives in a cave. According to tradition, when it was killed, the Crnojevic River appeared in its place. Another story says that the same river appeared when its ear was cut off. Ethnologists relate these traditions with the Illyrian deity of springs named Bindu, whose altar was discovered near Bihac. There is a goat's head on the altar.

There is belief that Witches, fairies, and clairvoyant old women ride goats. All of them could become goats when they needed to, except old women of course. Witches were often seen walking in the company of goats, and it was not surprising when some of them talked with a human voice; I have heard these accounts many times. We can say that among Balkan Witches, the goat is something like a "familiar" to their Western counterparts.

The snake

The snake is probably one of the most respected animals among the people of the territory of the former Yugoslavia. It is very hard to talk in detail about the snake and not to forget to mention something. The cult of the snake is also one of the most widespread cults in the Balkans. Bearing in mind the fact that any deep analysis of this sacred animal would require a book unto itself, we will try to point out only the pertinent facts concerning Witchcraft in the Balkans.

As with most anywhere in the world, the people of this area have an ambivalent attitude towards the snake. They respect it, but they fear it at the same time. The snake is a portent of good, but it can also be evil. Out of respect and, its name is not usually said aloud. It is said that the Devil himself created it, or that it changed from a hair that fell off from a horse's tail that fell into the water. It is also said that snakes have legs, but they keep them hidden. The snake pulls out legs only at night and if someone sees them, they die instantly. People also believe that snakes look differently than we see them; they are much larger and only horses and oxen can see them in their natural size.

There are good and bad snakes. People fight against bad ones first by magical means, and then by physical, but they respect the good ones. Some of bad ones are very bullet resistant, they could hypnotize their victims, drown them, and poison them. They usually represent evil demons from the underworld who assume the form of a snake when they want to visit our world.

Among good snakes, the first is the guardian snake that lives under the threshold or near the house. It represents the spirit of ancestors and protects the family from physical and magical threats. Sometimes when people went to work in the fields, they carried their children with them and placed them under the shade of large trees. They said that snakes came and stayed near the children or they lay coiled on their chests, not allowing anyone to approach them until their mothers returned. When their mothers returned, the snakes would quietly leave.

It is also good thing when you see **Aesculapius'** snake (*Elaphe longissima* or *Zamenis longissimus*) in the vineyard in the field because it means that will not be any elemental catastrophic on that area. Reason for this is belief that Aesculapius' snake fights with demons of elemental catastrophic and in that way guards its territory.

Many snakes are guardians of various goods, such as foods, medicinal herbs, etc. It is said that the snake that guards treasure kills nine searchers, and allows the tenth to take its treasure. Beside this, there is the Snake Czar that wears a golden crown and carries a small green branch in his mouth. The one who acquires the crown will acquire magical knowledge, learn the language of animals and herbs, will know how to recognize medicinal herbs, and many other things. There are many myths involving this figure. It is common belief that only snakes know the special herb that could revive the dead.

It is very good to help a snake, because it becomes the faithful ally of the person who saved its life, then teaches that person many things, especially about medicinal herbs.

The Snake itself is very powerful and scared animal, and by virtue of that many amulets and magical staffs are made from them. Earlier we described the process of making magical whip. However, that is not the only ritual of that kind; powerful amulets can be made of garlic in an almost identical manner. It is necessary to put few cloves of garlic in the snake's mouth instead of hemp, and wait for the garlic to grow. When garlic appears, it is necessary to take its seeds and carry them on their person. It is said that the owner of such an amulet could identify Witches and that they became clairvoyant. One who carries the head of the first snake he saw after the New Year could identify witches as well.

It is believed that it is enough to merely draw snake, and the item on which the snake was drawn became full of magical energy. Of course, they could be carved, chiseled, or hammered (Minted) snakes as well.

There is special, lower class of Witch men who can communicate with snakes. Many people witnessed this; a Witch man would sit down on a large rock, wait for few seconds, then suddenly, snakes would begin to appear out of nowhere and surround him. He would then tell them to go away, and they would listen to him. This is not a myth, rather an actual occurrence.

Witches often utilize dried snake parts in preparing medicines and magical rituals. Those parts are usually the head, tongue, heart, and shed skin. A white or albino snake has great value, because it is believed that one who eats the meat of such a snake gains the ability to learn the language of animals and herbs.

It is also believed that the Snake Czar lives around a thousand years, that six-winged snakes live in lakes and carry jewelry with magical powers under their wings, and that very old snakes could become dragons.

The wolf

Among the majority of the Balkan people, the wolf is a demonic animal. It can represent the souls of ancestors, underworld demons, and it could represent the deity of the underworld. The wolf is a respected animal and its name should not be pronounced out loud, especially after midnight.

Along with male goat, the wolf is considered to be devil's animal, as well as the devil himself, the wolf's creator. It is said that the wolf is so powerful that the devil himself fears it. It is said that every wolf has three of the devil's hairs between its eyes. It was supposed that the only way to be safe from the wolf was to ask it to be its godfather. Some people chose to offer sacrificial food, and based on that we can see, that sometimes the wolf represented the deity of the underworld. Rituals were performed at Christmas time when the family prepared the "wolf's supper" from all the dishes in the Christmas meal and put it a dish. After that, one of the children must wait until dark, then take the dish to a nearby crossroads and leave it there. After the child sets down the dish, they must turn and walk away without looking back.

Parts of the wolf's body were used to make amulets and in spellcasting, especially by Witches. The parts most often used were the eyes, jawbone, heart, hair, teeth, claws, and even the whole skull.

The raven

According to tradition, the raven is not a very important animal, but Witches used them extensively in the creation of healing potions and balms, mostly the head and blood. The raven is known as a bearer of bad tidings, bringing news from battlefields, announcing bad weather, and long winters.

The frog

The frog is a very sacred animal; the people of our country call Baba out of affection and respect. No frog should ever be killed, because if a person kills a frog, they also kill their mother. The frog represents the collective female spirit. A frog that lives under the threshold is very respected and is considered the guardian of the household and the family within.

Witches use them as a living amulet that is protection from all forms of evil. Many medicines are made from the frog, used to heal both people and livestock. The most respected frog is Baburaca, but I have spoken in depth of that previously.

The rabbit

The rabbit is a sacred animal that is identified with the Moon. Many taboos are associated with the rabbit, and a great number of rituals that include the rabbit must be performed during Christmas. Pregnant women must not eat or look at a dead rabbit.

Both people and Witches use many parts of the rabbit's body for making amulets, medicines, and in various magical rituals. The most often used are blood, tallow, skin, spleen, hair, bones, teeth, and paw.

The horse

The horse is almost unavoidable when we speak of sacred animals because it is closely connected to the underworld. Most supernatural creatures or creatures with supernatural capabilities, and even Witches have the ability to change into the form of a horse. The black horse is used in situations where the treasure needs to be discovered or when it is necessary to expose. Because the black horse itself is a denizen of the underworld, it is said that considered that it will never walk over the grave of a vampire.

The turtle

The turtle is one of the animals which people believe always knows where to find the Raskovnik, because it is the guardian of that plant. In stylized folk art, the turtle always have a protective function. Balkan Witches often use turtle's blood, meat, and eggs to prepare medicines.

Ants

In the territory of eastern Serbia Witches used to perform rituals on anthills. They are considered to have direct contact with underworld and can transmit instructions to those beings that reside there.

Other animals with lesser importance:

Mole – its paw is used as an amulet.

Butterfly – Witches have been known to use this form for travel.

Ram – The horns are used for handles for the Kustura – the magical knife is made of right ram's horn.

Eagle – the talons and beak are used as amulets for protection against the evil eye and demons.

Rooster – Medicines are made from some of its parts; the rooster warns demons to return to the underworld at sunrise.

Male turkey – Feathers of the male turkey were used as broom. It represents a demon of the underworld, and an old tom turkey can transform itself to a dragon.

Bear – the front and rear claws are used as amulets or talismans; there are traces of a bear cult in some regions of the Balkans.

Wild boar – its teeth are used as amulets for protection against demons.

Bat – it symbolizes the demons of the underworld, and parts of its body are simply unavoidable in making amulets and in magical rituals. The use of bat wings in love potions is almost mythical.

SACRED, MAGICAL, AND MEDICINAL HERBS

We say with certainty that no Witch who has ever existed has never used some form of sacred herb or plant. According to tradition, Witches could recognize various types of herbs tat could be used to help or to harm others. This belief is widespread in the Balkans, and it would be hypocritical of us to say otherwise.

Almost all peoples of the world have people somewhere in their history who were familiar with medicinal herbs. Those were the ancient phytotherapists, predecessors of today's doctors, which history remembers by its balms and teas. Still, they were not alone, and they had competition from people that practiced other methods of treating illness, whatever they were. It would be nothing new if we say that these phytotherapists saved many lives along with healers and those who practiced other disciplines, especially in those times when "scientific" medicine was based on bloodletting and drinking mercury.

 In ancient times in the Balkans, it was customary for each village to have its own gatherer of herbs. They learned this vocation from their parents and they keep its secrets in the family. Still, because their recipes did not always give positive results, people sought out magic practitioners as well. Those were Witches. They used both medicinal and sacred herbs in their rituals, using all available means to help those that came sought their help. People feared them, but at the same time, they were respected and sought out. A Witch did not have the right to make mistakes. A Witch was constantly persecuted and accused of lesser things, usually the figments of other's imaginations. It was most likely for that reason that Witches developed foolproof healing methods. Those methods have been preserved to present day, especially in eastern and southern Serbia.

The level of trust that people had for them is astounding, when we keep in mind that they treated many serious illnesses with poisonous herbs. To my knowledge, there is no evidence of any of their "patients" having any problems, which attests to their knowledge of herbs.

It is very difficult to make a clear distinction between sacred and medicinal herbs in the Balkans. At least one belief is related to each herb, and the only thing that makes one different from the other is the fact that some of them are "more sacred" than others. Each herb that helped someone in some way, reduced discomfort, or healed, automatically become sacred, because only supernatural has the power to do such things. That means that all medicinal herbs fell into the category of sacred, but not all sacred herbs are suitable for healing. Those not used for healing could be used as amulets or magical items in rituals. That is why is so hard to make a clear division and differentiate between the two groups of herbs.

The largest amount of these herbs were collected on the holiday that is dedicated to herbs, called "*Biljni petak*" (Herb Friday). *Biljni petak* (herbal friday) got its name because it is the last Friday before the 6th May, meaning that the actual date changes from year to year. The herbs must been collected manually, early in the morning before sunrise, because it is said herbs become medicines after midnight on Thursday. Collecting herbs was a community event; young women adorned themselves with wildflowers, and they sang and danced together while they collected the herbs. It was a celebration for the arrival of spring and the awakening of the spirits of the plants. The herbs were collected at that time because people believed that the ones that grew at that time were the most potent and had the most magical power. In eastern Serbia this holiday was continued in front of a cave, where bonfires were burned in honor of the underworld demons, that is, the spirits of vegetation. The collected herbs were dried and used throughout the year.
Besides this tradition of herb collecting, many other dates exist in

the Balkans that are very important for collecting a certain herb, for example, the "field broom" that we mentioned earlier. Some of the herbs were collected ritually, while others were collected at a certain time of day or night. More information about dates related to herb collection will be discussed in chapter eleven.

Witches acquired information about certain herbs in three ways. The first consisted of learning from an older Witch who had obtained her knowledge from a Witch before her, and so on.

The second way was to observe sick animals when they out to the forest or meadow to graze on certain herbs that would help them to relieve their pain. It was obvious that those herbs were not eaten in everyday grazing. It may sound strange, but for many years, was the most secure method for discovering medicinal herbs.

Third way to acquire information about herbs was by dreams, visions, or based on communication with supernatural beings. This information usually came from the Forest Mother and from fairies. It was not unusual for an animal to come to a Witch in a dream and show her a new medicinal herb, and give her advice how to use it. Imagine, if you will, the sheer scope of information that exists; since time untold, a Witch collects information her entire life, then passes her knowledge to younger one, then the younger one does the same, and so on. In my conversation with one old Witch, I found it amazing that there were no herbs that she did not know how to use, and she knew the related lore for all of them. She literally gave me a complete answer for every herb I pointed out or mentioned.

Let us just say that in folk's medicine and magic every part of the herb is useful, from the root, stalk, and leaves to its fruit and seeds. What will be used and in what way depends from many factors, and we will see that in following text.

"Raskovnik" Laser Trilobum, commonly known as Gladich

Laser Trilobum (laserpitium siler, siler trilobum) is probably one of the most important herbs in Balkan Witchcraft. Based on its name, "Raskovnik", we can conclude that this herb had power to "unshackle" things. It is said that this herb can open any lock, break chains, and even locate buried treasure. Nevertheless, those are just some of its functions. People say that it "breaks" spells, "opens" barren women and heals sterility, repels illnesses in people and cattle, provides protection from spells, evil, and many other things.

The most important property of the Raskovnik is its anthropomorphic attributes, in other words, its root is reminiscent of the human body. The Raskovnik is very difficult to find, especially one that has an anthropomorphic shape. It is said that the turtle is its guardian, and that one is always in its vicinity. Some people say that if you find turtle's eggs and build a fence around them, the turtle will return with a Raskovnik in its mouth and break the fence. Then you should take it from the turtle quickly, as it will eat the root after the job is finished. There is a similar story that involves the Hedgehog. It is necessary to find a young hedgehog and build a little fence around it; the big hedgehog will show up with a Raskovnik and free the younger one. People have tried to find Raskovnik by dragging a chain through a meadow; they would attach a chain to themselves or to an animal, and if the chain broke, they assumed that there was a Raskovnik nearby. I don't think it's a great secret when I tell you that these methods were not terribly successful.

The Raskovnik is a common plant, the only difference is that it grows in inaccessible areas and it is very difficult to find. As far as I know, it is now cultivated in southern Serbia because of the huge demand for it.

Special beliefs and uses are related to a Raskovnik that has an anthropomorphic shape. As we said in previous chapter when we spoke of dwarves, the root of the Raskovnik in the shape of a human body stops being an herb, and becomes a spirit of nature, an elf, a dwarf, etc. It is easiest to find by night because it leaves its herbal body in the ground and leaves in its astral shape. Some people claim that it is possible to see a creature one foot tall, or three flames suspended in the air. Of course, that is the right moment to dig up the root; that act puts this spirit of nature in your service. Essentially, the Raskovnik is to the Balkans what the Mandrake is to the west, and Ginseng is to the far east.

It is a very interesting fact that thieves had a custom to perform an unusual type of piercing. Namely, they sewed parts of the root under the skin of the palm. According to tradition, it would allow them to open any door they touched, though I do not believe that this was the main goal of this procedure.

In any case, the Raskovnik is a very sought-after item.. You do not have to do anything special with it, simply owning it is enough. A person could carry around or keep it in their house. In both cases, it will perform its duty of an amulet that protects its owner from various troubles and illnesses. Witches usually use one that has an anthropomorphic shape, so as to control an obliging spirit.

211

Mandrake

Mandrake (mandragora officinarum) is probably one of the most famous magical herbs in the world. Its popularity in Western Europe was followed only by its popularity in the Balkans. Some authors published the opinion that mandrake was brought to the Balkans by Jewish merchants, but I do not agree. I believe that mandrake has always been present in the Balkans, undoubtedly in the southern Balkans and near the sea. Also, we can't find any good reason why mandrake couldn't grow in the northern part of the country, especially if we know that it grows in Bulgaria and Romania.

Mandrake got its popularity because of many things but the most important fact is that mandrake, like the Rastovnik, could have an anthropomorphic root shape. Jews introduced the aphrodisiac usage of mandrake and ways of using it in love magic to the Balkan people, while the Balkan people transferred knowledge of Rastovnik to them. We assume that this is time when the beliefs converged that are still present in this areas. I had a conversation with an old, experienced Witch that lives in mountains. On that occasion she give me the advice to look for mandrake with the help of a hedgehog or turtle in the same manner that we use then when we want to find Rastovnik. This also supports the supposition that mandrake has always been in the Balkans.

The greatest value of the mandrake for Witches is the anthropomorphic aspect, which gave them another type of nature spirit that could serve them. Mandrake in itself can be an amulet that protects us from not only from evil, but also protection from bullets or any type of attack on its owner.

As Rastovnik and Mandrake were difficult to find and expensive to purchase, certain plants were sometimes used as substitutes. The best known replacements in the Balkans were the roots of the Celandine (chelidonium majus), and the Nightshade (atropa belladonna).

Toothwort (Gorska Majka, or "Great Mother" in Serbo-Croatian)

Toothwort (Lathraea Squamaria), or Jarba Muma Paduri (in the Vlach language) is one of the most respected herbs, especially in southern, southeastern, eastern, and northeast Serbia.

As you can see from its name, this herb is dedicated to Goddess itself and sometimes it represents a miniature Goddess. This herb is considered as female herb and usually only women use it. By itself it is considered an amulet, and can aid the person that carries it to maintain uninterrupted contact with the Goddess. This herb is known to do three things: it protects its carrier from evil, aids in maintaining stable finances, situation, and if the owner

213

is woman, to maintain her fertility or to make a barren woman fertile.

Toothwort is irreplaceable to Witches for their rituals, especially when they need to treat barren women. One of the famous rituals is performing in following way. A woman who cannot conceive refrains from sexual relations from some time, and then goes to find and harvest this herb. The easiest place to find it is near water, because it prefers such an environment. The woman must wait until midnight, then remove her clothes, then find and pick it in silence. When she leaves the place where she picked it, she must neither look back nor talk. This herb must be given to Witch who will perform ritual with it. The ritual consists of making a tea from this herb, and fumigation over the woman's head while reciting an appropriate incantation. Some physical diseases also treated with this herb in a similar manner, whether women or man. Further, the whole herb could be used, not just its above-ground part.

Garden Valerian or Garden Heliotrope

Garden heliotrope (valeriana officinalis), without exaggeration is the most powerful herbal amulet against all types of evil demons, and evil Witches as well. Various beliefs are related to the garden heliotrope; some claim that its power is so great that it cannot be controlled without another herb that reduces its effect. That other herb is called the Odumiljen (Herba ficta), but its existence has not yet been proven.

It is said that garden heliotrope protects male children, and that a newborn boy would not survive a single day if his mother does not put the root of this herb under his pillow, beside the bed, or in his diaper. People used to sew root of this herb into cattle, but adults wear it happily because it is said that it wards off the evil eye. It is said that its root needs to be kept in the house, as it will protect the entire family.

Witches also use garden heliotrope to make amulets for protection and health. When it is for protection, Witches wrap a red yarn around the root, then tie three knots and recite an appropriate incantation to protect the person for whom the amulet is intended. The process is almost identical when an amulet is made for protection; the only difference is that Witches use white yarn.

All manner of teas and potions can be made from the garden heliotrope; they are considered universal medicine for all kind of diseases, however, the emphasis seems to be on mental illnesses, menstrual pain, and hearth problems, although.

It is very often used in combination with Elecampane (inula helenium) and Rue (ruta graveolens) by soaking it with them in cold water, which the ill person must then drink. It is not necessary to boil the water to make tea, the water must be consumed to get the full effect of the herbs. It was not unusual for people leave those three herbs outside to soak overnight so that they could absorb cosmic energy.

Elecampane, or Horse-Heal

Elecampane (inula helenium) is also a very powerful herb that has immense powers of protection. Second to the garden heliotrope, the Elecampane root is the most used amulet against the evil eye. Like garden heliotrope, Elecampane is mentioned in many folk songs which exalt its power of protection.

Like most of the herbs here, Elecampane should be collected on "*biljni petak*" (Herb Friday), the Friday May 6, the only difference being that a ritual must be performed during the collection of this herb so that the herb won't lose its powers. The ritual must be performed in the following way: A spot where Elecampane must be found early in the morning on Herbal Friday. Because this herb has a large, thick roott, it is necessary to dig it up. It is forbidden to use any tool made by human hands, but it is necessary to find a piece of sharp stone, to free the earth around the root, being careful not to damage the root in any way. When this is done, you must throw the rock in the air as high as you can, and the root must be pulled from the earth before the rock hits the ground.

Thus picked, the Elecampane root is dried, and later must be sewn into clothes or used as an addition to various types of amulets. People give Elecampane root to cattle with salt for protection. Chopped and dried, it can be used for fumigation, to purge spaces of evil forces and demons.

Elecampane a very powerful medicinal herb and is often used in phytotherapy. Its main use was in treating tuberculosis; tea made of either its dried or fresh root and honey from conifer forests and consumed twice per day.

Sweet basil

Sweet basil (ocimum basilicum) is a herb with a wide range of functions among the people of the former Yugoslavia. I think that an entire book could be written about it, because it was used on almost any occasion, in every place and from all sides, even if they were in direct conflict. I will explain. Basil was used in all rituals actions related to birth, marriage, and death. Basil is also a very common herb in the Orthodox Church, where it used for holy water. Witches also use it very often, and both sorcerers and fortune-tellers consider it a necessary herb in many rituals.

Basil is considered very powerful protection, not only from evil demons, but also from vermin that could damage chicken coops, sheepfolds, and stables. Basil is also used for fumigation when you want to protect something. Witches could draw a magical circle with its smoke. Many parents put basil on their children to protect them from evil, and adults often wore it as well. Obviously, basil is a very powerful amulet. The ash that remained after a fumigation could be used to draw symbols of protection on the bodies of children and adults, most often on the forehead.

When Witches of eastern Serbia wanted to invoke spirits of nature, whether it was the Forest Mother or *Tartor*, they brought stalks of basil and few garlic cloves in case something went wrong during the summoning.

When an amulet is made from basil, a stalk is tied with red or white yarn, along with a lock of hair from the person for which the amulet is being made. This type of amulet had various functions, mostly for protection, health, happiness, and prosperity.

217

When a Witch extinguished live coals, she cut the water in the bowl with her *kustura* or she stirs it with basil.

Basil is considered a universal medicine for magical treatment of the sick. It could be used for fumigation of a sick person, drinking water in which basil was soaked overnight, or making amulets for recovery. It is often used for barren women because it is said that basil promotes fertility.

Garlic

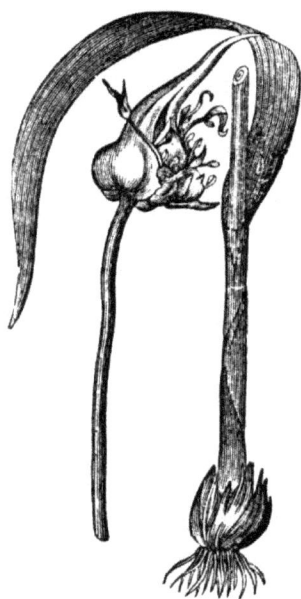

Garlic (allium sativum) falls into the category of protection herbs. It is considered extermely reliable when repelling Witches and various evil demons. In addition, a person who did not eat it was automatically guilt of practicing magic, but that is not true, of course. Witches gladly use garlic in many magical rituals and they are not afraid of it, as was once believed. As we just mentioned, Witches use garlic in several ways. We already said that garlic and basil could be carried as a safeguard when someone wants to invoke supernatural beings or spirits of nature.

Garlic that appears from snake's head cut off with silver coin has special power and provides the one who carries it to see creatures that common people cannot, specifically those of the astral plane. Any illness can be transferred to garlic, which can later be transferred to a tree or thrown away, in a stream or river, or in an abandoned well. Sometimes it is only necessary only bring garlic to the place where a sick person is and recite an appropriate incantation. It is also a part of many amulets related to protection and "chasing away" illness and disease.

Many of the remedies were meant to be ingested, and people ate it in various forms when the problem was of an inflammatory or infectious nature, but people have known of the antibiotic properties for a long time, and they put used it in all manner of poultices when there was a danger of infection, but they ate it when they were having various inflammatory processes in the body that were caused by bacteria.

Other sacred, magical, and medicinal herbs

Iris (iris germanica) is connected to the god of thunder because it is considered to protect from it. Its root, when shaped like a penis and testicles, was used in love magic and as an aphrodisiac. Fertility potions were made from its juice..

St. John's Wort (hypericum perforatum) is a herb that was once dedicated to the goddess, the mother of God is considered as strong protector of women from evil. If a woman believes that she is barren because someone has cast a spell on her wears it as an amulet and drinks tea made of it.

Madder (rubia tinctorum) is used in magic when you do not want the presence of others. It is believed that it has great power of protection, especially against vampires and evil spirits of the deceased. It is enough to hang it on the main entrance of a dwelling to keep them from entering.

Common Ivy (hedera helix) is used as a protection from evil demons and it is believed that it protects children as well. It is used in love magic and foretelling.

Danewort or Dwarf Elder (sambucus ebulus) is one of the herbs that is used in the ritual for invoking rain. It is considered to protect from snakebite, but it is its odor that repels snakes. It is burned in honor of deceased people who liked to smoke.

Scarlet pimpernel (anagallis arvensis) was once dedicated to the Slavic deity Svetovid, and is used today in rituals related to foretelling. It is considered that it is enough to keep this herb under the pillow, tell it what you want to know, and it will appear in your dreams.

Tansy (tanacetum vulgare) is a very important herb among Balkan Witches. It has power to return a place or thing to a previous condition, also to repel and reflect magical attacks. It can be worn, consumed in small quantities, or put it in boiled water and spilled over the threshold, reciting the incantation, "I don't track, I give it back"; we spoke of this ritual earlier.

Red Clover (trifolium pratense): like many other places in the world, it is considered lucky, especially if a stalk has four leaves. It is interesting that a great number of things are related to this herb in the same manner as Rastovnik. Specifically, the turtle was the protector of clover and that you could find

clover in the same way, by making a barrier around her eggs. It is necessary to have two types of clover to find buried treasure, four-leaf clover and two-leaf clover. The treasure is found with the help of the four-leaf clover, while the two-leaf clover helps to it from the earth. In addition, clover discovered with the help of a turtle can break any chain, and brings happiness in all aspects of life.

Dog rose or Rosehip (rosa canina) provides protection from diseases. An ill person must pass through a split stick made of dog rose if they want to get well and to clean their aura.

221

Sage (salvia officinalis) is a universal herb for protection that could protect from all manner of demons. Its primary purpose is fumigation, i.e. to clean ritual and home space. This custom has survived until modern day, although members of the Orthodox church converted to incense.

It is commonly used in amulets, often in combination with other herbs, like basil and wormwood.

Broom (cytisus capitatus) is considered strong protection from hostile entities and it is used mainly in the western Balkans and near the coast.

Geranium (geranium macrorrhizum) is one of the most important magical plants, used in healing rituals and for warding off disease in general. Amulets can be made from it, people bathe in the water in which geranium had been soaked as a healing remedy, and tea could be made from it. The dried root of the geranium is a very strong amulet whose purpose is to prevent diseases from infecting the person who wore it.

People adorned sick trees with geranium to heal them; they also put geranium in food so it would not spoil.

Mistletoe (viscum album) is a parasitic plant that mainly grows on oak trees, and it is considered very sacred. However, if it grows on a hazelnut tree, which is very rare, it is even more powerful. There are folk beliefs that say that golden apples grow on this mistletoe, and they are protected by a white snake. The person who picks this apple, boils it in water, then drinks the water will be able to identify every medicinal plant and herb in nature. Many common beliefs exist that include the snake, which is a guardian of something that lives under the hazelnut tree where mistletoe grows. The common thread for all these stories is the presence of hidden treasure or knowledge.

Mistletoe is also connected to Witches. It is said that some Witches makes their first brooms of mistletoe, and that is how mistletoe got its second name "witch's broom".

Burning Bush (dictamnus albus) is a sacred and miraculous herb. Above all, it is considered the fairy's plant. With this plant, you can make rituals of alliance with fairies when you want to cure a person of some disease. The reason for this is belief that fairies are familiar with alternative methods of healing all manner of diseases, and bearing in mind the fact that for any there is an appropriate herb to cure every disease, who knows better than fairies who themselves originate from nature.

The greatest number of these rituals were performed in Serbia at a place about fifty kilometers downstream from Belgrade, near an old town called Smederevo. The place where these rituals were performed is called Jasenak (Burning Bush), named after the large amount of them that grew in the area. News of miraculous healings spread in throughout the Balkans, and people from remote areas came to perform rituals that they learned from local people.

These rituals performed in following way, starting in the beginning of May. As the crowds were large and the ritual must be performed at night, people came early in the morning and left a towel under the chosen Burning Bush to reserve their spot.

When night fell, they would return with the sick person. They would lie them on the towel with their head near the base of the bush. Then, around the afflicted person, they placed a dish of honey, a loaf of bread, a glass of water, and a glass of wine. After that, they lit a candle made of beeswax. The sick person took a little of each, and the rest was left for the fairies. This kind of sacrifice is called the "fairy's supper". At the end, they were bound with the fairy. Then the afflicted person and the one who brought them there must lie down and fall asleep under "her" Burning Bush.

There were three possible outcomes. The first was that the sick person would see a fairy in their dreams that tells them what they need to do to be healed, the second one was that the person would wake and see that the tree had been damaged, which was the sign that the sick person would recover. The third one was to dig around the Burning Bush to find anything unusual that the fairy left during the night to be given to sick person to eat or drink so as to heal them.

The people then left, leaving the towels and dishes because they that they were not supposed to be touched. Today, the Burning Bush that grew there no longer exist, and a church sits on those grounds.

Carnation (dianthus caryophyllus) combined with basil makes an amulet that protects against all manner of evil forces.

Hellbore (helleborus odorus) falls into the category of very powerful amulets, especially its root. People used to put it in the cauldron to strengthen magical effects of whatever they were preparing. For this herb, one sacred rule must be followed, and that is that it cannot be held in bare hands or brought into the house before May.

Meadow saffron (colchicum autumnale): in the southwest Balkans, it is considered as the herb that gives birth to fairies.

Horseradish (cochlearia armoracia) is a plant whose root is considered protection from evil female entities that are well known as the "More" among Serbs.

Cattail (typha latifolia) is a plant with great magical power. Strings for catching evil entities were made from it. It is believed that no evil entity, whether vampire or werewolf, can break or tear this string. Among Serbs werewolf is an ethereal being rather than a physical one.

Gallic Rose or Apothecary's Rose (rosa gallica) is a very important plant that is used in the rituals related to health and communicable diseases.

For clear, soft skin, it is necessary to wash ones face with water in which its petals were soaked. Jaundice could be transferred to this rose as well; it is necessary to tie three knots around the stem with with yellow yarn, and silently recite the phrase: "I exchange yellowness for redness" while tying each knot.

Rosemary (rosmarinus officinalis) is herb of protection; all of its aboveground parts are used as protection from the evil eye and evil demons.

Rue, or Herb of Grace (ruta graveolens) is another herb of protection and its aboveground part is used as an amulet against evil demons.

226

Lovage (ligusticum levisticum) is above all a woman's herb, and it is most often used in love magic. Girls carried it with them or bathed in water in which Lovage was soaked as a magical way to attract attention from men.

Immortelle or Strawflower (helichrysum arenarium) is a woman's herb, but it is also considered a fairy herb. It is used as woman's protection from all manner of evil, and can attract love if worn as an amulet.

Onion (allium cepa) is considered protection from evil forces.

Wild teasel (dipsacus silvestris) is used for protection against vampires. People usually place it on the front door and in windows to prevent them from entering the home.

Lappa Burdock (arctium lappa) is an herb used in love magic and in rituals to bring couples together.

Summer Savory (satureia hortensis) has two uses. In combination with basil, it is used for protection against evil forces, and it is also used in rituals related to promoting good health.

Houseleek (*Sempervivum tectorum*). — *a*, fruit.

Common Houseleek (sempervivum tectorum) that grows around a home protects the family inside from misfortune. If none grew around the home, people planted it on the roof. It is said that this plant protects a home from burglars. Sometimes children wear it as an amulet to ward off illness.

Secret herbs of the Balkan Witches

Witches used the herbs that we mentioned above, whether they were used in rituals, in the making of amulets, or in the preparation of various medicines. However, common people used those herbs for the same purpose.

In contrast to these well-known herbs, Witches used herbs about were not spoken of, and whose magical effects they kept secret. This does not mean that no one except Witches knew about them or used them, but those cases were rare.

It is very difficult to find and identify these herbs. Additional barriers are posed by their given names, because they differed from place to place, and were given names based on their function. However, there are relatively few, because we have already identified most of them. Let's take a look at what we have.

Belladonna (atropa belladona), was used by Balkan Witches in many ways. Because this herb is very poisonous, people were afraid of it and each method of preparation required a level of knowledge that only Witches had.

228

It is generally known that this herb is one of the many that were used for making Witch's grease for flying. Further, its root, ground with a piece of white quartz, was given to sick people in very small quantities of course, to provoke vomiting, diarrhea, sweating, and other reactions that are considered good for purification of an organism. Besides this, Witches used this herb to provoke a miscarriage in a woman that did not want to have a child. This application gave it a very bad reputation, because abortion is considered a mortal sin in traditional Christian communities.

Belladonna root was used as a substitute for mandrake root. People wear it as an amulet for love or protection, and the root itself could be used as a kind of voodoo doll if it had a human shape. Witches mainly used its root and then the flowers and seeds.

Henbane (hyoscyamus niger) is another herb we know was used for making Witch's grease for flying. It is used for to make healing balms for toothaches and eye related diseases.

Thorn apple (datura stramonim) is another poisonous herb that has been mentioned was used for making Witch's grease and balms. In the forest, it is a sacred tree that acts as a medium with which to cast magic on another person. It was performed in following way. First, the Witch must acquire a

personal item or piece of clothing of the person on which she wants to perform a magical ritual. The Witch then goes to the thorn apple, puts the item on it, and recites a previously prepared incantation three times. It can look something like this: "When your fruit falls, let (The intended person) have good days (Prosperous times), may (The intended person)'s joys be as numerous as your seeds ."

Darnel or Cockle (lolium temulentum), or so-called "crazy grass" is one of the most dangerous and poisonous herbs that Witches used. When a Witch wanted to hurt someone, it was enough to make a small amount of powder from dried darnel stalk and put it into their food or drink The person would most certainly become mentally incompetent. Higher doses were lethal, so this herb was used very carefully.

Alske Grass (Gramina Draconis) were used by Witches for healing a great number of illnesses, but only in amulets or a necessary component for the performance of a ritual. Gramina Draconis grows only in sacred places and is dedicated to a supernatural creature named Ala who looks like huge snakelike dragon. It is believed that people who do not know how to use this herb should not collect it, because they will be punished by higher forces if they do. From this, we can conclude that this plant is reserved only for Witches.

Sweet Annie or Sweet Wormwood (artemisia annua) is a very powerful herb according to Witches; they used little brooms made of its stalks for ritual cleaning of spaces and unclean items.

Wormwood (artemisia absinthium) is used for many things. This plant is considered a very strong amulet, and possibly the only means of defense against bad fairies. Potions, teas, balms, and oils were made of this herb. It is said that water in which wormwood sits overnight has cleansing properties, so it was very often used for washing. With the help of wormwood, rusalje come out of their trances, and it is used as protection against *rusalke* fairies.

Coffee (coffea arabica) was brought to the Balkans a long time ago, and it was adopted very quickly. Roasted and ground coffee was used for reading and foretelling, as we mentioned in chapter seven.

Beside this, it was used in ritual treatment of mental illnesses in the following way. Ground coffee and sugar were placed on piece of blue paper that were lit; the sick person was then fumigated with the resulting smoke while reciting an appropriate incantation.

Coffee steam was considered as very good in rituals promoting female fertility.

Finally, coffee grounds are related to black demons, and are used to invoke them.

Monkshood or Wolfbane (aconitum napellus), hemlock (conium maculatum), hellebore (veratrum album) along with opium poppy (papaver somniferum) and fly agaric (amanita muscaria) are other herbs that were unavoidable for making Witch's grease for flying.

Marijuana (cannabis sativa) is an herb that plays a large role in Balkan Witchcraft. Its flowers and leaves were basic ingredients of Witch's greases for flying, especially in the central Balkans. The Witches magical whip was made from the stalk, grown in the ceremonial manner that we discussed earlier. Eggs were buried in the place where someone wanted to plant marijuana, as a sacrifice. Usually three eggs were buried, rarely just one. Its seed soaked in wine were used as an opiate.

Vervain (verbena officinalis) was primarily used to treat mental illnesses and epilepsy. Medical potions were made from this herb, and it was also used for fumigation to chase away demons.

Early Purple Orchid (orchis mascula) and Green Winged Orchid (orchis morio) are two herbs that belong to the Orchidaceae family. Early Purple Orchid's root, which is reminiscent of testicles was used for making aphrodisiac potions, while when dried were used as a fertility amulet for men. The Green Winged Orchid, whose root is shaped like a hand, was called the Goddess Hand; they are favorite amulets of Witches, and their function is universal.

There is an interesting myth connected to this plant that explains its sacredness and very powerful nature. In Eastern Serbia I found an

232

old woman that told me that the Green Winged Orchid is actually the Hand of the Goddess. As the story goes, she was once captured by foes and tortured, and in the end, they cut off her hand her. She went to the forest to dig up its root and put in the place where her hand used to be. It "took" and since then she has an orchid's root instead of a hand. That is why every orchid represents her hand and has her powers.

Field Poppy (papaver rhoeas) is a type of wild poppy. Its flowers can be used for making opiates and were often used as a fundamental ingredient for Witch's grease for flying. Let me explain. All herbs that we cited were included in the composition for Witch's grease, but they are not all parts of the same recipe; most recipes consisted of two or three of them combined. Field Poppy is an herb that is considered to be completely dedicated to the element of fire and that is why it is said that evil Witches use it when they want to make fire by magical means.

Greater Dodder or Hellbine (cuscuta europaea) is considered to be hair that has fallen from a fairy's head. This herb is very important within Balkan Witches because it gives them an altar where they could summon fairies.

This herb is the most sought-after for treatment of illnesses of every kind, because people believed that fairies were sympathetic to the ill. Witches tell sick people to put a loaf of bread made from flour that was sifted from an upside-down sieve, a bit of sugar, a bit of honey, and a small piece of cloth (Representing the sick person) under this plant overnight. If the bread is bitten into or the honey is eaten, it means that the fairies took the sacrifice and that sick person will get recover. If nothing happens, the Witches tells the sick person that he must perform this ritual 39 days in row, and if the fairies still do not accept the sacrifice, on the fortieth day the Witch goes with the sick person to that place and performs the following ritual:

A Witch accompanies the sick person to that place at night, after midnight and before the sunrise, and begins the ritual in following way. She first draws a circle around her and her "client" with her magical knife. After invoking of fairies, she sprinkles the sick person with water in which wormwood was soaked. She performs the sprinkling with her mouth, hand, or with a stalk of basil that is tied with red yarn. With this act she removes the illness and cleanses the body and spirit of her client while the fairies look on. When the sick person is free of illness, the Witch gives them a signal to leave, and they leaves, without looking back, of course. The sickness that was removed from that person stays in the circle and cannot go after the person. The Witch stays a little longer, observing fairies and keeping them together so that they could not go after her client. At sunrise, the fairies depart and the Witch can go home.

Silver thistle (carlina acaulis) is a large, flowering plant whose bloom can reach the size of sunflowers; it thrives in dry areas rich in limestone. Although its leaves have thorns, they are hardly visible, and it is a truly beautiful plant.

Witches use this flower in several ways. The first is as an amulet, that when carried, prevents others from slandering the wearer. The second was to keep it in the house as a ward the household against all manner of evils. The last one involves using this flower as an altar to commune with fairies. It is said that the fairies became the guardian of the family when this flower was kept in the house.

Dahlia (dahlia album) is an herb that Witches use to make potions for women if they want to give birth a daughter. As a result, it falls into the category of female herbs. When used as an amulet, it provides prosperity and fertility in all aspects of life to the bearer.

Bog Asphodel (narthecium ossifragum), and Vratolom are not plants that we could necessarily classify as magical herbs used specifically for rituals. These herbs were mainly used for evil purposes, to hurt someone or to bring them to a place against will. In an old folk song, an old woman puts both of them in her cauldron along with water, and recites an incantation. When the water starts to boil, he appears on her threshold, regardless of where he is or what he is doing at the time.

Daisy (bellis perennis) is an herb whose seeds were used for making a special circle (Not a witches's circle, rather a small circle to look through.) to look at the person that you want to fall in love with you. Essentially, it was used in love magic.

235

Velvetleaf (abutilon avicennae) in combination with white horehound (marrubium vulgare), ironwort (sideritis), and Gerinthe minor (No known translation) were used for warding off the "dark" night demon. It is completely black, translucent, and looks like the dark from which it comes. Ethnologists incorrectly concluded that it is the night itself, which is not the case. It is a completely different creature, a "night ghost"; it isn't really a dangerous creature, but children are afraid of it.

A Witch expels this creature by putting the dried and ground herbs onto live coals or in water, in which case the water must be spilled on three red-hot rocks. Each rock must be a different color, one white, one red, and one black. In that moment, is necessary to recite an appropriate incantation, and the ghost will flee.

Purple starthistle (centaurea calcitrapa) is an herb that was mainly used in the central and southwestern Balkans. There are many stories that exalt its power. It is believed that this herb is self-aware, like Laser Trilobum (Raskovnik), tries to flee when someone tries to pick it. Because

of that, this herb must be collected in the following ritual way. The harvested root must be placed in a copper pan quickly to prevent it from escaping. The herb itself is mainly used in love magic. Juice squeezed from its root crystallizes, and resembles an actual crystal that refracts light into different colors. That "crystal" can be used as a love amulet. In addition, it was combined with other herbs in love magic rituals.

Geranium (pelargonium) is only used in hunting magic. When a hunter cannot get any game, he asks a Witch to help him. She crushes this herb with a mortar and pestle, soaks it in water, and leaves it outside overnight. At sunrise the next day she washes the hunter's rifle with the water and pours it down its barrel three times. Each time, she recites an incantation that contains wording to remove mist from the eyes of the hunter, to calm his hands, to bring him luck, etc.

Ground Ivy (glechoma hederaceum), Rock Fern (ceterach officinarum) and lesser snapdragon (antirrhinum orontium) are some of the herbs that Witches use to cure people of panic attacks, irrational fears, and shock. The majority of older traditional Witches that I spoke with used Stone Fern exclusively. It must be soaked in water left outside overnight so that the "*vedrina*" could take it. When I asked what "vedrina" was, they told me it is a celestial sphere of power. I concluded that they wanted to expose that dish to cosmic energy that stars emit and that the water helps to accumulate that energy. At sunrise, they sprinkled the afflicted person with the water, washed them with it, then gave the rest of it to them to drink.

The area near Visoko (A town in Bosnia) that is known for magical rituals similar to those in northeastern Serbia, observe a somewhat different ritual for treating the above-mentioned maladies. A pot with virgin water must be put on the fire and Ground Ivy is added. Then pot is then covered until the water boils. When water boils, the pot must be brought to the afflicted person, who is sitting beside a metal washbowl. Then the pot is uncovered, and turned upside-down into the washbowl. If no water is spilled, that is the sign that sick person will recover soon. This action must be performed three times, and at the end, the afflicted person must first be washed with the water, then made to drink a sip. The water remaining in the washbowl is taken to a crossroads and poured out, preferably at night.

In the territory of Montenegro, an almost identical ritual was performed; the only difference that the containers that were used were much smaller, and the afflicted person washed themself.

Yellow archangel (Lamium Galeobdolon) Yellow Archangel closely resembles a small nettle, with the only differences being that it doesn't sting, and that it has white stripes on its leaves. This herb is used to remove magic from a person who is believed to be under magic influence. Yellow Archangel should be soaked in virgin water, spring water if possible, and must be left outside overnight. It is also possible to make a magical oil from it; huge quantities of this herb must be submerged in sunflower oil and left to steep for forty days. Dried, it could be used for fumigation around the body of a person under the influence of magic.

Trava od namere (Grass of Intention) is one of the secret Witch's herbs, which, unfortunately, we have not yet managed to identify. It is a low-lying vine with half-circle, fan-shaped leaves. The Witches I spoke with told me that if this plant is carried or worn, it is never necessary to perform any sort of ritual; the plant itself does the work for the bearer, needing only their wish or intention to perform one. It could quickly recognize all forms of danger and an provided an appropriate response, so it represented a sort of amulet as well. Essentially, this plant does everything we want, or anything we imagine or intend to do. If it actually has this sort of power, it is no surprise that it has remained a secret to ethnobiologists.

Wild angelica (Angelica Silvestris). I received one if its' roots as a gift from a Witch to protect me from all manner of evil. Its root is orange in color and reminds me of dried bell pepper with vertical folds.

Sacred Trees

Here we give a brief list of the most important respected trees within the Balkans among Witches and people in general, as it is very difficult to clearly differentiate between the two.

Certain trees were respected as deities; they represented substitutes for idols, or even a kind of "temple". People decided the manner in which they would be used and what would be made of them based on their "sanctity". Various taboos are related to them, such as being forbidden to cut them down or to sleep under them. Let us take a closer look.

Pine tree (pinus silvestris) was identified with God in some parts of the Balkans, so people often swore on it. It is said fairies gather in its treetops. Rods of this wood that had been burned on both ends were used by male Witches in their battles.

Birch wood (betula) is a very powerful tree. Brooms made from their branches could sweep away any evil, whether by jumping over them, or cleaning a space with them. Young girls (witches) invoked fairies with those brooms to persuade the fairies to protect them.

239

Rowan tree (sorbus torminalis) is also a very important and respected tree, especially among Witches. It is prohibited to cut it, or even to touch it. Remember the myth I spoke of earlier regarding the Rowan tree, the one about the deer that helps the woman across a stream? I think that everyone understands that this story is about a forest Goddess or spirit of nature that protects deer. The Rowan tree itself probably represents this deity.

Elm (ulmus campestris) is known as the fairy's favorite tree, unapproachable by evil demons. "Live Coal" could be made from its wood, and ill people could go under its roots to "remove" their illness. Finally, if a person suffered from chronic fatigue, a Witch could transfer it from them to this tree.

Beech (fagus silvatica) is one of the trees whose branches is believed to give birth to fairies.

Juniper (juniperus communis) is a tree that people believe protects against evil spirits and vampires. A vampire stake must be made from this tree, and a diseased person must be touched with a broom made of this so as not to become a vampire.

Willow (salix) has multiple roles as sacred tree. People and cattle were flogged with its branches so they would grow to be sound, and people adorned their homes with its branches to ward off thunder and lightning. Sick people bathed in its vicinity, and after that, they left an article of clothing on one of its branches, then depart without looking back. It is very good for treating headache and fever. A Sick person must roast an onion and then go to a willow tree early in the morning. They must shake the tree three times and say "I'm not shaking away your morning dew, I'm shaking away my fever". After that, they must leave the onion under the tree, and go away reciting "The fever will take me when this onion sprouts".

There is another custom where a Witch transfers an illness to the tree. She brings a sick person under its canopy at night, and recites the following words: "as this tree bends, so does (The afflicted person) stand tall".

Hawthorn (Crataegus) is small tree that is very sacred in the Balkans, and so powerful that it can provide protection against all types of evil forces. A stake for killing vampires and werewolves can be made of hawthorn, and its thorn must be stabbed into a corpse so it could not become a vampire. A magical staff is made of hawthorn is used for defending and chasing away evil forces.

Witches use parts of hawthorn, especially its branches and thorns, in rituals with the goal of chasing away anything negative, including illnesses.

Dogwood (cornus mas) is a very popular tree in Serbia, even today. It represents health; its branches, leaves, buds, and berries are ingested to promote health. People could also wear a piece of dogwood as an amulet to promote health. Magical rods or staffs could be made to use in healing rituals.

It also serves as a protection from werewolves and other demons. People decorate their houses with its branches as a barrier against unwanted demons. With a dogwood staff, spells could be removed from a person under the influence of evil magic, and it would heal sick people who walked through a wreath made of its branches. It is present in rituals of fertility and prosperity. A "living fire" must be lit that later must be spread to every house. It is an essential tree in Balkan Witchcraft

Elder (sambucus nigra) is a demonic tree, which means that supernatural beings reside inside them, and they are filled with magical power. It is forbidden to cut this tree because there are almost always fairies among its branches and in its flowers, most of which are invisible to people. Dodole (young girls who perform rituals to invoke rain) decorate themselves with elder and magical flutes are also made from it.

Field maple (acer campestre) is considered a very powerful tree whose parts can be used as amulets to ward off hostile magic from other Witches. Witches also perform rituals to banish illness near the maple.

Sycamore (acer pseudoplatanus) is tree that was once dedicated to a deity. People offer sacrifices to it and leave clothes on its branches so the tree helps them with all manner of problems.

European ash (fraxsinus excelsior) is considered fairy tree. They often reside there, and evil cannot come near this tree. Spells cast by others on a person could be removed with the help of this tree.

Fir (abies pectinata) is the tree in which forest fairies live. There is an interesting story found in folk literature that says that people used to eat and then pray under the fir. To this day, no one knows to whom these prayers were addressed.

Hazel (corylus avellana) is one of the most sacred trees, especially for Witches. I think it's common knowledge that almost every Witch carries a stick made of its wood. Among ancient Balkan Witches in there are myths that a stick of hazel could kill the devil himself, turn people into other creatures, revive the dead, and could be used to make a Witches magical circle. We mentioned earlier that Witches splash the water with a hazel wood stick to invoke Tartor.

Hazel is the tree of wisdom, knowledge, and understanding. Sometimes the mentally ill were made to walk three times around a hazel tree to cure them, and schoolchildren were beaten with hazel wood switches to help them learn.

It is very interesting that people made their confessions to a hazel tree rather than to a priest. It is also believed that lightning cannot strike this tree, and it is safe underneath a hazel during a thunderstorm. We have already spoken about the mistletoe that grows on the hazel and the snake that sleeps underneath, so we don't need to touch on those again.

Linden (tilia) was sometimes respected as sacred tree. It was forbidden to cut it, except when it was necessary to obtain a "living fire" from it.

In all likelihood, it served as a Pagan place of worship, and it is well known that Pagan idols were made from it.

English Walnut (juglans regia) is unlike any other tree. It is a tree of Witches, demons, and underworld spirits. It is the sacred tree that people have great respect for, yet they fear it at the same time. Underneath it's large canopy was favorite meeting place of Witches; it is said that they gathered there to celebrate their holidays.

It is strongly forbidden to fall asleep under the Walnut tree, because a sleeping man is very vulnerable and his soul wanders from him. If that happens, Witches could take it, or other creatures could take it somewhere he doesn't it want to go. We can assume that this is the underworld, the tree itself represents some sort of portal. It is no surprise that this tree is connected with supernatural beings. This tree is vital of the cult of the dead or the cult of ancestors, which adds credence to our assumption. In Pagan times, the walnut was the residence for souls of the ancestors.

People still walk across its exposed roots to cure or prevent illness, and if the firstborn child is a female, the placenta is buried underneath this tree so that the next will be boy.

As we have said, the walnut tree is probably related to great horned spirit of nature, because he appears underneath it at noon. Finally, according to data collected by Cajkanovic , male magi and Witches performed their magic underneath it. Its leaves were placed on graves, it was planted in graveyards, and its nuts were placed in corners of rooms as a sacrifice to the deceased during Christmastime.

Yew (taxus baccata) is very respected among the people of the Balkans. It and the hawthorn are considered the strongest trees for protection against any evil. Both children and adults wear little amulets in the shape of a cross or an upside-down triangle made from wood of the yew, as well as a magical stick that serves as protection from evil demons. Fairies are often found in yew, and people put horns from their cattle on the tree to protect them from hostile spells.

English Oak (quercus robur) is the most important tree, especially to the Slovene people. It occupies a special place among cults because probably represented a forgotten Pagan God, but it is assumed that was either Perun, Dabog, or Veles. Even now, priests lead an old ritual of making a food offering to the oak into which a cross has been carved, the so-called *zapis* (wooden cross).

It is forbidden to ever cut down an oak, because it is believed that great evil will befall the person that does. It is believed animal spirits in the shape of a bull, dog, goat, big rabbits, etc, appear near the tree after midnight, and that they are probably protecting this sacred tree.

The wood of the oak is rubbed with that of the linden to make "living fire". An old Witch consecrates a younger one with a broom made of oak's branches. Witches gladly use oak in rituals of extinguishing live coals; they put three, seven, or nine pieces in a fire until they glow.

244

Turkish oak (quercus cerris) also could be carved with the *zapis* (wooden cross), if it is large enough. Its branches must be brought into the home during Christmas, as it it represents the Sun God, the sun that is born again. It is very interesting that they must be taken by night, which leads Serbian ethnologists to believe that the old Serbian deity was in fact an underworld deity. A great number of Christmastime rituals are related to the *badnjak*, which a ritually cut piece of Turkish oak, but we won't go into detail, as it is outside the scope of this book.

Sacred fruits and vegetables

There is no real way to omit fruits and vegetables, nor would we want to; many myths, stories, and beliefs are related to them. In addition, fruits and vegetables are used daily in many rituals. They could be amulets, ritual items, or offered sacrifices. Regardless, it is necessary to know that they fall into an equally valuable category of sacred plants along with herbs and trees.

Quince (pirus cydonia) is mainly used in love magic; girls like to wear Quince leaves coated with honey as an amulet to provide them with male affection.

Apple (pirus malus) is considered the most important sacred fruit in the Balkans. Above all it is a symbol of goodness, health, fertility, and happiness. It is considered to have great magical powers and it protects from every evil.

In almost all rituals that are related to life of an individual, the apple is needed to bring happiness, fertility, and prosperity. It is the one of the key sacrifices that should be offered to both gods and spirits of nature.

There is an old custom that metal coins must be stabbed into apple during a wedding so the newlywed couple will be financially stable.

It is used in all kinds of rituals to bring improvement in any sphere of life. The red apple is the most appreciated because it is the symbol of health. Because of that, its branches are also sacred and can be used in similar rituals to provide prosperity.

Wild Strawberry (fragaria vesca) is symbol of justice and progress. Little wreathes made of strawberry leaves are used in love magic; you must look through the wreath at the person whom you want to fall in love with you. Strawberry is also used as a sacrificial offering in rituals to make contact with the deceased.

Pear (pirus communis) is a fruit that is connected with evil forces. Witches and demons gather underneath the pear tree. It is forbidden to sit or sleep under it. During their holidays, Witches gather near a pear tree, and because Witches are considered dangerous creatures by Christianity, it is dangerous to be in their vicinity.

However, it was not always like that. Ethnologists can clearly differentiate old beliefs from new. It is clear that the pear used to be a cult tree. Sometimes people made sacrifices to the tree and they prayed underneath it, instead of in a church. There is a story in which young girl released a deer from a trap by flogging it with three pear branches and three apple branches given to her by her mother, an old Witch. For Witches, pear and apple had equal value.

Blackberry (rubus fruticosus) is very important herb in Balkan Witchcraft. The Blackberry bush is considered a residence of female supernatural beings and deities, and a preferred residence for fairies. People would walk through its branches in a ceremony to ward off sickness.

A sort of black magic was performed with its branch in following way: It was necessary to catch a frog, cut it in two, and tie the halves to two different branches of blackberry. When the intended individual passes nearby, it was necessary to recite the following text "Shrivel like the blackberry, hang yourself like the frog." People keep blackberry root in their home as an amulet for family prosperity. People also call blackberry "devil's grapes", because it is believed that the Devil created them to strike back at God for creating grapes.

Bell Pepper (capsicum annum) has wide application in both folk and Witch magic. Red colored bell pepper is especially appreciated. Together with garlic, basil, and a personal effect, it is a very strong amulet against all manner of evil forces. The smoke of dried, ground bell pepper can chase away demons. All kinds of illnesses could be treated in a ritual manner with bell pepper. A Witch puts three bell pepper seeds, three kernels of corn, and three beans on the abdomen of s person with stomach cramps.

Bell pepper can be used in love magic which must be performed in the beginning of May. A girl has to take a bit of earth on which her beloved has stepped, put it in a kerchief, add some one of his personal effects and one bell pepper. The bundle must be taken home, put in the fire, and covered with live coals. As the bundle burns, she must continually recite the words: "Just as you burn, so his desire burns for me".

Spinach (spinacia oleracea) is the herb mainly used to put someone to sleep magically. All you need to do is dry several leaves of spinach, ground them, then fumigate the person you want put to sleep. This can also be done over someone's picture.

Pumpkin (cucurbita lagenaria) has a wide scope of application, especially in Witchcraft. We have already described how protection rituals are performed with the help of pumpkin. It is also a universal amulet against all types of female demons. To create it, it is as simple as to hang it over the oven with an iron nail until it is dry.

247

All kinds of evil demons were caught in a pumpkin in following way. It is necessary to cut top of the pumpkin to make a lid, then put the lid on the pumpkin the moment you feel an evil presence. It is believed that the pumpkin sucks in the demon and once the pumpkin is closed, it must remain there.

Plum (prunus domestica) sometimes fell into a class of sacred tree because the *badnjak* could be made from it, and because people were offered sacrifices to it. Besides that, the custom of burying the dead among plum trees is still observed. One can hang personal items on a plum tree to receive its' help, and the water from a baby's first bath must be spilled on the plum tree to ensure the baby's health.

Grains

In conclusion, we should say something about grains, because they certainly play a role in Balkan Witchcraft. In contrast to other herbs that we described one by one, there is no need for such attention with grains, because their role in magic is very similar. In folk magic, there are some differences; corn and wheat are grains that are very much respected, while others like rye, barley, and oat are much more seldom used.

In Witchcraft, these grains were used in several ways. The first and most used is as an offering to supernatural creatures. The second is the ritual need for a certain number of grains, mainly odd numbers with emphasis on three and nine. Numbers of grains are used in various rituals, such as healing, love, or some other magic. A certain number of grains is used in ritual foretelling, but we mentioned that in chapter about divination when we described the method of reading grains. We could also see how grains were offered as asacrifice to Tartor when we described the "*skoace draci*" ritual.

NUMBERS, COLORS, SYMBOLS

As we have mentioned before, ancient Balkan Witches did not use correspondence tables, colored candles, names of planetary intelligences, etc.

However, that does not mean that they were not using some of their own, whether personally fabricated or learned patterns with ancient origins. These folk correspondence tables originate from old myths, legends, stories, and incantations.

To be precise, Witches learn the "Rules of the game" in three ways. The first was by learning from some older Witch, the second way was from intervention by higher forces through dreams and astral projections, and the third one was through the collective heritage of the people, i.e. tradition.

According to this, we can conclude that each Witch has their own "tables" that may or may not resemble those of another Witch, depending on several factors, such of the heritage of a given witch or their origin within Bosnia. We must emphasize that the term "tables" is one that we use here for convenience, because they never existed in written form, and ancient Witches were probably not familiar with their existence. This set of rules was passed down through oral tradition, and Witches never questioned them. When someone asked them a question like like "Why that color", or "Why so many times", the reply was a succinct "That's the way it is".

If we look at this book backwards, we will see that we could make tables that would aid us greatly in the performance of traditional Balkan Witch's rituals. All we need to know is the time at which a certain ritual must be performed, its structure, what what components we need, which herbs, which colors, how many times we must perform an action or recite an incantation, and how to finish it. I sincerely hope that I have explained everything clearly. The following pages provide additional information related to numbers, colors, symbols, symbolic actions, and movements.

Numbers

In ancient Balkan Witchcraft, numbers played and still play an important role, not only in rituals, but in everyday life as well. Each number has a previously determined meaning, and the number itself represents a certain magical force that has the power to influence adjacent things. Numbers can be written on paper, cloth, wood, rock, or almost any item or material, but as a number signifying the repetition of some action; an exact number of grains, or days, months, or years that had to pass before something occurs. In the performance of group rituals, it is necessary to pay attention to precise number of participants, as well as how many circles or steps are going to be made during the course of the ritual.

There are both good and bad numbers. The good numbers are usually odd, except for thirteen, while even numbers are usually bad, except for the number two.

Even numbers usually predict something bad, so in the Balkans, people never give an even number of flowers to another. It is only allowed to bring an even number of flowers when visiting a grave. The strength of numbers could be evidenced by the fact that no man who doesn't know you will ever tell you how many children, sheep, pigs, etc. he has, because he believes that you can somehow hurt him with that information. Odd numbers dictate the daily lives of the country folk, down to small things like how many eggs they will put under a chicken to hatch, how many trees they will plant, how many guests will be invited, etc. Let's look at the most important numbers in further detail.

1

The number one has no great role in Witchcraft. A ritual act is rarely performed just once. On the other hand, it represents the unity that a very small number of people have, but it is often mentioned in incantations that mention celestial bodies; there is one moon, one sun, one Forest Mother, etc. When we talk about ritual harvesting of herbs or killing sacred animals like a snake or black rooster, this number has a totally different meaning. All these actions must be performed at once, with one stroke. The reason for this is the opinion that is not humane, and that by repeating these actions, herbs and animals would be tortured and lose their magical energy. Some rituals were performed just once, except in special circumstances, such as illness, when they could be performed forty times.

2

The number two represents a couple, a man and woman, and then twins, to which supernatural characteristics are attributed in almost all world cultures. The number two was rarely used in magic, except in the context of love magic, when two figures must be made, or two herbs must be provided, one each to symbolize man and woman. The number two is also present in rituals of cleansing with the help of fire, when people or livestock pass through two candles or two burning hazlenut pillars. In addition, two-leaf clover can be very valuable in the search for buried treasure, as we discussed earlier.

3

The number three is the most important number in Balkan Witchcraft. Almost every ritual action must be performed in threes, while others must be performed nine times. According to Witches, there are three worlds, the upper, the middle, and the underworld. A dead man could become a vampire three days after its death; to prevent that, three white river stones were placed in his grave. Incantations must be recited three times, and it is necessary to walk around sacred tree, rock, or something representing an altar three times. Witches most frequently extinguished three live coals, and in rare occasions, seven or nine. With three branches of a sacred tree, a great number of magical actions and gestures could be performed. For example, with three pear and three apple branches, a girl sets free a trapped deer. With three dogwood branches or three elder branches, people draw symbols on the round bread that must be made for Christmas. Further, people must drink a Witches potion in three draughts, whether it is water in which she practices sorcery, or water in which live coals were extinguished, or water that an herb was soaked in. This list is almost endless. Essentially, if you perform a magical action three times, you could almost be assured that you did it correctly.

4

The number four is only used in one case, and that is the number of strokes that a Witch swings her magical stick to dismiss a meeting of Witches. In addition, a four-leaf clover may be used as an amulet or as a means to find treasure.

5

The number five is rarely used in Balkan Witchcraft. On rare occasions, a Witch used five seeds of grain for ritual treatment of ill people. Each male child used to wear a silver earring his first five years as an amulet to protect him from hostile spells. There is a very old folktale that speaks of the "Czar of all people and animals" that had five souls and that had been killed five times and died five times. This could be an old myth that has been mistakenly identified as a folktale.

6

The number six is never used in Witchcraft. Balkan Witches do not value most even numbers.

7

The number seven, on the other hand, is very important number and can be used in almost every ritual, though as we said before, Witches usually chose three or nine. A Witch could extinguish seven live coals, use seven herbs or grains in healing rituals, prepare seven amulets, or take water from seven springs that become a strong means of protection when combined. According to ancient mythology, on which a great number of Witches rely, the upper world is composed of seven layers. One of magical tools that is used in agrarian magic is a hoe that was not used for seven years.

8

The number eight is never used in Witchcraft, just like the number six.

9

The number nine is another very important number for Balkan Witches. When it is necessary to perform some ritual that has special power, all actions must be performed nine times, not three. Three magical knots must be tied; however, with a complex ritual nine must be tied, and the corresponding incantation must be recited nine times. In one method of ritual water purification, water must be spilled over nine white stones. A ritual is used in black magic; nine branches must be tied together with a black yarn that has nine knots. A magical medicine that can cure every illness is made from a mixture of nine herbs, and love amulets are also made from nine different herbs.

Water taken from nine different springs has magical powers like the water that is taken from seven springs, and a Witch can extinguish nine live coals and use nine grains in healing rituals. It is known that Witches use a magical bag that is nine units of measurement long. Nine grains of corn, nine grains of barley, nine grains of rye, etc, are usually made as a sacrificial offering. The number nine is represents eternity, along with the number seven. In many incantations when something needs to be chased away it is said "Over nine mountains and nine hills, over nine seas etc"; the number seven could be used for the same purpose and the appropriate text is "Over seven seas and seven mountains etc". There is a folktale about a Witch that had nine different brooms, and a popular version of the upper world consisted of nine layers.

10

The number ten represents the end of something. For example, according to tradition, a dragon that protects treasure will kill nine people, but tenth will get the treasure. Ten could represent a deity, perfection, or a perfect couple. It represents the unity that originates from two digits: one and zero. It is the first two-digit number, and it therefore represents the beginning of something else, often divine or supernatural. It also represents the completion of every complex magical operation; it is also the number of achieving a goal. Here we can see something that, unfortunately, ethnologists failed to notice; that is relationship between the number of sacrifices offered, and the realization or completion of an action or a Witch's intentions.

It means if we say that if nine sacrifices were offered, those sacrifices need to be realized so that the one who represents the number ten would appear. Therefore, in the story dragon has to kill nine persons so the tenth will get the prize. Even when these numbers are multiplied, the situation is the same. Just remember that *Tartor* has ninety-nine servants, and he is the hundredth. Ten represents the being or thing that comes after, similar to the relationship between the numbers 12 and 13.

12

The number twelve seems very important number in ancient Balkan Witchcraft, but that is not actually the case. That fundamental confusion is made because of ancient myths and stories where twelve Witches, twelve fairies, twelve swans, etc. are mentioned.

We can also see the story about the twelve students that gather on threshing floor to consummate their initiation. All this information could lead to the incorrect conclusion that ancient Balkan Witch's gatherings consisted of twelve members, while western covens were connected with the number thirteen, which is also incorrect. The answer lies with the number thirteen.

13

Thirteen is a number that Balkan ethnologists concluded was a negative number that common people are afraid of, and in customs and rituals, this number is not mentioned at all. However, this is a big mistake. If we pay a bit more attention to stories and myths, we will see that another individual is always mentioned. For example, we already talked about the twelve Witches and yellow-beard, which leads us to the conclusion there were a total of thirteen; at every Witch's meeting, there was at least one more person present, the deity himself. When we talk about twelve students that consummate their initiation on the threshing floor, it was clear that a thirteenth presence, the supernatural being, would come.

Let us make it simpler; at every meeting, the thirteenth person is always a man, the horned God, or the Goddess. Even the beginning of these meetings, as well as rituals in general, herald the symbolism of the number thirteen, because all of them begin "deep in the night", i.e. at 12:01; that means $12+1=13$. From this, we can conclude that thirteen is the number of other world, that second reality but also a number of supernatural eminences at meetings, and the number of initiants.

40

Number forty is very important number when we talk about ritual actions and the cult of the dead. As we mentioned before, it is necessary to repeat some rituals for forty successive days to guarantee success. A Witch gives instructions to an ill person for what they should do for thirty-nine days, and if the sickness or

255

malady has not abated, the Witch completed the ritual on the fortieth day.

The ethereal body (Soul) of a deceased person wanders the earth for forty days, and it is easiest to contact them during this time. After forty days, their body could set free of its last connection with material world. The ethereal body must feed itself somehow, or it leaves this dimension. If deceased person continues to feed itself with the energy of the living, they become a vampire and a Witch will probably have to perform a ritual to destroy it..

41

Forty-one is the number for any sort of grain that is used with an indirect method of foretelling, reading grains. This number does not mean number of grains, but number of spirits of vegetation that help to finish this process successfully. As we said before, there are forty spirits of vegetation, while forty-first grain represents the person on which the foretelling is performed. My own experience tells me this is true; an old Witch gave me a recipe to make some medicine. She told me to pay attention to number of prune stones that I use, and that I put forty of them in a flask of Rakija(the rakija has a value of one, so together with stones, I have a total of forty-one), then I shake it well and leave to sit for forty days.

When I asked her why forty, she gave me the standard answer of "That's the way it is," and when I asked "What will happen if I use thirty nine?", she said "Nothing, absolutely nothing". I think that we can conclude with great confidence that the number of spirits of vegetation is either forty or forty-one. In conclusion, let us remind ourselves of Bogumil's myth of human genesis, which we discussed in the chapter related to divination.

(**Translator's note**: Rakija (Pronounced Rak-ee-ya) is a liquor distilled from fermented plums found in the Balkans.)

44

Forty-four is a very important number for Vlach people in northeastern Serbia and is directly related to the invocation of forty-four unknown saints; ethnologists conclude that this is probably related to supernatural beings of the underworld.

Witches also perform this ritual also, on the behalf of the deceased or ones that died suddenly, far away from their community. The first thing that must be done is a ritual to make a paradise candle. It is made of beeswax that a Witch creates by hand, after a ritual bath, dressed in white. The ritual starts after midnight; she must be alone, and she must not talk out loud. From liquid beeswax, she makes forty-four beeswax threads to create a complex intertwined sculpture that she will glue on a previously prepared wooden cross, which is placed in front of a mirror. At the end, this artfully decorated cross will have forty-four strands representing the forty-four saints; between them will be the mirror that functions as a door that connects the two worlds. The candle must be completed before dawn.

Colors

Precise selection of appropriate colors is a special skill in ancient Balkan Witchcraft, and without it, it would be impossible to perform a great number of rituals. Colors have always represented visual symbols whose meanings are similar across the entire world. Nowadays they are characterized as emitters of energetic vibrations whose effects on the body have become demonstrable with technological advances and the parallel development of alternative medicine. Today we can say that color has two effects on humans. The only medical effect is when waves of certain colors react with the human aura, which leads to physiologic changes within the body. The second effect is visual; certain colors stimulate parts of the mind to create a great number of responses, both wanted and unwanted. We are interested in the second effect of color, that on the mind, although in this case we can eliminate the differentiation between physiological and mental effects, because no such difference is made in magic.

The reasons for this are as follows. Color, even in the form of a small piece of colored cloth, is like an emitter of a certain energetic frequency that can amplify the energy of the thing that we put on that cloth. That same color, in the mind of a Witch who performs a certain ritual, opens a specific channel that will put her in touch with special spheres of the unconscious; that will open a certain energetic channel for which she will be the conductor. That means that the chosen color will always have a dual power, and helps the Witch who performs a ritual to succeed. As a result, color selection is very important for Witches all around the world, not just for those in the Balkans.

Among the people of the Balkans, white was the color of mourning, sorrow, and old age for a long time. Old women, and women in mourning wore white kerchiefs. If we want to be precise and analyze, we can conclude that white is the color of the underworld, or at least one of them. Werewolves and vampires used to appear with a white mantle. During certain celebrations, especially those that are connected with the cult of the dead, animal sacrifices must be white. Nowadays, all those meanings are associated with the color black.

Still, the color white is the color of healing, purity, and chastity. White is the color of the light of day. Many healing rituals include the colors white and red. In one early custom, a sick person wearing a white overcoat and goes to the crossroads while the sun is going down; the setting sun took the sickness with it.

All amulets that have the goal of protecting the wearer from illness have white yarn or white cloth integrated into them; herbs, personal items, and pieces of clothing were wrapped with white yarn, then tied with magical knots into white linen. Reading this book, one can see see that white rocks and garlic are mentioned several times, especially in those situations where illness must be transferred to them, or water must be spilled over them for purification. White color is the color of purification and removing all impurities, whether those of demons, sickness, or evil forces in general. The color white is mainly used in combination with red.

The color yellow, as with white, was looked at in two different ways, both positive and negative. The positive is that it is the color of the sun, sunlight, gold, ripe corn, ripe wheat, etc. In that aspect, it symbolizes progress and prosperity. We can compare it to the number ten, i.e. the successful end of something which was started. In this case, it is the end of what the color green started, the color of vegetation, and the culmination of that is ripe corn, yellow grain, etc. On the other hand, it is the color of the deceased, the sick, of jaundice, and of clay, the soil where the dead must be buried. When necessary, you should fight against this color with white and red together. White is the color of purification and light, and red is the color of protection and health..

Blue
Blue color is above all the color of masculinity, and the color of distance (Far away places), and infinity; the color of the sea and sky. The color blue calms us, and protects anyone that wears clothes of this color from evil intentions. Despite all that, it was rarely used in rituals of ancient Balkan Witchcraft because it is too calm and passive to satisfy the dynamics of ritual.

Green
Green is a very important and positive color. It is the color of vibrance, nature, and the spirits of vegetation. I recommended it in rituals for invoking spirits of nature. Green is a color of the underworld and its residents. As a color of protection and celebration, it is used in many rituals and celebrations. A green

branch of rosemary or basil provides protection during celebrations. Aside from that, it is obviously the color of fertility, because it represents nature and growth. In conclusion, it is the color of the Forest Mother, fairies, and other, though no less important, spirits of nature. It is the color of the Great Mother and ancient Goddess, our planet Earth.

Red

The color red is one of the most important and certainly the most used in ancient Balkan Witchcraft. There are several reasons for this. The first is that red is the color of protection, which protects and chases away all negative forces, demons, spells, and evil magic directed toward an individual. Red cloth or r yarn were used for making defensive amulets and performing rituals of protection. It is the color of love, so red cloth, usually silk or cotton, was extensively used in love spells. Red-colored rocks, apples, wine, and similar things can be symbols of love or serve as a sacrificial offering.

Red is also the color of health and good welfare, so it and white were used equally in rituals of healing or for making amulets that were universal protection against illness. In these rituals, the most used textiles were red cloth and red yarn. Lastly, we must emphasize that it symbolizes blood and militancy; it is the color of heroes and devotion. Some item of red color must be sacrificed in any ritual. Nowadays it is wine, but even now old Witches usually slaughter a chicken for that purpose. You, the reader, might find this cruel, but in the Balkans, it is an everyday event. People who live in the country do not buy pre-packaged meat at the supermarket; they raise livestock and slaughter it when necessary, so it does not present a problem when a Witch makes a sacrifice when something important must be done.

Black

Black is very interesting color for ancient Balkan Witches because it is considered a sacred and basic magical color. This doesn't mean that it is negative or that it is connected with black magic, as people used to think when they saw someone wearing black or when something black was used during a ritual. It came into these associations later, mainly because4 of influence from the west and the church. Sometimes the color white had the role of representing things dark and horrible, because it was color of the mourning, grief, and death. White became the representative of light and healing later on.

It most likely represents and symbolizes magic as a skill; black is the color of wisdom and the mysterious, of hidden and sacred things; it is the color of the other world that intersects with ours at midnight, and it is the gate. Just as day and light belong to us, dark and night belong to supernatural creatures. The underworld is black, as are its residents; according to tradition, sun shines there. Based on that, everything black has a secondary power, through which magic manifests itself.

Some of the most valuable Witch's tools must be black, such as the *kustura*, and it is not rare to see staffs and brooms made of black hawthorn. Charcoal that is made from oak and hazel has additional power after the process of charring, which represents purification by fire. When it becomes black after being extinguished in specially prepared water, it becomes a magical item with extraordinary power. That power could be transferred to the water that the person for whom the ritual of extinguishing is performed must use for washing and drinking. From that moment, the live coals themselves become a kind of amulet that protects the wearer from all types of misfortune.

Black is the color of protection in a broader sense of the word. Every knife that has a black handle that wasn't ritually made like *kustura* could also be means of protection, and could be placed under the pillow, beside the bed, and in other places so as to protect the family from all manner of demons. People place the head of black ram or horse above the main entrance to their homes, or they put them in fields and courtyards so they could protect those areas from evil forces.

However, things of that power and strength could not avoid being used for negative magical purposes. Black linen that is has been worn out and thrown away could be used for making magical dolls that represent individuals that someone wants to hurt. Also, knots could be tied in black yarn while reciting incantations to hurt someone.

It should be known that when animals were sacrificed, such as a black rooster or chicken, it means that they were offered to underworld demons, who are also black. Amulets made of sacrificed rooster, cat, or dog were some of the most valued items that Witches could own.

Grey
Grey is the color of wisdom, old age, and experience. The interpretation of these traits is often related to gray hair and a gray beard. It is also the color of mystery and oddities.

Violet
Violet is the color of happiness, love, cheerfulness, and youthful enthusiasm.

Russet
Russet, for some unknown reason, is the color of cruelty, seclusion, and resistance. Some people believe that many supernatural beings have reddish hair, including vampires, fairies, and Witches in the old, vulgar meaning of the word.

Celestial bodies

Here we will present celestial bodies that play an important role in old Balkan Witchcraft. Everyone probably knows that we are mainly going to talk about the most important ones, those being the Sun, Moon, stars, and so-called *Danica* – the morning star, i.e. the planet Venus. There are many customs, stories, and beliefs related to their origin, but we will refrain from those and concentrate on their place in performing rituals. In the following chapter, there will be more about the Sun when we discuss important dates and celebrations.

Among the Balkan people, the sun has always been portrayed as a masculine entity. People call it brother, uncle, God, or God's eye. The sun is very well respected, but traces of its cult are saved only in some folk celebrations. Sometime it was believed that it has a mother, but no father. It sisters are stars, and among them is the planet Venus, which people used to think of as one of the stars. Venus is the closest to the Sun and has the best relationship with it, and based on that, Venus was sometimes considered to be his wife. Bearing in mind the fact that among the Serbian people the Moon is also male, he was considered the Sun's brother or uncle. He represented the Sun's opposite.

The Sun was respected as a deity, and it was understood that it had its own needs, friends, and enemies. It is believed that by night, the Sun travels through the underworld from the west to east, and during the day from the east to west. In some places it was believed that the sun dies at night, and that in the morning the sun is born like the mythical phoenix. Another belief is that it spends the night in the ocean so that it could come to the surface in the morning. People also believed that the sun transports itself across the sky in a carriage or that it rides a horse. Its biggest enemies are dragons, big snakelike creatures, werewolves, and in one myth, the master of underworld, who wants to eat it. Those attempts occur in the moment of a solar eclipse, i.e., people think this is the reason for an eclipse.

The sun is often mentioned during Witches' ritual incantations. The sun is the witness for some procedures, and is the one that chases or takes something away. Many rituals were performed at a certain time of a day because of the sun's position. If the sun needed to take something away, a ritual was performed while the sun is setting, and if it needs to be a witness or to provide its energy, a ritual was performed at the moment when sun is at its zenith.

The rituals that needed to be performed at night were finished at sunrise, because that was the safest way to disconnect from the dangerous creatures which had been in contact with the witch during the course of the night, because they are afraid of the sun, and that is their time to return to their "world".

A very interesting ritual was performed during the moments of a solar eclipse, it looked like this. Before the eclipse. a Witch brings a dish of virgin water outside. She caught the reflection of the eclipsed sun in that dish. In that moment, the water would become magically electrified with the energy of the black sun; What is more powerful than sun's power and black color's strength together? She would later use this water to make dough for *pogaca* (a type of flat, round bread) in the sun in following way. She would roll the dough very thin, and put it on a hot stone heated by the sun. Bread prepared in this way is considered a medicine for all illnesses, and a food that provides huge amounts of energy.

In folk arts and crafts and magical rituals, the sun could be presented by symbols. Those symbols are the circle, spiral, many-pointed star, concentric circles, wheel, rosette, ring, wreath, *kolo*, sunflower, apple, eagle or falcon, rooster, horse, or ox, and in human form as young man made of gold a with golden apple or apples in its hands. Golden and yellow colors are also symbols of the sun.

The moon is a very important celestial body in ancient Balkan Witchcraft, and in some aspects, it is actually more important than the sun. When we talk about the moon, we must first make two separate distinctions. Among the Balkan people of the former Yugoslavia, the moon is masculine in gender and that is how it should be addressed. According to tradition, he is the Sun's brother, the husband of Danica (the planet Venus), and the old grandfather. Some people refer to him with respect by calling him father or grandfather. He is considered a source of good welfare, happiness, and joy. He also symbolizes and provides health.

In some areas he is called the oldest oldest ancestor, and thus, people consider him their father or grandfather. However, within the Vlach people in northeastern and eastern Serbia, the moon is called Luna and is feminine in gender. According to a Vlach myth, once there was a man who wanted to have intercourse with his sister, to commit incest. She committed suicide by throwing herself into the water, and God, having seen what had happened, and lifted them up to the sky. He made the sun from the man, and the moon from his sister. This myth is much more complex in its original version, but we don't have time to occupy ourselves with it now. Regardless, among the Vlach people, the moon is perceived an the same way as the other Balkan peoples and is considered a source of good, happiness, and health.

The moon is the most used celestial body in Witchcraft. People requested that the moon be present, to help, to bless, or to transfer its powers (energy) to something or someone. Since a great number of rituals were performed at night, it was normal to pay attention to its various phases. Most rituals were performed during the new moon, so the strength of spells would increase correspondingly with the strength of the moon. The period of the full moon was

265

used for finishing a procedure or ritual with one stroke. That means that a ritual was not repeated, and did not follow the rhythm of the waning moon, because people avoid the waning moon for most actions. We can conclude that most rituals were performed during the new moon, and a few of them were performed on a full moon. There are a few exceptions, specific rituals that were performed just during a lunar eclipse. We spoke of one of them already, the consecration of the *kustura*, the magical knife.

In those moments, rituals of healing, removing of spells, etc., and could be performed, with an incantation along these lines: "Just as you (moon) are triumphant … and appear again…so can (The intended individual) … let them triumph…" must be used.

In a human form, the moon is always represented as a young man, while it is symbolized in the shape of a horse, or cow, which is particularly interesting if we remember that the moon is masculine gender. In folk riddles, the moon is called a cow, and it is believed that Witches pulled it down from the sky to earth in that form. Besides that, every mythological creature, including deities, that are presented with some physical defect such as a limp or blindness, it is believed that they are lunar in orientation because those defects show the moon as it falls down and rises again.

In old folk beliefs, facts can be found that conclude that stars have influence on the life of an individual. It is considered one star exists for every person that follows them everywhere and observes their every motion. That star protects them while they sleep and protects it from evil things. Their star has a direct impact on their life; if it is strong and bright, it will be healthy and prosperous, and if that star is weak, their life will be short and unproductive.

Clusters of stars in a clear night sky could represent dangerous forces that could hurt people and put them into a state similar to a fever attack. Reason for this is the power of cosmic energy, is

266

too strong for most unprepared people. This is also why Witches leave water, herbs, medicines, and other things outside overnight, to absorb this ciosmic energy, or as they say, to catch "*vedrina*".

One of the famous stars is *Danica*. In contrast to ancient times, today we know it is the planet Venus. It is considered the sister or wife of the moon or sun, sometimes even their daughter, which was usual in the context of stars. Its role in rituals was not large, except in situations when it was necessary to testify, confirm, or to help perform rituals, However, among the Vlach people of eastern Serbia, this star is of masculine gender and its name is Lusafur, a transliteration of the Latin word" Lucifer" which means "*svetlonosa-* the one who carries the light". Based on that, he is very important, because it is believed that he himself brings the sun and the light that is necessary for every living thing on this planet. Just as he brings light, in the same way, he takes something away. What he takes away is symbolized by white quartz. What remains of this belief about Lusafur among the Vlach people can be evidenced in posthumous rituals, where white quartz must be sewn into the clothes of the deceased so Lusafur could take it into the world of the dead, which means that he has role of a psychopomp – a soul's guide to underworld.

Metals and crystals

We can say with great certainty that only two precious metals were used in ancient Balkan Witchcraft, silver and gold. To avoid any confusion, I must bring attention to the fact that Witches gladly used lead and tin because they were easier to find, they were much less expensive, and they melt at much lower temperatures, which was very important, especially in rituals of pouring molten metals into water, which we mentioned in the chapter about divination. Mercury was also used, i.e. liquid metal, especially in making potions.

Gold and silver represented the same things that they represent in western occultism, those being the sun and moon. If she were able, while she was making various types of amulets, magical bundles, and similar things, a Witch would happily add little nugget or some item made of gold. There is gold in the rivers of eastern Serbia, so in this region gold was often added. It was not uncommon that instead of gold, a gold-plated or gold-colored item would be substituted. The essence of using gold and items of similar color is not in nature of the metal, rather its color and what that color symbolizes, which is the nature of the sun; gold is source of the light, fire, positive energy, health, fertility, and prosperity in general. The sun gives additional potency to some rituals by not only providing its energy, but also including all that which the sun represents.

In contrast to gold, silver is the moon's metal, and bearing in mind that it was never very expensive, Witches used it much more often. Silver is the metal of magic and Witches. Because it is a symbol of moon's energy on the earth, all the moon's traits were transferred to it, as is the case with the sun and gold. Pieces and things made of silver were placed in magical bundles so they could speed up the culmination of its magical intent, and to relate with the moon's energy and to mirror its growth in the sky, this time with the function of a "catalyst" to the ritual.

Silver amulets were made in a ritual manner. Male children wore silver earrings to ward off hostile spells, and all silver rings are inherently magical, without any special process or sanctification. In addition to being an amulet of protection, a silver ring increases the magical powers of the one who wears it.

Mercury is a liquid metal that had no particular place in Balkan Witchcraft except in the case of one type of ritual healing. Namely, mercury was considered an element of purification. Every illness was treated with mercury, even those which were considered magical. Both male and female Witches prepared mercury potions that a person needed to drink. Only professionals performed this technique, because it was considered a very risky procedure.

Rock crystal is the most used crystal in the Balkans. The reason for this is probably the fact that this crystal is very easy to find. Its main function was to enhance the strength of whatever was being done. A piece of this crystal was placed in bowl with water where live coals were extinguished, in amulets, and in magical bundles. Sometimes, instead of this crystal, other crystals, and even rocks of unusual colors and shapes were used, but Witches did not know their names. In any case, there was no differentiation between them; all of them were used for the same purpose, to increase the power of the magical ritual that was being done.

Left and right side

The similarities between the perceptions of right and left in western and Balkan Witchcraft are fascinating. We can say that the right side is considered as active, the left passive; the right side is considered masculine, and the left side feminine; the right side is the outside and the left one inside, etc.

Besides this, the right side is considered solar and left is lunar; the right side belongs to God, and the left to the Devil and forces of darkness. This did not prevent people and Witches from using their left hand, because if we read between the lines, we will see that the left side is the side of the world of the supernatural creatures as well as of magic. The fact that left side is the side of the moon and of the Goddess and all supernatural creatures attests to this.

All magical rituals that are performed that include supernatural beings in their performance need to be done with the left hand. A protocol exists for putting clothing on a deceased personas well; it is necessary to put on the left sleeve first, then the left trouser leg, left shoe, and so on.

All ritual actions from the cult of the dead, from fumigation, to moving and dancing the *"mrtvacko kolo"* (The circle of death) that people dance in honor of a deceased individual, must be performed moving to the left, because that is the direction of death, while the right is that of life. In many parts of the country, there is a belief that the little finger on the left hand has magical powers. Those powers need to be renewed in the springtime of each year, in the following way. One must first find a moving snail, one whose eyestalks are fully extended. It is then necessary to touch one of the eyestalks with that finger, and in the moment when the snail starts to pull them in, recite the following phrase *"Ustu bice, moje bice jace"*.

Many ritual actions need to be performed to the right, and they are usually those that must be undertaken during the day. Still, this side is more related to religious gestures whose origins should be sought in the elements of Witchcraft stemming from Slavic heritage and Christianity, from which we can see that an angel sits on right shoulder, and the devil on the left. As a result, anything touched should be touched with the right hand, especially when it concerns food, money, or health, because then one can be assured of the help of angels. When the kolo at celebration, it must always move to the right, symbolizing the sun itself, which people believe spins to the right. In addition, you should always shake hands with your right hand, cross yourself, wave, and so forth.

Cardinal directions

When we talk about cardinal directions, we must say that within Balkan Witchcraft, as in folk belief in general, the most used are east and west. North and south are only used in Witchcraft while dismissing supernatural creatures, with gesture of swinging a magical staff to the four sides of the world, from below to above, as a necessary ritual benediction. We must add that those creatures cannot be invoked separately, so there is no differentiation according to cardinal directions, which is the case with elementals in western Witchcraft.

East and west are realized as the Chinese Yin & Yang. East is white, west is black; east is additive, and west is subtractive.

It has always been considered that the benevolent God lives in the east, and that his opposite lives in the west. The God of life, birth, and prosperity lives on this side, while God of the dead and the underworld resides in the depths where sun goes at the end of the day. The sun which was reborn was seen as a victor over darkness and the carrier of light, without which there would be no life.

In the context of Witchcraft, we cannot give any specific advantage or preference to either direction. Both of them where used equally, depending on the needs of the Witch. If a ritual was performed in daylight, it is normal that the altar, or better said, the place where it would be performed, be turned to the east. If a ritual must be performed during the hours of darkness, everything must be oriented to the west, because another God, or more precisely, others deities and supernatural beings are in control.

Witches always collected their medicinal herbs at sunrise, and they oriented themselves to the east, i.e. to the sun. This custom is applied to the ritual cutting of the *badnjak*, because in the moment that the person cuts it, they face east, making sure that the *badnjak* falls toward the east, and finally, it must be taken home moving in an easterly direction. The *Badnjak* is the incarnation of the young God reborn after winter, and it symbolizes his resurrection on the eastern side of the world from the black depths of darkness.

271

All negative things were banished to the west. When a Witch removed an illness from a person, she threw it away to the west. The spring water that Witches use in various rituals must usually be taken from the west side, because that water originates from the underworld, whose symbol is the west. As we have already said, west is the side of the dead and the direction in which their souls go. Almost all rituals related to the cult of the dead were performed by a person oriented westward; the deceased person must be placed with their head turned to the west, with a burning candle beside their head. This was so that the soul could find its way to the land of the dead, while the candle lit the way.

The north is a secret to the Witches. Let us just say that God comes from the north.

Symbols

Symbol is a word of Greek origin, and its literal transliteration means something such as an object, picture, written word, sound, or particular mark that represents something else by association, resemblance, or convention. Symbols are mainly artistic renderings of objects that embody the essence of something or somebody.

Looking through the prism of occultism, they form certain keys that could lead the one using them to a connection with the other world. Doors to certain parts of the human psyche are opened with them, through which one can establish two-way communication with the thing that the symbol represents. Knowledge of the nature of symbols was, at times, a secret that was reserved for a small number of 'chosen" magi, priests, Witches, etc.

Today, their essence is well known. In almost every bookstore, one can find dictionaries of symbols that interpret them in several ways, from religious to occult, even psychologically. Symbols could be

272

collective, but individual as well. We can recognize different types of symbols in the scope of different religions, religious movements, sects, cults, lodges, etc. Those symbols belong to a certain group of people, and they have no special meaning to others.

Still, it is very difficult to draw a line between collective, individual, and "group" symbols. All the "major" symbols are mostly universal. It is very hard to find a religion, cult, or lodge on the planet that does not use the symbol of the circle, pyramid, cross, pentagram, or Star of David. It is better to differentiate and say those that some symbols belong to a group of people, while others are just used by that group.

Everyone, including the Balkan Witches, use certain symbols in the scope of their system that do not belong to them, although there are some stylized animal renderings that were used as symbols, whose usage does not exceed the boundaries of certain regions. The origin of these symbols in ancient Balkan Witchcraft is complex. Some of them, especially those that include stylized animal renderings, have roots that reach back to the Neolithic era. Simple geometric shapes are also very old, but their origin is known, and we know that they originate from different religious systems, and from peoples that came to the Balkans and settled here. All in all, we are talking about one general mixture whose origin should not be subject of our discussion; it is much better to analyze the symbols used in Balkan Witchcraft closely, and determine what they represent and how they are used.

The cross is definitely one of the oldest and most widespread symbols. The first appearance of the cross came very early, at the beginning of Stone Age. It was inscribed and worn by people long before Christianity and monotheistic religions in general. It is very interesting that within the Serbs there is clear distinction between the church cross and the "folk" cross". The church cross is Christian, of course, but its origin and meaning are well known to everyone. So what is this so-called "folk cross"? It is of Pagan origin, of course. Long ago before accepting Christianity, it was known that Slavic were using the cross as a symbol in different ways. People inscribed it in clay pottery, embroidered it on linen, and wore it around the neck like some type of amulet. The situation was similar among the other peoples of the Balkans. The cross was mainly used as an amulet of protection that ensures the presence of a supernatural force.

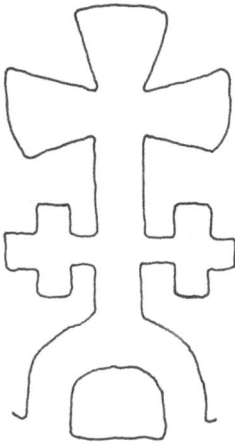

In its oldest version, the anthropoid cross was a Pagan idol. It was a simplified version of some deity, and often new lines were added so it would more closely resemble the deity it represented. Generally speaking, old "folk crosses" are different in appearance from the Christian ones by some addition, be that a head on the upper arms, or crescents, the sun, a crown, etc. In addition, the anthropoid cross had another arm, which made it resemble a crossroads, the place where the two worlds intersect. As a result, crossroads were considered special ritual places where Witches performed their rituals. Water in which live coals were extinguished was cut with the *kustura*, making a sign of the cross. The magical gesture of making three identical crosses in a row, whether in the air or water, did not enter the Witch's religion after accepting Christianity, rather, they were already present before it's appearance. The goal of this gesture is to make a point of the dimension intersection at the place where a ritual was going to be performed.

As a means of protection, a cross could be made of linden branches, hazel wood, hawthorn, dogwood, pine, and similar sacred trees. With soot made from burned basil and sage, a cross could be inscribed on the forehead of a child to protect it from evil. On doors, it was inscribed with tar to chase away evil demons. People placed it in their fields to protect their crops. Items inscribed with the cross were considered sacred, as were pieces of cloth on which it had been embroidered. A cross made from the burned remains of a *badnjak* (Yule log) was especially powerful, which clearly infers the presence of the old Pagan God. Its power was irrefutable from many reasons. The *badnjak* was cut in a sacred ritual way, then is brought in the house in special way, and was eventually purified by fire, and with this ritual, the God was reborn. That is the reason why crosses and little idols were made from that wood, as they especially represented the newborn God. A similar situation exists with the straw cross that people place under the dinner table during Christmas holidays. According to ethnologists, it represents either the sprits of the family ancestors or the deity itself. The purpose of the cross was to transfer its powers onto next crop of wheat to ensure a bountiful harvest.

The cross as a symbol represents either a deity, or the point of intersection of the two worlds, from which otherworldly power originates. As we said before, its purpose is to protect and to ensure presence of divine forces, whatever they are. Every usage of the cross for any purpose is, in fact, invoking the deity that it represents, whoever that may be. It is not strange that the cross is present in many rituals used in Witchcraft, even as an item that needs to be present. A special foretelling method exists in which it is necessary to throw a wooden cross into the water three times in a row, and to pay attention to which side it falls. If it falls on a side that we marked as the "face" two or three times in a row, it is a good sign, but if it falls just once or never, then the sign is bad. This kind of foretelling is performed with a special cross that is often made of some sacred tree and its "Results" are considered absolutely accurate and beyond refute.

The circle is one of the oldest symbols; it is impossible determine its origin, because it appears equally throughout the world. In ancient times it was written down, inscribed, embroidered on various items and linens, and carved in objects and in ritual places.

The symbolism of the circle never was an enigma. Whether that was ring, earring, amulet, drawing, herbal wreath, or some other item, the circle always represented the sun and its power of protection.

The power of circle could be amplified in several ways; one of them was to draw little circles inside the big one, usually an odd number of concentric circles, or inscribing the circle with a cross, lighting candles as a sacrificial offering, etc. When drawing or embroidering a circle, people were careful about the color they used. Usually red and gold colors were used, as they have very strong supernatural energy and power.

Above all, the essence of these symbols implies protection. It is believed that the cross provides two kinds of protection to the person who uses it. One is as a small cross that someone will carry, such as a piece of jewelry or knitted symbol that will be placed somewhere on the clothes. The second is one of the ways that we spoke of earlier, to place it on or around a ritual space, in the home, in or on a cradle, etc. The econd way not only protects, but also creates barriers through which no supernatural being could pass.

In the Balkans, above all, the triangle represents a trinity and the power of the number three. By the concept of trinity, people usually mean the number where the most supernatural creatures appear. Its appearance on dishes, linen, and drawings in general played the role of protection, but in this case, protection was provided by the supernatural beings whose presence were invoked with this symbol.

A triangle cam be shown with its tip pointed either up or down, and it does not change its meaning, as it does in the West. It is known that in earlier times, amulets of yew were made in the shape of one or three upside-down triangles. It is a common phenomenon that three triangles were put together to form a triple trinity, hence signifying the power of the number nine, which we already was used only in emergencies. On some old tombstones and amulets, we can see a triangle with an eye inside, but in that case it represents God himself, i.e. the eye of God. We believe that this symbol came to Balkans much later, but it is difficult to say who brought it.

The Star of David, or Solomon's letter, as it was once referred to by the people of the former Yugoslavia, as a symbol, is probably much older than we know. It is believed that this symbol came to the Balkans with Jews who settled down in every big city, and the proof for that theory is the name of this symbol. This could be, but it isn't necessarily true. The

symbol of hexagram falls into the category of universal symbols, one used by many people, and among those the people of the Balkans. It is very often found on old tombstones, pendants, and earrings, and people say that *Mato Glusac* (A Montenegran Seer, b1774, d1870) carved this symbol into wood, and that Witches used it to decorate their sacrificial offerings of round bread.

It is difficult to find any concrete data that will shows how people were interpreted this symbol. From certain indications, we can conclude that this symbol represented a star as a source of cosmic energy, sometimes the sun, and above all, a symbol of protection.

Despite all efforts, I could not find any usage of the pentagram as a symbol.

The swastika an ancient symbol that was gladly used in the Balkans, until Hitler used it to represent his ideology, and in that way alienate all of its previous meaning. On many excavation sites, archeologists found dishes from the Neolithic age with swastikas engraved on them, which means that the indigenous Balkan people knew about this symbol long before the arrival of Indo-Europeans. People often used to call this symbol the Bent cross or the hooked circle. Until the Second World War, this symbol was present everywhere, especially on clothes and items. It was represented as active by the points facing the right, and passive with hooks that faced the left.

The swastika is just like the circle and other similar symbols that represented the sun, and more importantly, the sun's brightness and heat. It is a symbol of fire, and fire is the symbol of sun. In this domain, we can easily interpret the essence of this symbol. It was used as protection, and as a means of purification. A person who wears it is protected from evil forces and will be purified from all internal negativity (such as illness) as well.

As a symbol, the crescent or half-moon was presented in three ways. In the first two, it is in a vertical position with the points turned to left or right side, although mainly to the left. The horizontal position is always represented with points turned down, never up, for reasons that we do not know. On rare occasions the moon was represented as a circle, but only in complex symbols.

The moon had a decorative function, and was placed on clothing, kitchen dishes, and jewelry. Even then, it was not solely decoration; the symbol of the moon should be interpreted in a way that the human relationship to the moon as to heavenly body. Above all, the moon is a source of otherworld magic and supernatural creatures. The moon itself is a deity, and whether it is perceived as male or female, it is a source of magical power and protection. By carrying its symbol, a person invokes its powers and magical characteristics, and at the same time makes contact with given deity that it represents. The moon is a fundamental symbol of Balkan Witchcraft. It is symbol of Witches, their powers, and their affiliation.

The crescent was a prerequisite part of any amulet that a blacksmith created; it and other symbols created a series that were important to the person for which the amulet was created. On old amulets, the new moon was always depicted with its points down.

Animal symbols are a special type of symbol whose meanings are derived from renderings of sacred animals or their essence, and what they mean. We can find them just about anywhere, on clothes, carvings, dishes, carpets, rugs, drawings, etc. They are also an integral part of any ritually made blacksmith's amulet. You can also find them on Christmas breads, earrings, pendants, etc.

In the artistic sense, they could be depicted extremely realistically, but also in a manner as to be completely unrecognizable, and the

only thing you can do is take a guess at which animal it represents. That is case with the "zeljka", an ornament representing turtle. It can be found on rugs from Pirot (city in southeast Serbia). Animals could be rendered in their entirety, or just the part of them that represents their essence, such as claws, an eyetooth, a wing, etc.

These symbols could have one of three functions, or any combination of the three simultaneously. The first is decorative, the second is for protection, and third involves transferring traits of the animal to the carrier of its symbol. Here are some of the symbols and a bit about them.

The snake is usually represented in two ways, as a spiral and as a winding line. The snake is always considered a reliable guardian, so its primary function is defensive.

It is very hard to describe the turtle in words; it is depicted as a sloping rhomboid with flat corners, with legs bent like ram's horns on the upper and lower corners. It was never shown in a realistic manner. The function of this symbol is protection, as well as decoration. In addition, it represented all aspects of progress and prosperity.

The paw was also one of the integral parts of metal amulets. It could be a rabbit's paw, which represents not only happiness and prosperity, but protection as well, because the rabbit is a symbol of the moon. That could be bear's paw, and in that case, it represent the power of life and protection.

Deer were chiseled into tombstones, as one function of this symbol was to take the souls of the deceased to the underworld. It is also symbol of fertility and wealth, so it was embroidered onto clothes and engraved in dishes. The symbolism of deer is very complex, because all renderings are a mix of Celtic beliefs, Balkan natives, and Slavic settlers, so it could have different meanings in different situations.

Bird symbols were usually depicted very realistically, though occasionally they were stylized. The bird symbolizes several things, those are innocence, purity, and the human soul. The last one is related to symbol of the pigeon. As a result, a motif of the bird is very often found on tombstones, and in its other functional capacity, as a symbol of purity and innocence, it could be seen in women's clothing and jewelry.

In conclusion, let us mention something very interesting. It is related to a small group of symbols that actually represent weapons. Blacksmiths made these amulets and men wore them, mostly soldiers and law enforcement; based on this we can conclude their basic function. They were either represented as simplified stylized versions of miniature weapons or in a realistic way. The strength of these amulets and symbols was increased in following way. If it was a saber, it was rendered as s snake in the shape of saber, which directly invokes the snake for protection. The basic function of this symbol was to protect its carrier from that type of weapon. Keep in mind that the diversity of weapons continually grows, so the number of weapons that it symbolically represented grew as well. These amulets were forged in a ritual manner and were usually made of silver.

THE WITCH'S CALENDAR

You've probably noticed that throughout this book, in one way or another, that certain times of the year and several concrete dates have been mentioned. That is unavoidable, as they relate directly to some of the fundamental pillars of ancient Balkan Witchcraft. With great regret, we can conclude that no holy days or holidays that were specifically for Witches in the Balkans, at least none that left any remnants of their existence. However, if we look at the entire Pagan tradition, we will see that there are certain indications. Another thing that makes it even more difficult is that Pagan religions and Witch's traditions from those areas no longer exist, and some of them have been incorporated to Christianity; it is a known fact that many folk customs become part of a church's doctrine, so that people would more closely relate to the new religion.

Therefore, if we look closely at the celebrations Witches did participate in, and which dates they consider important, we will be able to get some picture of the Witch's calendar.

Bearing in mind that there were three different Witchcraft traditions in the Balkans , the Vlach, the Visocka, and Slavic tradition. We are certain that there are more, but it is difficult to differentiate them, because they intermingled with others over time. This means that important dates could be different, based on the tradition to which a Witch belongs. We also cannot disregard the fact that some Witches could have their own, personal, important dates, in addition to the fact that some important dates were actually only important to the inhabitants of a small geographic area. That being said, there are some things that will be better understood if we start from the very beginning.

When we take a close at ethnologic literature collected from the territory of the former Yugoslavia, we will find a lot of corresponding data, and a general agreement about when Witches are active; that is, on what dates they gather the most and do different things.

The most frequently reported is the claim that Witches are active on March 1st by the old calendar; that is, March 14th by the new; also during Christmas, then during the autumn equinox, and carnival. We will look at each of these days separately. It is believed that the Witch's day is Tuesday, and that their part of the day is at night, which is understandable considering the importance of the moon during rituals, and the fact this is the time when the two worlds overlap and when Witches leave their bodies. All of this is true, and we will go through them in an arbitrary order, the only parameter will be the importance of the celebrations in Witch's tradition.

Let us begin with March 14, a holiday that only Witches, sorcerers,, and other magic users celebrate. Today, this date is dedicated to Saint Evdhokia, a woman born in the Phoenician city of Iliok, where she had wealth and riches and led a debaucherous life. A German converted her to Christianity and she entered a convent, giving all her wealth to the church. She was tortured and killed in ad1152.

It is very difficult, though not impossible, to determine in what connection she has with this date. Ethnological facts collected from people give us a completely different picture. According to them, only women celebrated Saint Evdhokia, took her as their patron, and respected as her as a giver of health. In central Serbia, only women that practiced sorcery celebrated her. On that day, a ritual of "purification" of livestock was performed in the following way. Cattle were herded between two "living coals" or between two candles. It was for forbidden to pronounce her name, because it was believed that wild animals would appear. This last fact helps us to conclude that, at some point in time, this date was dedicated to a Goddess of the forest and wilderness, and that the prohibition of saying her name is a characteristic related to all Pagan deities and supernatural creatures.

Also very respected, especially by women, was the celebration of today's Saint Petka, celebrated by women on October 27th. She was nun and saint that died in the 11th century. She lived near Constantinople and her relics were transferred to the city of Jasi in Romania. At one time, her relics were in Belgrade by order of empress Milica.

We have already said that her name often mentioned in many rituals, especially in southern Serbia. Many stories and myths are related to her that have no connection with her true Christian life. Many supernatural powers are attributed to her, especially her ability to cure barren women and women in general. She is considered the patron of women, just like Muma Padura in eastern Serbia. On that day women don't do anything except rituals to ensure fertility among people and livestock. Ethnologists relate her appearance and ways of showing her respect with Mokos, a female Slavic deity, and I must say that their opinion was unanimous. We can therefore conclude that this deity had a meaningful role in the Slavic Witch tradition, while saint Evdhokia probably belonged to an even older current.

For everyone, especially gatherers of herbs, Witches, and doctors, "*biljni petak*" (Herb Friday) was a very important holiday. It was celebrated on the Friday before May 6, today's St. George's day. On the night before this day, it was thought that herbs received unusual powers, be those herbal or magical. During the night, people start collecting herbs, and when they finished, they celebrated with music and dance. Since we have already discussed *biljni petak* in detail, we won't discuss the customs related to this celebration, but we will mention some conclusions that ethnologists have made.

Ethnologists assume that all celebrations related to herbs were, at some period in time before Christianity, related to female deities and female spirits of nature. All of them, especially *"medjudnevnice"*, were celebrated in the same period that female deities were celebrated. Among them are St. George's day, St. John's day, and *"biljni petak"* (Herbal Friday), in adition to *"medjudnevnice"*. The difference today is that St. John's day and St. George's day are related to male Christian saints. It possible that a good reason for this exists, perhaps that those dates were indeed dedicated to a male deity or spirit of nature, like the European Green Man.

As we already said, St. George's day is a major holiday celebrated by many Christians in the Balkans. Based on available facts, it was one of the most beautiful and festive Pagan celebrations before the advent of Christianity. It represented turning the point between the approaching summer and the passing winter.

This holiday celebrated the revival of nature, life, and the powers of creation and birth. Many ritual actions performed during this time of year had the goal of transferring all those cited powers to people and their families, cattle, and properties. People used to wash their faces with the water in which basil had been soaked, and they bathed in the rivers, and people, especially youth, carried sticks made of willow or dogwood, and they also flogged themselves with nettles. Every household slaughtered one lamb as a sacrifice. People placed young hazel trees or wooden crosses of that wood in their fields and vineyards to ensure the presence of divine forces. It is not difficult to conclude, based on these ceremonies, that hazel represents this deity, and from that we can extrapolate that it is the deity of the forest, herbs and fields, protector of cattle and wild animals;in other words, it is the Goddess of nature, something like the European Green man.

286

It is totally possible that St. George's day and Herbal Friday were much more closely related in times past than they are today, and we can also explore the possibility that Herbal Friday was related to the Goddess, and St. George's day to her friend and lover, one of the versions of the horned God. Maybe that period between these two celebrations never existed, but they were the beginning and end of the spring celebrations. These now correspond with the Western European holiday of Beltaine.

The period between the Nativity of the Virgin Mary and the Assumption is called *"medjudnevnice"*, the calendar period between August 28 and September 21. These days are hallmarked by the last ritual collection of herbs for the year. During that time, everything stops and nothing new must be started, especially marriages. It is said that during this period, snakes are at the height of their and that their poison is the strongest. Because of that, it is necessary to avoid them by all means possible and to try not to kill them.

As I mentioned before, ethnologists believe that this period was once reserved for the celebration of female spirits of nature and female deities. If we combine the period of time when these holidays were celebrated and the significance of the snake, it is not difficult to conclude what manner of deity it was. The snake is the spirit of vegetation, but also an underworld "demon". The celebration time itself falls into the period of slowly decreasing daylight, after the Autumnal Equinox, when nature is slowly dying down, and life forces are ending their cycle on earth and returning to the underworld.

This is the time of third aspect of the Goddess, represented in the form of an old woman. It was necessary to carry out the last "harvest" of herbs before autumnal equinox, because after that herbs lose their power, because nature is dying out and the Goddess is retiring to the underworld and taking life force with her. She is not the same Goddess that appears in the spring, but rather a feeble old hag who rules from the depths of the Earth. We already said that autumnal equinox is known for Witch's celebrations and Witch activity during that time. For people interested in western Witchcraft, is no surprise that the autumnal equinox is time of celebrating Modron, one of the Witch's Sabbaths. Although those dates do not precisely match those of western Witchcraft, we should mention that many Pagan holidays were moved from the original date of their celebration so that they could be connected to a Christian saint or holiday whose date was close by.

Between the autumnal equinox and Djurdjevdan (St. George's day), people celebrated Ivandan (St. John's day). This holiday is celebrated on July 7th on the new calendar, and it represents the middle "harvest" of medicinal and magical herbs during the year. Although this holiday is dedicated to Sv. Jovan (St. John) it is almost impossible that it has any correlation with Christianity, hence its celebration outside of the church.

It is very hard to say which deity is being celebrated. Some ethnologists think it is a deity of the Slavic Pantheon named Kupalo, and others think this holiday belonged to a female deity at some point in time, because its essence is hidden in the fact that people collected herbs at that time, and it is known that those holidays belong to female deities and spirits of nature. It is also believed that in bygone times this holiday was actually dedicated to the celebration of the summer solstice, although Christianity moved it away from the original date so it could be related to this saint.

In any case, nowadays people call this saint Metlar, Biljober, Narukvicar etc, depending on the type of ritual action the saint is connected with. As we said before, people collected herbs twice per year, but there are two herbs that stand out and need additional attention. One of them is yellow bedstraw (Galium verum) that is used for making wreaths for decoration that are hung on fences and houses, and the second is field broom, whose ritual harvest has already been discussed earlier in the book.

Fires must be built at crossroads, houses, and on hilltops during this holiday; they purified those places and chased away evil spirits. The fact that young people jumped over them gives us a clue as to their function. In some regions of the Balkans, wood from the juniper tree was burned, lit with a flint so that it would be "Living fire", a symbol of the sun's energy. Animals were made to jump over these fires as well, so that they could be strong and sound.

It is believed that the sky opens three times the night before Ivandan (St. John's day), that some herbs attained magical powers, and that places where treasure is buried glow with bluish light. Many magical rituals are performed during this time because it is believed that there are much greater chances of success.

Carnival is celebrated by huge feasts the night before major Christian fasts. There are many of them, and their names come from the fast which must be performed. The biggest ones are for Easter and Christmas. According to tradition, Witches are most active night before White Carnival on white Sunday, which is the last week of wintertime just before the Easter feast.

The celebration of White Carnival has many Pagan traits. Its framework is made of processions of men and women that wore animal skins with blackened faces, or clothing made specifically for the occasion, and it was a loud and boisterous occasion. The procession accepted gifts from the spectators, and licentious behavior was encouraged. Ethnologists assume that this procession represented the spirits of nature who emphasize their return with noisy entrance, and accepted the gifts as offerings so they would bring good crops to the people. The last day of the week was an organized public celebration where people ate, drank, and danced, and played games. On that day, lascivious jokes were encouraged and no one criticized them. It is a well-known belief that during this week the Earth slept and that no one should bother it; that is, till the soil until after the celebration.

There are two reasons why Witches are associated to this holiday. The first reason relies on the theory that Witches are actually "the ones" who commune with demons, and they appear together one last time before the end of Winter. This is related to an ancient belief that all demons are exceptionally active during the winter months. The second is that they celebrated the end of Winter and that it is an integral part of their tradition.

Another folk belief says that Witches are active on Christmas Eve and on Christmas day. Ethnologists think that essence of Christmas is on the day and evening of Christmas Eve, the time that a large number of rituals must be performed.

We have already said that Christmas is one of the biggest Pagan holidays celebrated in the past. It contains the remnants of the ritual respect and worship of the ancestors, supernatural creatures, and according to some ethnologists, the worship of a higher Pagan deity. This could be evidenced by the sort sort of the food that was consumed, the custom to eat on the floor, and the invocation of deceased ancestors to supper, all of which are hallmarks of the cult of the dead.

On the other hand, bringing the Badnjak (Yule Log) into home after sundown and placing straw on the floor points to the remains of worshiping spirits of vegetation; that is, chthonic demons. I must emphasize again that the word "demon", in anthropological sense, does not mean an evil monster, rather it is the universal name for all supernatural creatures. Finally, God himself is expected on Christmas Eve. People invoked God with their words to join them for dinner. Sometimes a piece of ritual bread and the first glass of wine were dedicated to him. Based on variations in celebrating Christmas Eve and Christmas Day, it can be concluded that the God was Dabog, an ancient Slavic deity, who is well-known as underworld deity whose holiday was celebrated at the time of today's Christian Christmas.

Another holiday that is not directly connected to Witches, but was definitely intended for them, was celebrated on January 8 under the name "*babin dan*" (Grandmother's day). On that day, women along with their children who had been born in the previous year visited midwives and gave them food, flowers, kerchiefs, towels, and similar things. In return, the midwives gave hemp to the children to make them sound, and placed wool on their heads (a symbol of gray hair) so they would grow old. Besides the fact that this holiday was primarily intended for some supernatural creature or creatures that midwifes symbolized, it begs the question, what connection does this hoiday have with Witches?

The answer is very simple. The majority of midwives were Witches. Their scope of activities consisted of various healing methods that are known today under the name "alternative medicine". Back then, they did not have a bad reputation, and people believed that they were a good substitute for doctor and obstetrician.

Good Friday is Friday before Easter. According to Christianity, it is the day when the Jesus were crucified. However, people celebrate this holiday in very specific way. On Friday people fasted, and on the next day they ate an egg, a red-colored one if possible. They then took Communion with the bud of hazelnut tree. Another very interesting fact is that on that day, people cannot eat garlic and the house must be cleaned in an almost ritual manner. The broom that was used had to be disposed of in a body of water. It is said that on this day, Witches perform various types of magic, and you must be careful not to fall under a Witches' influence.

"*Meckin dan*", or St. Andreas' day, is a very interesting holiday that was celebrated on December 13th of the new calendar (on November 30 by the old) and that is dedicated to Jesus' contemporary St. Andrea, who was crucified at the age of 17 on the type of cross which now bears his name. There is little information about him, except that which says he was brother of Apostle Peter, that he was pupil of St. John, and that later he becomes one of Jesus's constant companions. He was crucified in the city of Patras, in Greece.

The thing that is interesting about this holiday is the fact that it used to belong to a Pagan deity that was somehow related to the bear as sacred animal. Ways of celebrating this holiday, myths, and stories about it clearly show that a bear cult existed in the Balkans at some point in time. The folk name for this holiday, "*Meckin dan*" (Bear's day). speaks in favor of this. It is also very interesting that in some renditions, Veles was shown riding a bear.

There is a myth that is related to St. Andreas, in which a girl accidentally ate a human heart, become pregnant, and gave birth to him. He was often shown as riding a bear with a snake for a bridle. On that day, people cooked corn as a sacrificial offering to the bear. Cooked corn must be taken to the roof and left overnight, then in the morning it was taken into the home, and all household members had to eat it on empty stomach, like some sort of Communion. In some areas, instead of corn, people made sacrificial loaves bread (*meckina povojnica*) which functioned identically to cooked corn, to keep bears attacking cattle. Many prohibitions are related to this holiday; goal was to restrain bears from doing bad things. From all of this, we can conclude that St. Andreas has the role of a Pagan deity, the patron of cattle and the cattle breeder.

Thing that relates this holiday to Witches is fact that it was the most appropriate day for performing rituals. One of them is ritual treatment of fear, especially in children, by a method of fumigation with slightly burned bear's hair. Another is the ritual melting of lead that we mentioned before. No one knows why the melting of lead is related to this holiday, but bearing in mind that it is part of the tradition, we'll assume that the reasons were known at one point, but they have been lost and forgotten through time.

Pentecost is a holiday that is celebrated on the fiftieth day after Easter. Today this holiday is celebrated as a Christian holiday, although it is very clear that it belonged to Pagan tradition at some point in time. On this holiday, the rusalje of several villages in the area of Zvizde fall into trance. Because we have already discussed this, we will mention other customs related to this holiday, which is observed mainly in Serbian territory.

On that day, herbs were harvested and taken to the church, were wreaths were made while the people knelt. The wreaths were taken home and placed in windows and doors to protect the members of the household from evil demons. It is a very interesting fact that people should not sleep during that day, because it was believed people were exceptionally vulnerable, and that spirits could possess and hurt them. There are many customs related to the walnut tree. In some places, people collected walnuts and placed them on tombstones on that day. The walnut tree is connected to the underworld, spirits, and demons. Serbian people say that the walnut tree is "*senovito*" (shady).

It is believed that during wintertime, there were several popular periods during which Witches, demons, spirits, and other supernatural or creatures with supernatural powers had the ability to extend their stay among common people. The most significant among them is the period known in the Balkans as The Unbaptized days, that lasted from Christmas until Epiphany. During that period, many people did not want to leave homes, especially at night, to avoid contact with those "forces".

After them follows *"Mesojedje"* (Shrovetide). They started from either Christmas or Epiphany, depending on the area, and lasted for six to ten weeks. Back then carnival parades, travelling performers, marriages were organized, and all kinds of entertainment events during that time. One particularly interesting custom was performed. A big fire was lit in the middle of the village, and women danced and sang around it. The fire was built by women, and men were completely excluded from this event. This custom was called *"Bukara"* ,named after the fire, and ethnologists assume that the basic function of this fire was to increase the sun's power in the period after winter solstice when the days begin to grow longer.

During The Unbaptized days - that is, the period from Christmas until Epiphany - *Kolede* was organized, a festival in which people wore masks that represented spirits, mainly those of the forest and of Lesnik, their leader. We provided more information about this when we talked about the horned God. Also, in some parts of the country, young men dressed in wolf's skin and wearing masks walked in processions. They were called *"vucari"*. Sometime they carried around a dead wolf stuffed with straw. In the territory of Kosovo processions were lead by two men, one of them dressed as *"baba"* (grandmother) and the other as *"deda"* (grandfather). It is believed they were represented ancient deities, Baba and Deda, the oldest deceased ancestors that live in the underworld.

One of the so-called minor holidays is *"vodena nedelja"* (Water Sunday) on May 13. As its name says, this holiday is dedicated to water; that is, water demons – spirits from which people need to induce mercy in the springtime when the snow is melting, rains are falling, and the possibility of floods is increased. It was sometimes believed that water spirits have special powers at this time of year, so the rituals related to them were performed then. Anglers also know this holiday very well.

294

Beside this holidays that we mentioned here, there are great number of others whose origins are understood, to a greater or lesser extent. Not all of these holidays were equally related to Witches, although they are all Pagan in origin. The one thing that is sure is the fact that Witches that observed them performed their rituals the day preceding those holidays, because it was thought that the rituals had more power then. On the day of holiday, they avoid performing rituals, except ones that need to be done on that day. That is the case with *Vidovdan* (St. Vitus' Day, June 28th). On this day two things must be done; the first is treating eyes; that is, problems with sight through magical actions, and the second thing is seeking of prophetic visions, in reality or through dream. Both actions were performed with the help of herb named *Vid* (anagallis arvensis – Scarlet pimpernel) that is dedicated to St. Vid, a deity whose role was taken over by this Christian saint.

The situation is similar with Physicians holiday that is dedicated to healers Damjan & Kuzman. This holiday is celebrated on November 14th and July 14th. Shortly before these dates, rituals related to health must be performed, while on the holidays themselves, all magical actions must be avoided. There are two possible reasons for this; it is possible that Witches avoid rituals on those days in respect to those saints, and it could be that they performed those rituals at night, in other words, the night before the holiday. If you find this respect of Christian saints by Witches too confusing, let us just say that traditional Witches were always women from villages, for whom it was normal to invoke the Forest Mother in the middle of the night, then go to church the next morning. In many original rituals, the many Christian elements are the result of religious syncretism over the centuries. You can imagine what the clergy thinks about that!

Today, the Ascension is also a Christian holiday that is celebrated on August 19th. Sometimes it was the period when the transfiguration of nature was celebrated; that is, from summer into winter. However, this holiday was "reserved" for a very interesting love ritual that was performed by young women. A group of them would gather in an empty or abandoned building and light a fire in the center. One of them would remove her clothes and climb up on a beam in the ceiling. Rest of them would take rolling pins in hand and walk around the fire, so that boys would pursue them. Simultaneously, they start to kick the fire and say "As many sparks, so many boys". This ritual was performed by night, only in this day.

Among the various peoples of the Balkans, various types of ritual whipping of adults, children, cattle, and plants existed. Whipping was done on holidays, mainly in time of *Mesojedje* and the spring holidays. The reasons for magical whipping differed, but the main function of whipping was to chase away evil and to bring good. A barren woman was whipped to conceive, a child was whipped to grow, a sick man was whipped so the illness (evil spirit) would be chased away, a fruit tree was whipped to bear plentiful fruit, etc. There is great number of these examples, but that should suffice. Having mentioned the importance related to holidays, something should be said about the days of the week. You have probably noticed that some days of the week have been mentioned several times, but we have not mentioned all of them. So, let us look at what beliefs are connected to them.

Monday is considered the first day of the working week so it is very good to start any business that day. A great number of people avoid paying bills on Monday, lending money, and similar things so that these expenses would not follow them through the whole week. It is considered that person born on Monday will be very happy in their life.

Tuesday is the opposite of Monday. Children born on Tuesday will be unfortunate. You should to avoid any business on Tuesday, even cutting nails or washing hair. Still, it is considered a magical day, and that is why it is most appropriate day in the week for performing rituals. People believed that this is the day of supernatural forces, and that is the reason for being most appropriate day.

Wednesday is a very interesting day. It is considered very good day to start business ventures, but some actions, such as baking bread, bathing children, or shearing sheep are forbidden, or to be more precise, people avoid doing them. People fast on Wednesday just as on Friday. Women pay special attention to this day and call it St. Wednesday, considering this day as the embodiment of a female saint. Many sick people swear by this day to be healed. According to tradition, a girl that did not have respect for St. Wednesday was spinning wool, and when saint saw what she was doing, he tried to cook her in his cauldron. You can make your own conclusion, but it could be the day of some Goddess of this region.

Thursday, by all accounts, is one of the best days of the week. People say, "Each day is a good day, but Thursday is the best". Above all, this is the farmer's day, as far as I could conclude. It is a very good day to start plowing, sowing, reaping, etc. It is possible that at one time Thursday could have been the day of a deity of fertility and nature..

Friday is a day of fasting and a day of many prohibitions. It resembles Wednesday, but it is not related to any saint. People believe that the dead should not be buried on Wednesday because they will become vampires. It is also believed that people are safe on Friday, because supernatural forces rest on that day.

Above all, Saturday is the day of the dead. It is believed that no enterprise or business should be initiated on Saturday, because it will inevitably fail. It is also believed that a child born on Saturday will have some supernatural powers, such as to see ghosts, vampires, and Witches (in their astral forms), etc.

Sunday is also considered a saint's day; people take oaths on it and ask help from it. Sunday is a day of relaxation, and it is strictly forbidden to do any form of labor. There is a very interesting belief related to the *"mlada nedelja"* (Young week); that is, weeks during which the moon is waxing. Namely, it is said that this is the best time for performing various types of rituals and that is the best time for visiting a Witch, sorcerer, fortune-teller, etc., to ask for help.

There is one story related to Kraljevic Marko (Prince Marko, a medieval Serbian prince), who tried to hunt on Sunday. St. *Mlada nedelja* (Young week) was angered and turned him into a four-headed dragon with six wings to punish him because he wanted to hunt on her (The Saint's) Sunday (when the moon is increasing). This story has an educative function; it informs us that we can recognize the Young week as a young Goddess, because based on these facts we can see that she is related with the waxing moon, which is her representative, and in this case, her essence..

BIBLIOGRAPHY:

ŠPIRO KULIŠIĆ, PETAR Z. PETROVIĆ, NIKOLA PANTELIĆ, *SRPSKI MITOLOSKI REČNIK*, ETNOGRAFSKI INSTITUT SANU INTERPRINT, BEOGRAD 1998

DR. RADOVAN N. KAZIMIROVIĆ, *TAJANSTVENE POJAVE U NAŠEM NARODU*, DEČJA KNJIGA, BEOGRAD 2000

VESELIN ČAJKANOVIĆ, *STARA SRPSKA RELIGIJA I MITOLOGIJA*, BEOGRAD 1994

VUK STEFANOVIĆ KARADŽIĆ, *SRPSKI RJEČNIK*, BEOGRAD 1935

NIKOLA BEGOVIĆ, *ŽIVOT SRBA GRANIĆARA*, PROSVETA, BEOGRAD 1986

SLOBODAN ZEČEVIĆ, *MITSKA BIĆA SRPSKIH PREDANJA*, VUK KARADŽIĆ, BEOGRAD 1981

GRĐIĆ L. BJELOKOSIĆ, *NARODNA GATANJA*, SARAJEVO 1896

DUŠAN BANDIĆ, *CARSTVO ZEMALJSKO I CARSTVO NEBESKO*, BIBLIOTEKA XX VEK, BEOGRAD 1997

PEJŠNS KEMP, *BALKANSKI KULTOVI*, LUTA, BEOGRAD 2000

JASNA JOJIĆ PAVLOVSKI, *ČUDA VLAŠKE MAGIJE*, BEOGRAD 2000

J.CHEVALIER, A.GHEERBRANT, *RIJEČNIK SIMBOLA*, ROMANOV, BANJA LUKA 2003

GWYDION, *VIKA-DREVNA RELIGIJA VEŠTICA*, ESOTHERIA, BEOGRAD 1994

SIMA TROJANOVIĆ, *VATRA U OBIČAJIMA I ŽIVOTU SRPSKOG NARODA*, PROSVETA, BEOGRAD 1990

PEJŠNS KEMP, *SLOVENSKA MAGIJA*, LUTA, BEOGRAD 1993

HELMUT HARK, *LEKSIKON OSNOVNIH JUNGOVSKIH POJMOVA*, DERETA, BEOGRAD 1998

VID VULETIĆ VUKOSAVIĆ, *VJEŠTICE U JUŽNIJEH SLOVENA*, KARADŽIĆ ZA OKTOBAR, ALEKSINAC 1901

VESELIN ČAJKANOVIĆ, *O VRHOVNOM BOGU U STAROJ SRPSKOJ RELIGIJI*, GRUPA IZDAVAČA, BEOGRAD 1994

VESELIN ČAJKANOVIĆ, *REČNIK SRPSKIH NARODNIH VEROVANJA O BILJKAMA*, GRUPA IZDAVAČA, BEOGRAD 1994

BORIS RIBAKOV, *ANCIENT SLAVIC PAGANISM*, MOSCOW 1981

TIHOMIR ĐORĐEVIĆ „*VEŠTICA I VILA U NAŠEM NARODNOM VEROVANJU I PREDANJU*", BOGRAD, 1953.

VUK STEFANOVIĆ KARADŽIĆ, „*SRPSKI RJEČNIK*, 1818.

INDEX

Atropa, 67, 215, 230
August, 289, 297
Autumnal Equinox, 289-290
Axe, 101-102

B

Baba, 37, 175-177, 205, 296
Baba Korizmu, 177
Baba Martu, 177
Baba Pethru, 177
Baba Rogu, 177
Baba Rugu, 177
Baba Yaga, 37, 176-177
Baba Yegu, 177
Babajic, 175
Babetino, 175
Babica, 175
Babin Zub, 175
Babina, 175
Babina Gora, 175
Babini, 179
Babino Polje, 175
Babino Selo, 175
Baburaca, 205
Baburacha, 176
Badnjak, 247, 250, 273, 277, 292
Balkan Baba, 176
Balkan Cults, 49, 52
Balkan Hecate, 173
Balkan Peninsula, 98
Balkan Traditional Witchcraft, 1, 3-4, 11, 36, 58, 76, 85
Balkan Witch, 36, 251, 257
Baltic, 98

Bandic, 33, 58, 102, 180
Banisteriopsis, 66
Basil, 67, 164, 166, 218-220, 224, 227, 229, 236, 249, 262, 276, 288
Bat, 18, 67, 207
Bear, 31, 143, 160, 190, 207, 283, 294, 298
Beech, 20, 242
Belgrade, 18, 38, 49, 56, 225, 287
Bell, 104, 138, 143, 241, 249
Bell Pepper, 138, 143, 241, 249
Belladonna, 67, 215, 230-231
Beltaine, 289
Benadant, 40
Bigz, 189
Bihac, 201
Biljni, 210, 218, 287-288
Biljober, 290
Bindu, 201
Birchwood, 22, 90, 116, 241
Bird, 39, 80, 160, 283
Bistrica, 20
Black God, 189
Black Hawthorn, 97, 263
Black Plague, 23
Blackberry, 248-249
Blacksmiths, 35, 92-93, 115, 143, 188, 195, 284
Blagovesti, 179
Blue, 22, 84, 144, 233, 261
Bog Asphodel, 237
Bogomil, 163

Bogomils, 9, 163, 200
Bogu, 189, 302
Bogujevac, 39
Bogumil, 258
Boljevac, 26
Book of Enoch, 198
Borrowed, 146
Bosnia, 39, 52, 85, 102, 177, 239, 251
Bosnian, 9, 22
Bosnian Witches, 22
Bread, 226, 235-236, 254, 266, 280, 292, 294, 299
Brew, 18, 22, 119-120
British, 7, 188
Broom, 13, 36, 40, 43, 83, 88-92, 134-135, 139, 207, 211, 224-225, 242, 246, 291, 293
Brooms, 16, 20, 22, 37, 88-91, 99, 112, 225, 232, 241, 256, 263
Brown, 157
Bud, 160, 293
Bukara, 296
Bulgaria, 34, 214
Burning Bush, 225-226
Butterfly, 14-15, 207
Byzantine Christianity, 173

C
Caapi, 66
Candles, 102, 107, 116, 142, 251, 253, 278, 286
Cardinal, 272-273
Carnation, 227

Carnival, 14, 16, 286, 291, 296
Carpathian Mountains, 178
Cat, 22, 83, 142, 160, 264
Cathars, 9
Cattail, 227
Cattle, 19-21, 26, 28-30, 34, 54, 181, 191-192, 199-200, 212, 217-218, 242, 246, 286, 288, 294, 298
Cauldron, 13, 36, 48, 83, 86-88, 142, 227, 237, 299
Celandine, 215
Celestial, 239, 253, 265, 267
Celtic, 9, 191, 283
Celts, 8-9
Cernih, 20-21
Certain, 7-9, 15, 23, 25, 27, 32, 35, 38, 46, 48, 51, 57, 59, 63, 67, 82, 85, 90, 92, 102, 108-113, 124, 151, 158, 165, 172, 200, 211, 215, 241, 250-252, 259-260, 266, 274-275, 280, 285
Charcoal, 263
Charles Godfrey Leland, 7
Children, 14-15, 19, 23, 66, 86, 97, 102, 144, 150, 181, 198, 202, 205, 217, 219, 222, 230, 238, 246, 252, 270, 293-294, 298-299
Chinese Yin, 273
Christian Ascetic-scholastic, 19, 23
Christian Christmas, 293

God of Witches, 180
God Veles, 182
Goddess Bendis, 174
Goddess Hand, 234
Goddess Light-Carrier, 93
Goddess Mara-Morena, 179
Goddess of Death, 75
Goddesses, 179
Gods, 34, 65, 74-75, 87, 174, 184, 190, 192, 247
Gods of Dacian, 174
Gold, 22, 100, 148, 166, 187-188, 261, 267, 269-270, 278
Golden, 15, 89, 183, 199, 203, 225, 267
Good, 7, 23-24, 26, 28-29, 35, 37, 40-41, 61, 68, 76, 78, 81, 88, 102, 117, 123, 125, 148, 156, 160, 162-163, 165-166, 184, 187, 192, 195, 197, 202-203, 214, 229, 231, 233, 242, 252, 262, 267, 277, 288, 291, 293, 298-299
Good Friday, 293
Gorska Majka, 215
Gospel, 7
Grains, 28-29, 134-136, 162, 250, 252, 255, 258
Gramina Draconis, 232
Grand Magister, 51
Grandma Dokia, 178
Grandma Ruza, 53-54
Grandma Stanka, 28, 30-31
Grandmother, 25-26, 30, 56, 58, 62, 83, 175, 177, 179, 293, 296
Grandmother Joana, 25
Grandmother Stanka, 30
Grass of Intention, 240
Great Britain, 48
Great Mother, 35, 37, 58, 65, 75, 215, 262
Great Rite, 48
Great Spirit of Nature, 180, 184
Great Water Spirit, 25, 38, 175, 184
Greater Dodder, 235
Greece, 34, 294
Greek, 180, 191, 274
Greek Pan, 180
Greeks, 179
Green, 87-88, 164, 183, 203, 234, 261, 288
Green Winged Orchid, 234
Grey, 264
Grintavec, 22
Grljan, 30
Ground, 33, 76-77, 91, 96, 99, 116, 128, 137, 145, 156, 172, 213, 218, 231, 233, 238-239, 249
Ground Ivy, 239

H
Hades, 191
Hallucinations, 66, 68
Hand, 9, 11, 14, 20, 23, 49, 77, 84, 99, 101, 103, 123, 131, 133, 142-143, 145-146,

Whipping, 149, 298
White, 14, 20, 100-101, 108,
116, 123-125, 127, 129-130,
144-145, 157, 160, 167, 172,
185, 192, 204, 217, 219, 225,
231, 238, 240, 253, 255, 259-
263, 269, 273, 291
White Carnival, 291
Wicca, 7, 124
Wiccan, 8, 47-48
Wiccan Traditions, 8
Wild Strawberry, 248
Willow, 49-50, 97, 116, 242,
288
Wind People, 38
Winter, 178-179, 181-182,
273, 288, 292, 296-297
Winter Solstice, 181, 296
Witching, 28
Wolfbane, 233
Wolves, 13, 35, 87-88, 181,
188-189
Woman, 12, 14-17, 19-21,
23-28, 36, 53-54, 76, 89, 146,
153, 167, 172-173, 175-177,
179, 216, 221, 229, 231, 234,
237, 242, 253, 286, 289, 298
Women, 11, 14, 16-17, 19-23,
26, 32-33, 35-36, 43, 51, 53,
55, 89, 93-94, 102, 110, 115,
118, 127, 133, 139, 141, 143-
144, 173, 176-177, 181, 198,
200-201, 206, 210, 212, 215-
216, 220-221, 237, 260, 283,
286-287, 291, 293, 296-299

World Traditional Witchcraft,
48
World War II, 69, 169
Wormwood, 33, 224, 232-233,
236
Wort, 221

Y

Yaga, 37, 66, 83, 176-177
Yang, 273
Yarn, 87, 89, 100-101, 130-
133, 136, 144, 217, 219, 228,
236, 255, 260, 262, 264
Yellow, 22, 49-51, 228, 240,
261, 267, 290
Yellow Archangel, 240
Yew, 41, 97, 246, 279
Yugoslavia, 121, 161, 183-184,
201, 218, 267, 279, 286
Yule, 277, 292
Yule Log, 277, 292

Z

Zabari, 16
Zagorska, 19
Zagreb, 21, 69
Zaje, 118
Zajecar, 26, 29-30
Zamenis, 203
Zarije, 41
Zduhac, 39, 43, 90, 99, 191
Zecevic, 31, 38-39
Zivko, 39
Zvizde, 295

Professor Dusan Bandic, 102
Projection, 58, 68, 71-73, 78, 83, 91
Prophecy, 41, 56, 157
Prosveta, 189, 301-302
Protection, 39, 76-78, 89-90, 95, 97, 101, 107, 115, 138-139, 143-144, 160, 173, 205, 207, 212, 215, 217-224, 227-229, 231, 233, 243, 246, 249, 255, 261-264, 270, 276, 278-284
Prvanovich, 119
Pumpkin, 138, 249-250
Purple, 234, 238

Q

Queen, 37, 52, 58, 172, 193-194
Quince, 247

R

Rabbit, 160, 206, 283
Radan, 51
Radomir Radulovic, 26
Radovan N. Kazimirovic, 18
Rakija, 258
Rakitju, 21
Ram, 13, 29, 92-93, 139, 143, 190, 207, 264, 283
Ranko Jovanovic, 169
Rastko Nemanjic, 35
Rastovnik, 214-215, 223
Rather, 46, 61, 75, 80, 89, 96, 98, 110, 124, 139, 186, 194,

204, 228, 237, 245, 270, 276, 289, 292
Ravijojla, 194
Ravna, 111
Razane, 39
Red, 98, 100-101, 116, 133, 136, 144-146, 164, 167, 183, 217, 219, 223, 236, 238, 248-249, 260-262, 278
Red Clover, 223
Renaissance Witches, 11
Ritual, 5, 10-11, 13, 22, 24-29, 32-33, 36-37, 42-43, 45-46, 48, 50-51, 53, 60, 62, 64-65, 69, 76, 78, 85-86, 88-90, 92-95, 97, 99, 101-104, 107-109, 111, 113-123, 125-126, 128-139, 141-143, 145-146, 148-149, 151, 153-154, 163-164, 167-168, 171, 174, 180, 183, 187, 203, 216, 218, 222-224, 226, 231-233, 236, 238-240, 246-247, 249-255, 257-263, 266, 268, 270-273, 276-278, 284, 286, 288-294, 298
Ritual Skoace Draci - Artist Stasha, 27
Ritual Spaces, 108
RITUAL TRANCE, 5, 10-11, 33, 37, 53, 62, 64-65, 69, 107, 153
Rituals, 5, 10, 12, 21, 32, 35-36, 51-52, 86, 91-92, 95, 97, 100, 107-115, 118-119, 122-126, 130-131, 133-135,

315

www.ingramcontent.com/pod-product-compliance
Lightning Source LLC
Chambersburg PA
CBHW060247100426
42742CB00011B/1661